Thunderbirds!

Books by Martin Caidin

fiction

Marooned
Devil Take All
No Man's World

The Last Fathom
The God Machine
Four Came Back

nonfiction

The Ragged, Rugged Warriors
Everything But the Flak
Messerschmitt ME-109
Flying Forts
The Mission
This Is My Land
Thunderbirds!
Black Thursday
Samurai!
The Night Hamburg Died
Wings into Space
Barnstorming
The Winged Armada
The Mighty Hercules
Air Force
Golden Wings
Zero!
The Zero Fighter
Boeing 707
Thunderbolt!
Test Pilot
The Silken Angels
A Torch to the Enemy
The Long, Lonely Leap
The Long Arm of America
Flying
Cross-Country Flying

Let's Go Flying!
The Long Night
Hydrospace
The Power of Decision
The Greatest Challenge
Red Star in Space
Spaceport U.S.A.
War for the Moon
By Apollo to the Moon
The Moon: New World for Men
Countdown for Tomorrow
Vanguard!
Worlds in Space
Overture to Space
Rendezvous in Space
Man into Space
First Flight into Space
Aviation and Space Medicine
I Am Eagle!
The Man-in-Space Dictionary
Rockets Beyond the Earth
Rockets and Missiles
Jets, Rockets and Guided Missiles
Why Space?
Why Mars?
The Astronauts

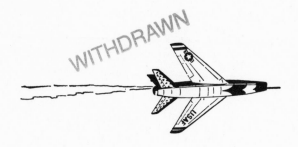

Thunderbirds!

BY MARTIN CAIDIN

Line drawings by Fred L. Wolff

E. P. DUTTON & CO., INC.   NEW YORK   1968

This book, with deep affection from
all of us of the Team . . .
is for DICK CRANE.

Contents

Illustrations

Drawings and Diagrams

Foreword

They came out of the east, distance cloaking their sudden passage in silence. Eight winged metal shapes riding the crest of a huge razored mountain ridge, maneuvered and held together tightly so that eight appeared to be one. Trailing red and blue smoke traced their swift rush down the mountain slope. Tens of thousands of awed spectators caught the bright sun-splashed gleam of massed wings. The formation arced up suddenly from the earth, reaching high in a swift and towering rush. Up; still up. Higher and higher, the dazzling wedge arrowed through the heavens, rolling over until the eight machines were on their backs and then plunging, recklessly it seemed, down toward the earth.

These were the Golden Centennaires of the Royal Canadian Armed Forces. The mountain reared high over the Nevada desert at the edge of Nellis Air Force Base, home of the famed Air Force Thunderbirds. It was an auspicious moment of flight that delighted and thrilled all who were present. The Canadians had come to honor and pay homage to their Thunderbirds compatriots of the United States Air Force. Theirs was a salute of superb pilots to the world's outstanding jet precision flying team.

There were others who also had come to pay their respects. Before the morning of November 18th, 1967, was done, the Blue Angels of the United States Navy had performed with the same breathtaking skill that for more than twenty years has marked their aerial demonstrations before tens of millions of people. In a sense the Blue Angels and the Thunderbirds are competitors. But not during moments such as these, when they are pilots together and there is the impression, unmistakable to all those who fly, of the mutual respect true professionals afford to one another. And the Blue Angels, as always, had even the old-time pilots of decades' experience on their feet and applauding.

It was a day of flight unexcelled. The occasion was the gathering of former pilots of the Thunderbirds and of those who serviced their powerful machines on the ground. Present to honor the Air Force team were members of the aerospace industry and private citizens who in one way or another were involved in the activities of the Thunderbirds. There were the Blue Angels and the Golden Centennaires; the internationally famed and competition-beating parachutists of the United States Army's Golden Knights skydiving team; there were skilled skydivers from as far away as England; and some of the world's greatest and best known aerial artists from all over the United States. Bob Hoover, Dick Schram, and Bill Fornof, flying everything from Piper Cubs to Mustang and Bearcat fighters, all helped to make it a day of flight supreme.

But of all that took place, nothing was more meaningful, more significant, more emotional, than the gathering of so many pilots who once had worn the red, white, and blue insignia of the Thunderbirds. Those who had led the team and for fourteen years of outstanding flying made up its formations were assembled beneath that deep blue sky. They had joined together to sustain what they and others had created, they were part of the legend, and, I am quite certain, unknowing to them, they were impressing upon our national history the continuance of that legend.

More than seven years before, I had flown with several of these men who had come to join with one another on these few days of November, 1967. In 1960, when for several months I lived and flew with the Thunderbirds, the team was made up of Bob Fitzgerald, Chuck Maultsby, Bob Janca, Neil Eddins, Herman Griffin, Dick Crane, and Bob Cass. Those intervening years had in many ways been a long journey for all concerned. Back in 1960 Neil Eddins, as a lieutenant, flew the Slot position of the Thunderbirds' diamond formation. Now, seven years later, Neil was a major, he had helped to fight a war, had served on several different continents, and he had returned, as only the second man ever to do so, to the team as its new Leader.

Chuck Maultsby could not be with us. He was on his way home from Vietnam where he had flown 216 combat missions. Try as he might, time and distance were against him, and he missed this particular rendezvous.

Dick Crane and Bob Fitzgerald were there only in memory, as they must always be. In the summer of 1960 a single fighter hurtled out of the Nevada skies. It was alone; no one saw the machine rush against a mountain. No one saw the brilliant flash.

Dick Crane was the pilot of that airplane.

Not quite one year later, Bob Fitzgerald relinquished the leadership of the team to its new Leader. Shortly afterward Fitz was flying with the team's new Narrator, George Nial. There was an error measured in the span of a split second. Again came that dreaded brilliant flash as their fighter slammed into the desert floor.

Other members of the Thunderbirds have been lost to us forever. Some of these men, our friends, died while flying with the team. Others gave their lives in combat. Military flight with machines of great power and high performance is demanding of the men who commit themselves to the high blue. So it is, as it always has been, as always it must be.

Who are the Thunderbirds? They are the members of a precision aerial team, men who fly great machines that perform in the heavens with a catlike agility and ballet artistry. They are pilots of our Air Force who are not daredevils but dedicated airmen, not stunt fliers but men of extraordinary skill and teamwork.

Never has a pilot in the United States Air Force been *assigned* to the Thunderbirds. Each man on the team, from the Commander to the enlisted ranks, must volunteer. That by itself, however, is not enough. If the man qualifies, he is only one among many who covet membership as one of the fifty-five officers and men who comprise the Thunderbirds. He must wait and, when a place is open, he must compete for that position. Every officer, every pilot, every member of the ground crew is a highly selected professional who is dedicated beyond question to the successful accomplishment of the team's responsibility and its mission as the USAF Air Demonstration Squadron.

Since their activation in 1953, the Thunderbirds (at the time of this writing) have performed before approximately

70 million spectators throughout the United States, and over the land of thirty-nine other nations. As America's "Ambassadors in Blue," they have flown more than 25 million air miles to complete nearly 1,300 dazzling aerial demonstrations.

But these are statistics. While they are important, numbers do not comprise our story. Join with me, then, in turning back the clock to 1960, when it was my privilege to share in the miracle of flight as it may only be experienced with the most exclusive flying fraternity in the world — the *Thunderbirds*.

Martin Caidin

December, 1967

1 Flight to Thunderbird Lake

It is one of those rare and wonderful days when the sky is *alive;* the air is gleaming gold and blue so intensely bright that it stabs the eyes. It is the kind of a day that delights pilots. Your feet itch and your heart yearns. You cannot remain on the ground. You must *fly!*

We are 17,000 feet over Nevada, floating above bleak ridges jutting starkly from the earth, great skeletal vertebrae twisting away to the horizon. We are acutely respectful of their razor edges, their unyielding mass. In an unwary moment they can smash a powerful fighter airplane into a shocking blot of angry red and black smoke.

We float above them; close, it is true, but sustained in the ocean of air by sweptback wings and a flaming engine from which streams a torrent of superheated air. Our magic carpet is very real; it is solid and made of aluminum and steel, and it weighs 30,000 pounds. Yet by the miracle of understanding this ocean of air, and by the knowledge of aeronautics and a thousand other sciences, we have been given a machine that in superb fashion defies both gravity and imagination. It has a name—Super Sabre—and even a number by which it is known: F-100F. It is a fabulous steed on which to ride, but what noble prince of the Arabian Nights could ever dream of rushing over towering mountain peaks—while seeming to float lazily—at better than 700 miles per hour!

Several feet before me is my pilot, Captain John Richard Crane, United States Air Force, a member of one of the most exclusive flying fraternities in the world. Dick Crane is a pilot of extraordinary skill with his fifteen-ton machine. He is one of seven fighter pilots who make up the Thunderbirds, the famed Air Force jet precision team that has demonstrated its awe-inspiring maneuvers before millions of people in more than twenty-three countries around the world.

Twenty minutes ago we were poised in the Super Sabre at the end of the main runway of Nellis Air Force Base in Nevada, our nose pointing almost due north. In front of us stretched more than two miles of black pavement, streaked with the tire marks of tens of thousands of landings made by heavy machines dropping from the sky. It was then late morning, that beautiful morning beseeching flight to all of us. To our right reared the ridges of Sunrise Mountain, named appropriately, it seems, for this day.

The call comes from the tower. "Okay, Thunderbird Seven, you're clear to roll." Dick eases the throttle forward; fuel surges through the lines, bursts in a needle spray into the great jet engine. Pressure and temperature increase, and the volcano chained beneath our feet trembles with power. Then the brakes are released, and the metal creature is free. We roll slowly at first, a storm of energy straining to cast the airplane away from the earth, but forced through an orderly progression of increasing thrust and speed. Suddenly, a solid, muffled explosion behind us; Dick pushes the throttle into afterburner. Instantly raw fuel shoots into the flaming jet blast, another massive controlled explosion results, and the Super Sabre leaps forward, tasting her freedom now, eager, rushing with unbelievable acceleration down the runway that shoves us hard into our seats.

We feel the plunge. The wheels rebound from the shock of movement, the landing gear legs react with a mechanical absorption of that shock, and the fifteen tons of accelerating airplane have a gentle trembling motion. But before we can adjust to this, the miracle of flight is upon us.

Dick applies a gentle back pressure to the control stick. The movement is barely perceptible, the gentlest touch, but it is enough. Sixteen thousand pounds of thrust from the howling jet impart lift to the wings. The sweptback sheets of metal grasp the air, secure their hold. We cannot hear the sound from the sealed cockpit, but all Nellis Air Force Base is inundated with the crashing explosion of our takeoff, a roaring howl that marks our movement, races out on each side, and comes back in a booming peal of thunder as it bounds off the flanks of the mountains to our right.

We do not take off from Nellis's runway in the accepted sense of the word. There is no pounding roar or vibration from pistons or propellers; neither is there the long, flat lift from earth so common to the jet. The instant that our wheels lift from the runway, Dick hits the gear control; the

8

two main wheels and the nose wheel respond by snapping up and inward. They fold neatly into wells in the wings and the nose, door covers bang closed, and the F-100F is clean, ready for her element.

The needle winds around quickly on the gauge, and Dick has the speed that he wants. He doesn't even realize that he is talking aloud, but through the helmet earphones I hear the whispered command to the great airplane. "All right, baby," he calls softly, "let's go upstairs."

And "upstairs" we go! The nose comes up sharply now, the mountain ridges plunge away. There comes the sensation of weight increasing suddenly, almost alarmingly, as the sleek fighter leaves an orderly path of flight. It is centrifugal

Coming home; flaring out.

force, of course, an increase in weight caused by the sudden upward movement at high speed. It is not so severe as to be uncomfortable, but I sit much heavier in my seat, my oxygen mask tugs downward, and the helmet presses on my head with more pressure. All this I know as though from a distance, for the world has disappeared and there is only sky above.

The Super Sabre rears steeply, the nose swings higher and higher, and we balance on the pillar of afterburner flame behind us. There is only rich blue sky, and then suddenly the world falls over on its side. And keeps falling! Abruptly the mountains flash into sight; they whirl crazily, a wide sweeping motion that flings them through line of sight. And then sky again.

We are rolling rapidly, almost vertically, a marvelous and sensational takeoff maneuver. Right from takeoff, allowing the fighter to accelerate rapidly, Dick has brought the nose higher and higher, pointing the F-100F almost straight up, then pushing the stick over sharply to the left. The fighter rolls quickly around her line of flight, vertical rolls that turn the world into a tumbling mosaic of jagged mountains and that brilliant sky above.

The airspeed drops off quickly in the rolls; exactly at a reading of 150 knots Dick eases her out. Wings level, there comes another strange sensation, this time the absence of weight. Afterburner still blazing, Dick pushes the stick forward. The mountains appear again, to our right and left now, in normal, sensible position. Nose up at thirty degrees from the horizontal, we rush away from the sprawling airbase behind us.

Three hundred miles per hour—then 400—and without effort, without any seeming intent, we plunge past five hundred miles per hour. On to six hundred! We no longer climb steeply; the throttle is back, afterburner off, and a "mild and gentle" push of only 10,000 pounds thrust kicks us through the sky.

And then, at this moment, the magic spell is cast. We are not encased in curving walls of metal with only limited vision to the outside world. We are not imprisoned by lack of sight as are so many who fly. To each side, before and behind us, and overhead, there is a gently curving canopy of plexiglas, a defense against wind and sound and cold, but not at all to sight. We seem, therefore, to have nothing about our shoulders. We look out upon a world from what seems literally to be a vehicle of magic. We do not feel the wind. Our earphones and helmets muffle sound. The plexiglas is under pressure, and we are comfortable in much denser air than that through which we rush at better than 600 miles per hour. Beyond that curving, transparent sheet, it is bitterly cold; on this side we are warm and comfortable. We talk to each other with ease; the masks contain the microphones, and we are interconnected through the machine in which we fly.

10

From this superb, almost unbelievable vantage, we command the earth below and the heavens about us. No clouds drifted in the sky over the airfield. Now, however, they float above our heads. Nothing seems to lie between us and the clouds, it is almost as if we could reach out and push our hands through the cottony masses. But they are still several thousand feet above us.

For a moment I push up the thick, colored plexiglas visor that bends around the forward part of the helmet. The glare is intolerable; it is this heavy, darkened glass that allows us to look out in such visual comfort, and quickly I snap the visor back into place.

At 8,000 feet we move past 600 miles per hour. But we seem almost to be standing still! Or doing little more than floating through space. We had climbed away from Nellis on a heading of 320 degrees; in front of us were mountains stabbing nearly ten thousand feet into the sky.

These mountains act at times like a great atmospheric trap. Taking off, we could not see a haze that hung in the air. Now, at 8,000 feet, we are in the lower fringes of that haze. It stretches up for several thousand feet more, and it has a strange and miraculous effect upon the sky. The air becomes visible. The clouds, which normally are like any other clouds upon which people gaze, gain a substance visible only to the flier, denied to the person on the ground. They drift along a great river within an ocean; it is visible, yet almost wholly transparent, a visual paradox that delights the eye. At 12,000 feet the clouds drift with the moving river of air. Not a single finger of cloud drops below this level. There are no strays. Everything fits within the pattern, every cloud obeys the laws of the atmosphere that prevail at this moment. The river of air that moves has no visible banks; it stretches forever away from us.

But we are not at the sides of that river, or even above the flowing mass; we are *beneath* the surface! We are like divers emerging from some incredible depth, with the surface of that river still over our heads.

We are, literally—and visibly—within this river. We hurtle through the liquid medium at unbelievable speed, yet we

11

cannot comprehend our movement. Not really, we are still too distant from the mountains to the sides, and too far beneath that level at 12,000 feet where the clouds rest.

Dick signals for me to take over, and I must confess I have suffered a rising impatience to control this steel creature myself.

The fighter is unbelievably sensitive to the touch. The slightest movement of the stick with my fingertips is magnified to the strength of a dozen men; these are power-boosted controls. When I move the stick or rudder pedals, I activate a power system. This sends a command to the ailerons in the wings, the solid slab tail, the high rudder. It is easy to overcontrol, and Dick laughs as the wings rock despite my attempts to fly a level course. Soon, however, I have the hang of it—in this metal monster you fly with your fingertips, and not with the heavy grasp of other airplanes.

It is a joyous thing to command such power, to gain access to this miracle of flight simply by moving the fingers. I want to go higher, to rush directly through the surface of the river, to flash through the clouds. I ease back on the stick with my right hand; with my left I push the throttle slightly forward. The Super Sabre responds, and we climb.

Now there comes the first true feeling of speed. To our left a peak stands exactly at 9,920 feet. We watch the height of the uppermost ridge as we ascend. The mountain slides past; we stand still; it is the mountain that moves.

What was a promise of speed builds up to a torrent. Eleven thousand feet, and we are deeper into the haze. The clouds are thicker now, closer together, and they float on the haze, deeper in shade at the base and the sides away from the sun; caught in sunlight, however, they are a rich pure white. I bank the airplane, and the visible air suddenly is speared with great shafts of light. The haze, from a changing vantage as we sweep around in a wide turn, seems thicker and heavier. Where the clouds allow the sun to pass through, the light itself becomes visible, sunlight stabbing through the river of dust and sand blown to these heights by a great storm many miles away in the desert.

Then we are at the base of the clouds, still swinging around in the turn. I level the wings, push forward on the stick ever so gently. The Super Sabre trembles from unseen currents. Every now and then we race into the underhang of a cloud. The world vanishes into a blurred creaminess of white; then we are out. Brilliance and gold and flashes of blue as we dash from cloud to cloud.

Our speed is fantastic! Seven hundred miles per hour, but now we have substance with which to realize that speed. We do not fly from one cloud to the other, we seem to explode along in our haste. It is fascinating and beautiful and a thousand other things. It is sensational movement, a race for the sheer joy of racing.

The urge is there, and why not answer it? I pull back on the stick, hard. Instantly a hand squeezes my body; centrifugal force asserts itself, and not with any mild discomfort this time! I am rammed down into my seat, my helmet seems to weigh a hundred pounds, and it is difficult to keep my grip on the stick. In that instant we flash through the clouds. I ease the fighter into gentler flight; the stick goes forward and to the left, and I apply a gentle rudder pressure. In a great soaring arc we sail above the river. We see its surface, more opaque from this position. It has an almost solid substance, the clouds rest visibly upon the mass.

Gone is our speed. At the top of our arc we are above 17,000 feet. More than a mile gained in height, and many miles of our wide turn, in bare seconds. Dick Crane has been flying for many years, with thousands of hours in fighters. Do not believe that the experienced pilot is not moved by a sight such as we have found. For ten or fifteen minutes, perhaps more, we hold our turn, absorbing the miracle given to us. The intense glare of light along the horizon; the hard steel-blue of the sky directly overhead. Through the thick, dark-colored plexiglas visor the sun is almost unbearable, a savage furnace of light. We watch the cumulus building up; within the clouds there is churning energy, and towering palaces and mountains evolve before our eyes, performing tricks with light and shadow and reflection. Through the spaces between the clouds appear the mountains of earth; sometimes we are especially fortunate, and we follow a shaft of light that pierces the haze, stabs quickly all the way down to the earth, and illuminates the edge of steeply-falling cliffs.

But we did not come up here—much as we enjoy the heavens in so spectacular a display—without purpose. Dick takes the controls; he throttles back, and we take up a new heading of 270 degrees. We are looking for a valley, a deep hollow between the towering mountains of Nevada.

Dick presses the radio switch on the throttle. "Thunderbird Leader, this is Thunderbird Seven. Where are you, Boss?"

The earphones crackle. "Hello, Richard. We're over the lake. Griff and Cass are over the bombing range, heading back. You characters coming down for a visit?"

The "boss" is Major Robert S. Fitzgerald, Leader of the Thunderbirds team. At the moment the four-plane diamond formation is over Thunderbird Lake. This is a roughly circular dry lake bed, lying deep within mountains that loom to all sides. But to the northwest there is a finger of desert flatland, often the route the swift fighters follow when they come low over the lake to practice their intricate maneuvers.

The Thunderbirds don't necessarily follow the desert lowland because this makes their approach easier into the mountain-ringed dry lake. Not these pilots! They could just as easily fall out of the sky in a perfectly held formation, sliding past the mountains into the deep hollow of the lake, and pulling out into a sweeping horizontal turn exactly where they wish to be. For the four pilots who fly the diamond formation that marks the Thunderbirds to pilots everywhere, rank as the best of precision fliers in the world.

Thunderbird Lake is their practice area, lying within the restricted airspace of the gunnery ranges northwest of Nellis Air Force Base. Nellis operations require a vast controlled airspace from which all other planes are barred. Every week of the year an intensive war is fought in what is known as the Indian Springs Restricted Area. In this desolate and forbidding vastness of the barren desert and mountains, Air Force pilots practice gunnery, rocket, and bombing attacks. The desert hills echo with the cough of machine guns and cannon, the blasting roar of exploding bombs, the sharp hissing crack of rockets, and the acetylene-torch sounds of guided missiles pursuing robot targets high in the air.

Because this airspace is well known to all pilots who fly

through this part of the country, it is perfect for the Thunderbirds. They can practice their intricate maneuvers from speeds of only 90 miles per hour—when they fall in perfect formation from the top of a soaring loop—to 800 miles per hour, when the team's solo pilot screams, bare feet above the desert floor, practicing his supersonic passes, with the knowledge that other aircraft will not fly into their area.

It is necessary that this practice take place at almost ground level. When the Thunderbirds demonstrate to massed audiences the precision jet flying representative of Air Force pilots, they do so at minimum altitudes in order best to show the marvelous skill with which they control their heavy jet fighters. All practice missions are flown right "on the deck," exactly as they are flown before an audience that at times has reached 2,000,000 people. Only, Thunderbird Lake is more demanding of their skill; here the maneuvering area is ringed with massive mountains that demand—on penalty of a fatal crash—constant attention.

The two other Thunderbirds—Captain Herman E. "Griff" Griffin, Solo Pilot, and Captain Robert Cass, Spare Pilot—listen in to our conversation with Fitzgerald. We are on a common channel, and all pilots hear the spoken words of any one man. Griff breaks into the talk: "We're at eight thousand, Dick," he calls. "Will you be coming in from the south?"

"Affirmative. We're at seventeen thousand and descending. We'll break out to the east, over the ridge."

"Roger. We'll be looking for you."

Griff and Cass know our position, our approach, and exactly where we will descend from beneath the clouds. Dick lowers the nose to a steeper rate of descent, and the F-100F streaks from the sky, dropping toward the clouds. We pull out exactly at the cloud tops, and the opportunity for this type of flying, which comes all too rarely, can't be denied.

Again we have plunged into the beautiful world of flight. At 700 miles per hour we skim the edges of the clouds, flashing in and out of foaming whiteness, exploding into sunlight and as rapidly plunging back into the clouds. We turn and head for the sun; because of the haze and the clouds the flaming orb in the sky becomes a clearly defined disk, still brilliant but not unbearable to the eyes. It has gained a new and strange levitation; the disk seems to be clearly outlined as it alternately appears and disappears because of the clouds. It hangs motionless; because of the impression of speed created by the clouds through which we race, it is we who hurtle onward toward that great fiery orb.

A touch of the stick, and we are into the clouds; a moment later we are through.

We burst upon one of the most stunning sights I have ever seen in many years of flying. Framed by the great vault of broken clouds above our heads, built up by towering walls of mountain, we enter upon a scene of cathedral-like majesty. I have never seen its like before, or since.

It is a moment out of time and space.

The sun spears great shafts of golden light through the clouds; these appear as luminous pillars that seem to rise out of the desert floor and the mountains, and rush away into space. The haze over the lake bed is thicker; because of the variations in light and shadow we seem to be swimming through water of unusual clarity. Directly beneath us is the lake bed, to our sides the looming peaks. The world has disappeared, leaving only this vast cathedral of flight.

It seems that we have descended close to the surface of the dry lake. But . . . no! Almost at the same moment Dick and I see the diamond formation flash. We are much higher than I believed. Miles away, rushing in almost at ground level from the finger of desert to the northwest, there appears a sudden flash of light, a glitter of sun off silver wings.

They are so small! The four airplanes are as one, barely distinct as sweptwing fighters. They appear to be no more than silver darts, but as we race toward them, closing at a combined speed of better than 1,200 miles per hour, they magnify in size. They are still tiny, but at least clearly discernible now as the F-100 fighters of the team. Fitzgerald's voice comes over the common channel. "Okay, gang, smoke on—*now*."

Behind the dartlike shapes a finger draws a line over the desert floor, a double finger. A growing lance of white, the fighters to each side and behind Fitzgerald's F-100 pour out a streamer of smoke. From here it appears as a single thin

16

band; the second line is the shadow of that smoke on the lake bed. Smoke that assists massed crowds better to follow the planes in their maneuvers. Now it has a strange quality of light and shadow that can be seen only from on high.

The Thunderbirds.

Nothing so emphasizes the feeling of motion through deep waters as this moment. The tiny airplanes are not what they really are; the wonder of our surroundings, the haze and shadows, the surrounding walls of mountains, all these turn the four heavy jet fighters into tiny silver minnows, flashing through still waters. It *is* an ocean, the observer swears. But then the Thunderbirds change their shape, and there is neither fish in the sea nor bird in the sky that can match the wonder of the next few moments.

We swing around the lake in a great turn. Dick has eased off on the throttle to a gentle 500 miles per hour. We are banked steeply, turning within the boundaries formed by the mountain ridges. At 500 miles per hour this imposes a constant force of two g's—twice that of gravity—on our bodies, but we hardly take notice. The team is entering its most famous maneuver—the Bomb Burst—and it is a sight that commands our attention.

Trailing their lance of white, the four airplanes—each one so close that their wingtips overlap, and barely five feet

17

separate one fighter from the other—reach the center of the lake bed. "Okay, Thunderbirds," calls Fitzgerald in his quiet voice, "let's make this a good one. Coming back on the pull . . ."

Four airplanes have become one. In perfect unison four pilots ease back on their sticks, then harder. The diamond formation breaks from its level flight, points higher and higher into the sky. It is a breathtaking sight. . . . They rush away from the earth, 600 miles per hour, the diamond going straight up. Higher, and higher.

"Prepare to break . . . Okay, break—*now.*" The Leader calling out the signals to his men. At the moment that Fitzgerald says *"now"* the diamond formation explodes, each Super Sabre bursting away from the other. I have seen the Thunderbirds perform this maneuver dozens of times, while I watched from the ground. But here and now, within this vast amphitheater of nature, the sight is . . . well, beautiful is the proper word.

Each fighter hurtles away from a single point of the climb They break with great speed in four different directions— the cardinal points of the compass. As they flash away from one another, soaring up and over in a tremendous sweeping arc, the pilots send the Super Sabres spinning through rapid aileron rolls. It is spectacular. As the jet fighters whirl through the rolls their wings flash like intense lights from sun reflection. Behind them the smoke corkscrews along the path of flight, revealing clearly the great arc.

Then each man stops the roll. Now the F-100's are inverted, on their backs. Every pilot has the stick back. The four airplanes increase the distance between them. Fitzgerald turned on his smoke as he called for the break, and as we circle above them, trying to keep each racing plane in sight, the pilots have reached a vertical dive. Each Super Sabre plunges for the earth with increasing speed. Faster and faster—700 miles per hour as they flatten out of their dives.

Then they are nearly level, rushing toward a common center over the lake bed. Each plane is aimed like a bullet— indeed, the speed of each F-100 is nearly 200 miles per hour faster than a .45 caliber bullet!—at a crossover point. From east, west, north, and south they scream toward that climax of the maneuver. Combined approach speed of the fighters heading toward one another—faster than 1,400 miles per hour!

Captain Neil Eddins, the Slot Man, calls out, "You're a little low, Fitz." Fitzgerald acknowledges, picks up a few feet in height. We watch breathlessly. Four lances of white smoke, a silver minnow leading each thread through the sky, barely thirty feet above the ground.

They cross! All four fighters, plunging with tremendous speed, flash over the same point on the ground with less than a second from approach to passing, and racing away from one another!

It is a fabulous sight. Dick chuckles. "How do you like *that*, Marty?"

"Whew!" What else is there to say!

The Super Sabres soar higher and higher; Fitz pulls up and over into a half Cuban Eight within the boundary of the amphitheater, exactly as he would behind a watching audience after the crossover. He rolls out and then, coming down the back side toward the position of his invisible audience, moves out to their front as the other three planes with blazing afterburners hasten to catch him. The Wingmen have chandelled right and left after the crossover to rejoin, and the Slot Man has soared through another complete loop. They all slide back into the tight diamond formation.

Suddenly another voice breaks in on the channel. "Richard, you have just *never* learned to watch where you're going. Don't look now, Dad, but you've got company." I look off our right wing. I should be startled, but I've had time to expect anything with the Thunderbirds.

A powerful, sleek Super Sabre sits—not off our wing, but literally almost on top of us. It's Griffin, the Solo Pilot. While we watched the diamond formation he and Cass have raced around without our seeing their approach, and slid in to the tightest possible formation. At least six feet of Griff's wing juts over ours, no more than a foot below. And to our left looms another big fighter—Bob Cass—helping Griff herd us from both sides.

In the gentle turbulence of the air the three airplanes rock and bob gently. Griff and Cass, if this is at all possible, slide

19

in a little closer. Dick squeezes the radio button. "G'wan, you clowns," he growls, "go chase yourselves—we got work to do!"

There is a blur of motion; Griff's fighter explodes away from us, rolling like a dervish, snapping out 200 feet away. On the other side Cass has duplicated the maneuver, precise, perfect . . . and then they are gone, joined in formation, dropping for the desert floor.

We remain over Thunderbird Lake for another hour, and it is without question the most wonderful sixty minutes I have ever spent in the air. For with Dick I join the Thunderbirds in their spectacular maneuvers . . . and it is quite the thing to be flying with the most famous jet precision team in the world.

2 The Mission

It was on Okinawa, late in 1959, that the Thunderbirds were provided one of their rare opportunities to "throw away the crutches" in flying their full aerial demonstration. The site was bleak and forbidding—the Easley Bombing and Gunnery Range on the eastern shore of Okinawa, north of the town of Ishikawa.

At Easley Range there is nothing that even remotely resembles flat land. Cliffs rise steeply from the shore road, and from their edge there is a plunge of 500 feet down to a rock-studded shoreline. The area is all gorges and gullies; behind these are towering mountain peaks. Here the Thunderbirds would perform for thousands of Air Force and Army personnel and their families, as well as many thousands of Okinawan natives.

On the day of the scheduled demonstration it looked like a fine time for staying home in bed. Among the mountain peaks the clouds seethed wildly, twisting and shredding as the wind flung them along. On the ground it was cold and bitter, and the wind blowing along the surface at forty miles per hour made the waiting throng miserable.

When the Thunderbirds display their precision wares in aerial demonstrations in the United States they do so under restrictions of which the audience is blissfully unaware. Nothing happens in the skies in this country without the blessings of the Federal Aviation Agency. The Thunderbirds comply with all operating restrictions imposed by FAA, and FAA in return is usually overwhelmingly cautious in their approach to air safety. With this theme the Thunderbirds have no argument, and they have never exceeded limitations.

But the pilots sometimes *do* chafe at the bit ... and Easley Range was one of those wonderful opportunities to fly as the team had trained to fly, and could do so with their marvelous skill. First, the area for the flight was a bombing and gunnery range, and the fighter pilots who fought their own private war here from week to week often came as low as you can fly without scraping rock. There weren't any operating restrictions; when the show was over, there wasn't a man or woman in that audience of many thousands without weak knees.

Herman Griffin opened the show from the north.

As usual, Herman made sure that no one saw him coming. Dick Crane was at the microphone, explaining to the crowd the aims, mission, training, and background of the Thunderbirds. He makes sure never to look in the direction from which Herman will approach. In fact, Dick is one of those rare public announcers who talks with a stop watch on the basis of second-by-second counting. And just as he was winding up his last few words, without an airplane in the sky—a visible airplane, anyway—Herman hit the viewing stands like a bomb.

In the United States the Thunderbirds stay just short of supersonic. The sonic boom can be an almighty blast of thunder that leaves home owners very unhappy, and so the supersonic F-100C's of the team only on rare occasions tear through the sonic wall. But at Easley Range there weren't any houses, and there weren't any operating restrictions in respect to speed.

Herman made a wide detour around the island, dropped the nose of the Super Sabre, and kicked into afterburner. Herman has a habit of timing his opening of the Thunderbirds' performance with his solo act to the exact second, and on this day he couldn't have timed it better.

He hit supersonic while over the water, still well below the rim of the plateau, then burst over the horizon as he rushed toward a point that would bring him just before and passing by the audience. Of course he was now moving so fast that his sound was well behind him. There was absolutely no warning. . . .

Frank Harvey, a close friend and one of the nation's outstanding aviation writers, was at the Easley Range that morning. Frank isn't easily impressed with flying. Although until this moment he'd never seen the Thunderbirds perform, he has seen other jet demonstration teams. He has also done a fair amount of flying himself, including towering climbs with loops at 650 miles per hour in a six-jet, 100-ton bomber. I mention these things because they add to the meaning of a letter Frank wrote me from Okinawa, describing his introduction as a spectator to the Thunderbirds. Frank wrote:

"It was like an artillery shell. It was twelve feet up. When Herman came over it was a star spangled blur and a vivid smear of afterburner fire and a shock wave of sound and fury that sandbagged me right to my knees. And then Herman was going straight up through a patch of bright blue sky, and he was rolling—one, two, three, four, five, six, seven, eight—growing toy-tiny, and *then*, without any warning, the four-plane diamond hit us from behind, slightly higher than Herman, but not much, in the screaming cry of full afterburners. . . .

"I've never known anything like it. I grabbed my ears and dodged behind a GI. The next thing I knew we were in a tangle of dust and arms and legs; several guys had thrown themselves flat and were spitting out dirt. There was that momentary roaring silence, and one awed, aggrieved voice split the air with an anguished yelp: 'Leaping catfish! I wouldn't be inna Air Force! Not if they make ya do that crazy stuff!'

"I kept my eyes glued to the diamond. They were beautiful; it's the only way I can describe it. The formation was barrel-rolling now, skimming the welter of gullies and knobs, and it was a wonderful kind of precision I didn't know existed. It was as if the four planes had all been mounted on a big sheet of glass and somebody was rotating the sheet. They tilted gently upward. They went smoothly over on their backs. They slid gently downward into level flight. They were wired, rigid, perfect.

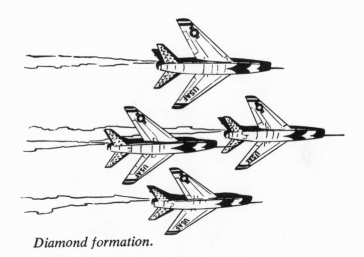

Diamond formation.

"I watched the tight diamond slide apart in a fluid motion, and then three red-white-and-blue birds were sniffing the tail of the leader in a close-order line and all trailing white smoke. They profiled the cliff and streaked low over the shining surface of the sea. They turned—four glinting specks—a centiplane with a cottony flowing tail, and headed back toward us. As they climbed the cliff I was privileged to look *down* on the Thunderbirds.

"I was just relaxing a bit, when Herman was back.

"He came by upside down. Right on the edge of sound. He was so low that I looked straight across the gullies and saw the smudge of his upside-down helmet inside the canopy. Still inverted, Herman kicked into afterburner and an orange torch full of blazing shock diamonds boomed from his tailpipe. Then the formation passed over us, in trail, and their white smoke drifted down across the rocky ground.

"Dick Crane was working the public-address system. 'The three-hundred-and-sixty-degree vertical turn is coming up.

Major Fitz will probably lead them a little high, to clear the mountains—'

"Marty, that's what Pappy Crane said, but believe me, Fitz did *not* lead them a little high, to clear the mountains. Fitz had his boys cocked vertically going into the ring of mountains, a diamond pattern of bright Vee-winged toys, a good two thousand feet below the rim. They were too low to get over. They were too fast to turn back. They *had* to pull their vertical turn, they just *had* to . . ."

Let me interject a word here for the moment. For Frank —and to the audience, of course—this was an incredible maneuver that put the Thunderbirds on the brink of disaster. Actually, it wasn't anything of the sort. But Frank never had the opportunity, as I did, to fly with the Thunderbirds in that deep mountain-created punchbowl in the Nevada desert.

"The fighters were reefing it in tighter and tighter as they sucked toward the wall of rock, and there was a limit to *that*. Fitz could black out, or any of his boys could—or they could load those heavy fighters with so many g's of centrifugal force that the monsters would stall, stumble at high speed and hit the cliffs out of control . . .

"And then I realized that Major Fitzgerald, if anyone did, knew about high-speed stalls, that he was a master at flying. He played it ice-cold like the top pro he truly is. He let the g-loaded Super Sabres sink as close to the flying blur of rocks as he could while still giving his boys the greatest possible margin of stall safety—and they burst out of what seemed like a trap of mountains, silhouetted against the blue horizon sky, and I cheered. Damn, but I cheered, and so did everyone else, a great roar that swelled up and drowned even the thunder of those four powerful jets.

"Marty, now I know what you've been telling me about this team. They are the most fabulous group of fliers I have ever seen in all my years in aviation. When the show was over—even though the audience knew that the pilots couldn't hear them—to a man they rose to their feet and applauded and shouted themselves hoarse. It was the damndest demonstration I ever saw. And I wish you could have seen Pappy

Crane at that moment ... he was the proudest-looking 'father' in the world!"

Since they were first organized in May, 1953, the Thunderbirds have demonstrated precision jet-flying—in the four-plane diamond formation and with the solo pilot—before some *forty million spectators*. Nearly 600 individual airshows were required to amass this incredible figure of personal appearances, and this does not include the aggregate of another 400 million people who have watched the performance of the team on nationwide television programs.

Citizens of the United States, Canada, Puerto Rico, Bermuda, the nations of Central and South America, of Okinawa, Japan, Taiwan and other Far East countries, and others, have for hours willingly endured the gamut of weather—blistering heat to bitter cold—in order not to miss the Thunderbirds.

Their appearances have created mass traffic jams in every country. They have been feted and acclaimed everywhere the diamond-shaped formation has flown. Their demonstrations have been preceded with banner headlines in leading newspapers, with running announcements on television and radio. Schools often close their doors in order to allow the students to see the most famous precision flying team in the world.

Military pilots—with many thousands of hours jet flying time—go out of their way to watch the Thunderbirds in the air. And they are just as impressed and excited as the teen-age youths who see in the split-second precision flying of the team the future they want more than anything else—to be a jet pilot, "just like the Thunderbirds."

Therein, perhaps, lies one of the many reasons behind the decision in 1953 to create the famed demonstration team. Officially, the Thunderbirds are the 4520th Aerial Demonstration Team, under the command of the Office of the Secretary of the Air Force, Headquarters, USAF, and supported by the 4520th Combat Crew Training Wing with headquarters at Nellis Air Force Base, Nevada. Brigadier General John N. Ewbank, Nellis commander, has a brilliant combat record with the USAF, and brings to the team one of its most understanding and staunch supporters. The wing itself is part and parcel of the Tactical Air Command, an organization which has been forced by two masters—the ominous threat of war, and the sharp bite of financial austerity—to keep itself in a condition of razor-sharp combat readiness.

This is a vital point in the makeup of the Thunderbirds. They are in themselves a superb combat-ready team. Their skill as individual pilots alone is sufficient to command attention, but of greater significance is their ability to function with such precision and *teamwork*.

Take this military designation—*4520th Aerial Demonstration Team*. Just what does this mean? To put on a brilliant, even dazzling air show? Is that all? Does this justify the effort and expense of organizing a group of fighter planes, each costing more than $750,000, plus the support aircraft, the mechanics and technicians and administrative personnel, the fuel and facilities, and all the other vital elements that make up a compact flying group, just to impress all those millions of people with the ability of Air Force pilots?

On its own, of course, this would hardly constitute justification for considerable effort and cost. It doesn't; an economy-minded Congress would have wielded the ax long before now if the Air Force could not show, dramatically and positively, that the Thunderbirds have produced results which beyond all question enhance a greater public support and a richer understanding of our national airpower among the free peoples of the world.

The Far East tour, for example, not only enhanced the team's capability to perform an Air Force mission in dramatic fashion, but it highlighted a significant change in that mission and the team's goals.

This was the first time that native Okinawans had ever seen a performance of this kind. To many Oriental minds, the team gave an aerial ballet that literally danced through the heavens as those fliers maneuvered their planes. Others saw the deeper meaning behind the Team's outstanding professional airmanship—the common goal of the Free World—an effective, highly polished "power for peace."

The Far East tour of the Thunderbirds, which opened the

floodgates to a cascade of congratulatory messages in the mail and the highest accolades in the press of the nations visited, lent special emphasis to the meaning that the Thunderbirds were truly a world-wide airpower demonstration team. Their mission was considerably greater than helping to promote a better understanding and appreciation of airpower around the globe; it assisted with the strongest effectiveness the advancement and support of the national policy objectives of our country.

"Buddy system" for refueling F-100 fighters.

Let's look at it yet another way. The American citizen is required to carry a staggering financial burden every year in taxes. A substantial portion of his tax dollar pays for his national airpower—and a crucial part of that airpower is made up by the Tactical Air Command.

Now tactical airpower doesn't mean the same thing it did in World War II when our pilots flew the old Maurauders, Mitchells, and Havocs. The Tactical Air Command that exists today operates under a vastly changed concept. It no longer has a fixed area of operation distinct from other organizations within the Air Force. The supersonic jet fighter and bomber, the atomic and hydrogen bomb, and a handy technique known as air refueling have made TAC a supersonic retaliatory strike force that reaches out to every point on this planet.

Reduced to its essentials, TAC's primary mission—should the whistle ever blow—is to deliver both atomic and thermonuclear weapons against enemy bases. Anywhere, and at any time. And not only enemy bases—for a single F-100C fighter plane, exactly like the one flown by the Thunderbirds, packs a wallop so devastating that it can smash an entire city. There's a secondary mission as well. This includes the full gamut of aerial war—it means air-to-air combat

Super Sabre ... in combat dress.

against enemy aircraft. It calls for the delivery of strikes with everything from cannon and rockets to small atomic bombs for air-to-ground support missions. It means doubling in brass as an intercepter defense for our own cities and factories. In sum—name any requirement of air combat from the treetops to 60,000 feet, from over Kansas to deep into Russia and China, Africa or Europe—*anywhere*—and you'll find that TAC is charged with that requirement.

A single F-100C fighter or the F-100D fighter-bomber (the Thunderbirds have flown with both) can carry a bomb tonnage payload that exceeds that of a World War II B-17 heavy bomber. More important, the destructive force hung beneath that fighter's wings is greater than the massive blow that could be hurled against an enemy target by an all-out heavy bomber mission of World War II.

Because the heavy jet fighters can be refueled in mid-air—

and have been refueled many tens of thousands of times, under all conditions around the world—TAC has long been a *realistic* global striking force. It maintains what are known as composite striking forces; in simulated and actual emergencies, TAC squadrons have deployed in a matter of hours halfway around the world—"cocked" for a shooting war at a moment's notice. At Myrtle Beach Air Force Base I have watched these men under alert; commanded by Colonel Francis Gabreski (leading ace in World War II in Europe, a jet ace with seven kills in Korea, he is the country's number one living ace), these men have been on their way overseas within only a few hours after the "red alert" was sounded.

I have also watched F-100 fighter pilots sharpen their combat claws on the gunnery and bombing ranges in the desert. I have been knocked off my feet as the Super Sabres screamed in twenty feet off the deck, blasting away at targets with a bristling array of weapons ranging from 20-mm cannon on up through simulated atomic bombs. At these ranges they make firing passes at targets towed by other fighters, and also at speedy jet drones. They attack dummy factories, buildings, trains, convoys and other targets.

Nellis Air Force Base—the 4520th Combat Crew Training Wing—is the polish and perfection station where the F-100 fighter pilots truly become killers with their powerful airplanes. Week after week, they start their combat training at seven in the morning.

Delivering an atomic bomb calls for some very special tactics. The F-100 pilot must provide himself an "escape time"—or be destroyed in the atomic holocaust of his own attack. So he learns to "toss" or "flip" the bomb on target, and be miles away before the mechanism in the falling bomb whirs, and that searing fireball leaps into existence.

Every TAC fighter pilot is skilled in dive, over-the-shoulder, and toss-bombing techniques. In the dive-bombing attack, the fighter comes in fast, diving from 35,000 or 40,000 feet down to 14,000 feet. At this point he releases his bomb, pulls out in a punishing zoom, and races away at supersonic speed while the bomb is falling toward the target.

"Down on the deck is where you stay alive," best describes the over-the-shoulder technique. It's a fabulous maneuver.

To elude radar defenses, the pilot streaks in at treetop level. Over the target he pulls straight up to 5,000 feet and releases his bomb, which zooms up another 5,000 feet—while the pilot soars upward into an Immelmann maneuver at 10,000 feet. It takes the bomb fifty-five seconds to strike; by that time the airplane is well out of blast range.

Toss-bombing is reserved for the heavily defended target. The Super Sabre races in at medium height, pulls up into a

Preparing F-100D for Pacific flight.

steep climb while still several thousand yards from the objective. While the pilot continues on upward and over on his back in the Immelmann—at the top of the loop he half-rolls into level flight—the bomb is carried by centrifugal force around a great soaring arc, and then falls into the target.

Every one of these three maneuvers requires tremendous skill. Before the pilot graduates from Nellis, for example, he must demonstrate that he can dive-bomb almost straight down at a target from 15,000 feet; come in at a target no more than twenty-five feet off the ground and skip a bomb squarely through the middle of that target; perform high- and low-angle strafing, and "thread needles" with tank-busting rockets.

It is impossible to believe the accuracy these men attain. I have seen an F-100D fighter-bomber hurtle low over the desert, and the pilot pick out a hatch in a tank through which he sent his bomb. He then came around, picked a second tank, and cleanly took the turret off with another bomb.

Nothing so effectively tells the story of TAC fighter-pilot skill in aerial combat than the record in Korea—approximately one thousand MiG-15 fighters went down for a loss of some eighty F-86 Sabres.

And right here we reach the heart of the matter, in respect to the actual Thunderbird demonstration. "The ultimate in precision flying" is a term quite often used to explain the Thunderbird maneuvers. And so it is. Precision flying in formation is just another way of saying teamwork. And teamwork is the key to successful air combat.

We learned this lesson in bitter fashion in World War II. Our concept of aerial battle resolved the early engagements into wild, free-for-all individual dogfights. Until we learned that the fighter plane was a much more effective *weapon*— when flown by men who were skilled and who would as a team co-ordinate their flying perfectly—we lost a lot of good men who otherwise would never have been shot down. This is the brunt of it. We learned this lesson at the hands of Japanese Zero fighter pilots, who delighted in any American flier who wanted to dogfight. The nimble Zero hacked our heavier planes to pieces.

One of the little known episodes of that air war took place over North Africa in November 1942. Navy pilots flying Grumman Wildcats flew against French pilots who flew old Curtiss P-36 Hawk fighters provided France under our foreign aid program. The French pilots were superb, members of the famed Lafayette Escadrille. Their airplanes were old—slower, poorly armed, generally inferior to the Wildcats. But in every battle the superior *skill in teamwork* of the French pilots broke up the Wildcat formations and scattered our men.

It didn't take long for the lesson to sink home. Precision flying, teamwork—these were the new rules of aerial war. We learned the rules, and whenever our pilots flew this way they achieved tremendous successes against their opponents.

Korea was the graduation class, so to speak. The MiG-15 fighter plane had approximately the same power as our North American F-86 Sabre, but it was much lighter in weight. It was faster than the Sabre, it could climb faster, it flew to greater heights, and at high altitudes it reminded our pilots of the Zero—it could turn in a much shorter radius than could our heavier Sabres.

But even with these considerable advantages on their side, the MiG pilots couldn't cope with the Sabre as a *weapon*. And weapon takes in many categories—it refers to structural integrity, to solid firepower, to reliability of components, and above all to the proper use of the fighter airplane by its pilots.

In Korea our fighter pilots flew as teams. The battle area was so delineated south of the Yalu River that the MiG's almost always enjoyed the classic position of attack: high above the Sabres, and diving out of the sun—blinding the American pilots who had to look into the glaring disk in the sky.

Yet we shot down more than a thousand Russian fighter airplanes for just about eighty Sabres. The key was teamwork and precision flying. Our pilots flew as though they were glued together. The basic weapon was the four-plane formation; it provided maximum offensive and defensive fire power and protection. The four planes flew as one; every pilot co-ordinated with his wingmen. It worked. The scoreboard is blazing proof of its fantastic success.

And this brings us back to the Thunderbirds. The men who fly the glittering Super Sabres of the Thunderbirds team haven't been especially selected and assigned to the team in order to develop their precision flying to the exclusion of their roles as fighter pilots. Far from it. The Thunderbirds pilots serve on the team for a two-year tour of duty. When those two years are up they move out to another assignment, and a replacement pilot moves in.

Two years is the limit. This is proof of the fact that the Thunderbirds whom the millions of people watch in the air are representative of the skilled Air Force fighter pilot.

Assignment to the team is, obviously, a coveted honor. Only the best are accepted. In this instance, however, the "best" is all-inclusive, taking in as it does areas of importance other than piloting ability.

Any unit, civilian or military, is only as good as the caliber of its individual men. The Thunderbirds are convinced that they have in their team members the best the Air Force has to offer. The team is the "showpiece" of the Air Force. To qualify, every man must possess outstanding skill and ability in his work, he must at all times have an irreproachable military bearing and appearance, and conduct himself always in a fashion that reflects only the highest credit on his Wing, his Air Force, and his country.

Every man on the team—from the grease monkey to the leader—is a volunteer. The catch is that there are about a thousand highly qualified volunteers for every vacancy that comes up. Pilots who measure their jet time in *years*—not in hundreds or thousands of hours—who are combat veterans and perhaps aces, who wear a fistful of decorations, who have a record for superb skill in the air . . . these are the volunteers for the Thunderbirds.

The only way for a man to join the Thunderbirds is first to be sure he has the basic qualifications on his flying record. But that isn't enough. For the ability to fly impeccably only opens the door. He must be able to maintain an appearance beyond reproach, to meet with the public from exuberant kids to the elderly, to get along so well with his flying mates that there isn't any chance of friction among the pilots. Because the slightest rub between these men can wreck not only a show, but perhaps the formation at a critical moment, and kill a man.

I discussed this subject at length with Major J. A. "Robby" Robinson, who led the Thunderbirds team before relinquishing the Leader's position to Fitzgerald. Robby's background in the air includes outstanding performance as a radar-bombardier with the Strategic Air Command, as well as his brilliant flying record. With the 4th Fighter Group, he took the first F-86 Sabres into Korean combat, flying seventy-four missions. He has also served with the 48th Fighter Group in France and the 36th Fighter Group in Germany. Robby is a gifted, skilled pilot—more important, he is an outstanding leader.

"One of our worst enemies on a long trip," he explained, "was ourselves—and this doesn't change from team to team. When we're on the road for show after show, flying day after day in demonstrations, and practicing steadily in between those shows, we just about live in each other's pockets. We live, eat, sleep, work, fly, travel—we do everything together. It's impossible for men to live under these conditions without getting tired of one another; it's just human nature. You know how close we have to stay, when we must all dress alike, go to this dinner or to that television interview, and so forth. Privacy is a word that gets more and more delicious with every day. If there is the slightest rub between anyone, well, the tension mounts as the trip progresses, and the greatest care must be taken by the leader to watch everything. A guy gets lonesome for his wife and his kids, and we can't let that go too far. One bad disposition could spoil a lot of the things we are trying to accomplish.

"And it's nothing short of wonderful, I suppose, that the team—all the teams—have been just as much a team on the ground as they have been in the air.

"The manner in which I picked my team had an awful lot to do with the future success of any man. I often threatened to interview the wives before I did the guys. This is how important I consider them. We were often gone for long periods, and it was absolutely essential that a wife be tolerant of her guy when he came home—bushed physically, tired emotionally. The wife was just as much a member of the team as her pilot husband; she had to share in the team's pride, in it's accomplishments. She had to *want* the team to succeed, and that called for some sacrifice on her part as well.

"If a pilot was made unhappy at home, every one of us would suffer. And the record of these girls has been tremendous; just marvelous.

"I always picked the fellow for the team with the first proviso that he could get along with people, that he was a type who could appear as the clean-cut kid—except for Baldy Griff, of course!—and only then we considered flying ability. As far as I was concerned, his flying ability was resolved on the basis of one thing—on the first try, our first flight together, he had to stick to my wing, keep me in sight, no matter what I did. Everything else would come through training.

"If he showed the desire—and this was really the crux of the matter—we taught him the fine points. After the practice we put the new pilots through, and we kept at it day after day after day, they could fly wing right through a hurricane.

"I always made it a strict, standing rule never to miss a

day of practice. We practiced on weekdays, on Saturdays and Sundays, on holidays. The longest stretch of time we ever took off in two years was after we had been gone for many weeks; and at that we took exactly forty-eight hours off and no more. It was amazing how rusty we could get after even a short layoff.

"I always felt that we were trying to put on the best show we possibly could, and the rest of the business came after we were down from flying. And never once, not on a single occasion, did my boys ever do less than their very best. This may sound a bit corny, but the two years with the Thunderbirds are the best I have ever spent in my entire life. When you're flying with that outfit, you know you're part of the best team ever."

We've learned that the key to successful air-to-air combat is teamwork, that precision flying comes only from teamwork, skill, and constant practice. The precision exhibited by the Thunderbirds before their massed audiences is a direct product of the Air Force's tactical flying programs. It is related directly to the combat effectiveness of airpower. The modern airplane is the most destructive weapon ever conceived—yet any instrument, regardless of its capabilities, is less than effective in the hands of an unskilled operator.

These are the facts of life. The more precisely a pilot can fly, the more effective he will be with his weapon.

When the Thunderbirds' diamond formation sweeps through the skies in their dazzling, knife-sharp performance, they are demonstrating to the American public—every element of that public—an important part of the power of their Air Force. The public pays for that airpower. The Thunderbirds are a unique manner of demonstrating their return for their dollar. It's *their* Air Force, and this is the most effective means of bringing that Air Force home to them.

Not a single phase of the Thunderbirds' performance is created especially as a crowd thriller. When the Thunderbirds fly their close-knit diamond formation, they are demonstrating an adaptation of the four-ship formation that has been used with such outstanding results in combat. Not only for air-to-air work, but to provide a broad frontal wave for ground attack—the four-ship formation has an appalling effect in a napalm strike, for example, literally inundating its target with an ocean of searing fire.

When Herman Griffin makes his opening pass in front of the audience, he isn't carrying out a stunt. His maneuver is virtually a duplicate of the sneak run for the over-the-shoulder bombing strike. When he streaks low over the ground in inverted flight, or holding his fabulous eight-point roll, he demonstrates the capabilities and maneuverability of his weapon—the airplane.

Later in this book we will meet the pilots who fly the Super Sabres of the Thunderbirds. Suffice for the moment to say that most of these men, and the majority of all pilots who have earned their place on the Thunderbirds roster, have flown in combat either as fighter pilots or as fighter-bomber pilots. Every man is an expert at using his F-100C as a superior weapon. There are no stunts or tricks involved; the entire aerial demonstration is that of *airpower*.

When millions of American citizens see the Thunderbirds perform, they have a greater understanding, a richer appreciation of what the weapons of the Air Force look like, how they perform, what are their capabilities. Many thousands of American youngsters are provided the impetus to become air cadets, and the over-all Air Force recruiting program gains from the demonstration. Members of the Air Force, and of the other armed forces, are among the most enthusiastic in the audience—for this is *their* team as well.

But the mission is not restricted to the United States, or only to our own people. The Thunderbirds have flown in many countries around the world. As such, their performance is a tangible, vital demonstration of our airpower capabilities. You cannot stand on the ground with your head back and your eyes following the dazzling flight of the Thunderbirds without being deeply impressed. People of foreign lands who watch the Thunderbirds—and many of them never before even saw any jet airplane—are watching airpower in action. American airpower, swift, powerful, extraordinarily skillful. It is a tremendous boon for our national prestige, for new respect engendered for our country.

Every move is taken to assure that the watching throngs receive a maximum benefit from the flight demonstration. All of the team's maneuvers are executed at low altitude and within a one-mile radius of the demonstration area, and the audience is informed by the team narrator that these are the same basic maneuvers taught all new pilots by the United States Air Force.

The Thunderbirds perform slow rolls, loops, clover-leaf turns, corkscrew rolls, the whifferdill, and a tight 360-degree turn in a vertical bank while maintaining—under a constant, punishing five-g force—their perfect diamond formation.

The solo pilot performs a series of maneuvers, including four-point and eight-point rolls, inverted passes, vertical rolls, and others.

The climax to the aerobatic demonstration, of course, is the Bomb Burst which has gained international fame. In this maneuver the diamond formation (as seen from the ground) climbs vertically in front of the audience, trailing the white smoke streamers. At the leaders' signal each airplane, with a sudden booming roar from the afterburner, breaks out and away from the diamond like an exploding skyrocket. Each F-100 then executes a series of rolls, snaps out on its back and, executing a giant split-S maneuver, dives toward the ground to pull out at minimum altitude. Roaring directly toward each other from the four points of the compass, each pair of fighters closing at better than 1,400 miles per hour, the four Super Sabres cross simultaneously in front of the audience with only a few feet separating each airplane.

It is a fantastic maneuver, unbelievable even when it is personally seen. The airplanes seem to explode out of nowhere over that single crossover point, and in an instant the sky in front of the stands is filled with flashing metal, crisscrossing smoke, the crash of violent thunder, and blurs of afterburner flame. It is a maneuver that is, to put it mildly, critical; it demands absolute perfection in timing and precision flying.

There is yet another—and important—demonstration of the airpower capabilities of the Thunderbirds. Despite opinions to the contrary, they are not dependent upon any organization but their own, in respect to maintenance, servicing, and logistics. When the Thunderbirds leave their home base at Nellis, they travel "complete." The aircraft of the team includes six F-100C fighters, one F-100F two-seat fighter, one C-54 Skymaster four-engine transport, and one twin-engine C-123 Provider transport. Mechanics and specialists in at least one of the transports always fly ahead of the team, meeting the heavy fighters as they land for refueling or servicing. Except for fuel and major overhaul items, the Thunderbirds are self-contained, carrying their own equipment, tools, parts, and facilities.

They are a self-contained combat-ready unit. Their Super Sabres are standard fighter aircraft, with only slight modification to fit them to their aerobatic mission. The four twenty-mm. cannon, for example, have been removed; this was not to reduce the weight of the airplane, for lead weights replaced the cannon in order to maintain a center of gravity. However, space that was saved by this move allowed the installation of special oilcans which feed a thin stream of oil to a pipe in the tail; this pipe squirts the oil directly into the flaming jet blast, creating the smoke used in demonstrations. There are several other minor changes; the gunsights, as another example, have been removed, being unnecessary for the Thunderbirds' aerobatic flying.

Within several hours, however, the Super Sabres can be ready for war, armed to the teeth, in perfect mechanical condition—and flown by one of the deadliest team of pilots anywhere in the world.

3 Leading the Team

Several years ago four sweptwing jet fighters were weaving magic patterns in the sky near the city of Baden-Baden in Germany. The sleek airplanes were the heart of a jet precision team renowned in aviation circles for their superb airmanship. As one machine, they swooped over the earth in a sun-splashed pattern of glinting metal. They raced near the ground, the wingmen watching the leader intently, following his every move. The ground came closer; hands and feet moved in the cockpits, preparing to lift the formation up and away in a graceful soaring climb.

For a reason we shall never know, the leader erred. His fighter dipped too low; the next instant all four of the beautiful airplanes smashed into the earth and in a terrifying blast were torn to pieces.

There was another team, world-famed, skilled in the air and masters at showmanship. Before a scheduled performance, a pilot became ill; he was in no condition to fly. A spare pilot on the team stepped forward, volunteered to take his place. The team leader hesitated; then, spurred on by the fact that hundreds of thousands of people were waiting and would be disappointed by any cancellation, he assented.

It was an error—and a fatal one. The spare pilot lacked the training and the long practice necessary to give him the split-second proficiency he needed for the intricate, delicate formation flying. The team swooped up and over on their backs, flashed gracefully toward the earth, whistled upward again, sliding into new positions. It was beautiful. But then . . . something happened. Turbulence? A slip of the hand on the stick? No one knows, and really it doesn't matter.

Two fighters met, metal crumpled like paper, fuel tanks ruptured. Flame spurted greedily, tasted the fuel, then mushroomed outward in a savage eye of glaring fire. In the shattered, blazing wreckage that plummeted to earth were the bodies of the two pilots.

There is a moral, of course, in these two fatal incidents. Flying with a jet precision team is a terribly unforgiving pastime. It is unforgiving of the team member, it is worse for the team leader. He is the man who makes the decisions. No matter what the reason, when something happens, it takes place under his leadership. It is a heavy, relentless responsibility to shoulder; it does not permit—ever—of negligence.

The Thunderbirds have enjoyed the leadership of superb pilots—and, equally as important—each of those pilots was an outstanding leader. From May, 1953, to October, 1954, Lt. Colonel Dick Catledge took the original Thunderbirds through their paces, and built the foundation upon which all future team members would stand. After Catledge, there appeared Major Jack Broughton, who remained at the Thunderbirds helm for two and a half years. In March, 1957, Major Robby Robinson took over to add some of the more colorful pages to the Thunderbirds' history. The fourth and current team leader is the most experienced of all the men who assumed command, with a long record of skilled aerobatic flying—Major Robert S. Fitzgerald, who had the unique distinction in 1946 of organizing, with 1st Lieutenant J. Fenton, the Air Force's first aerobatic team—the famous duo of *Fenton and Fitzgerald.*

Fitz—or Boss, as the Thunderbirds pilots call their team leader—isn't the easiest man in the world to know. He's a ruggedly handsome Irishman, quiet, fabulous in the cockpit—and a hard driving taskmaster in the air and on the ground. I had the great fortune to live with this team, and so I came to know Fitz quite well.

The Thunderbirds have never been so hot as they are right now; without fear of criticism, I'll state flatly that their almost unbelievable precision stems from the ceaseless drive, training, understanding, and leadership of one Bob Fitzgerald.

Fitz isn't just a flier, or even an outstanding pilot—he seems to be flying itself.

There are some men to whom there can be no life without flying. Fitz is such a man. Ever since he was old enough to reason—an age he labels as beginning at seven years—Fitz has wanted nothing so much as to fly. Flying became the primary motivating factor in his life. He went through what may be described as the routine for all youngsters with skydust in their eyes, building models, hanging around airports, gazing with both rapture and hope at the airplanes that bumped and soared around the grass strips and the concrete runways.

Flying was always all around him. He grew up only fifteen miles from Mitchel Field on Long Island, New York, and there were other airplanes and fields to beckon to the boy. Jamaica Sea Airport, Zahns, Curtiss Field, Flushing Airport, Roosevelt Field, and more.

In 1941 Fitz scrimped and sweated and saved until he had accumulated the great sum of twelve dollars. With the change and crumpled dollar bills jammed into a pocket, he dashed off to Flushing Airport to buy his first airplane ride. His forty-five minutes in an ancient Aeronca stirred a clinical, rather than an emotional, reaction—still a sign of the Fitz-gerald today.

What he had believed about his life in flying was confirmed the moment the fabric airplane's wheels left the cinder runway at Flushing. To Fitz this was only another proof that the road ahead was long and demanding of dedicated work. Flying cost money; money came dearly. It was a precise analysis of his future—but then Fitzgerald has always believed, and practiced, that everything in flying is done with the scalpel of precision. Anything less is sloppy.

We talked in his small office at Nellis Air Force Base after a training mission about his early aviation career. Fitz deftly lifted my tobacco pouch from my pocket, tamped the evil weed into a battered pipe, and happily blew a cloud of sulphurous smoke into the room. His words drifted through the blue haze. "My motivating ambition has always been to be a military aviator," he mused. "Everything I've ever done has been along that line. My schooling, even the sports I played. That was designed to get me a scholarship into a college, which I knew I needed to meet the requirements for a military aviator."

A sergeant staggered through the smoke to drop some papers into Fitz's *IN* basket, and groped his way out again. Fitz grinned, and went on. "Perseverance paid off, I guess. I got that scholarship to Ohio State University. . . ."

Waiting to enter college, Fitzgerald didn't allow time to waste; he simply had too much to do. He spent his summer days working in a machine shop to save the money he would need in college. Spurred on by the crying demand to earn his wings one day, Fitz attended summer school at night, and spent every spare minute he could squeeze out of this schedule to travel to Warwick, New York, where he flew in the Civilian Pilot Training Program to earn his private pilot license.

Never one to let an opportunity pass by, Fitz drove to Mitchel Field and enlisted in the Army Air Corps. The recruiting sergeant raised his eyebrows when Fitz insisted—in writing—that he not be called to active duty until he completed his private flying training.

But, as happened with several million other young men,

a war—a big war—tossed all of Fitz's carefully laid plans into the nearest wastebasket. He never had the chance to use that scholarship, because he reported for duty as an aviation cadet. Regrets? Never. Fitz was right where he always wanted to be—behind the control stick of a military airplane.

It's difficult to reconcile the past with the Major's amazing skill with a fighter plane today, but Fitz never flew in World War II as a fighter pilot. Instead, he sat in the left seat of a lumbering four-engine B-24 bomber of the Fifth Air Force, droning far out over the Pacific in single-plane, long-range reconnaissance missions. Sometimes, however, there was a need to come in fast and low, and Fitz relinquished the heavy B-24 for a twin-engine B-25 Mitchell in which the mode of flying was somewhat different—in this case you tried to stay above the treetops. Most of his missions were staged out of Nadzab, New Guinea, and places Fitz had never before heard of—Hollandia, Biak, the Halmalneras, Morotai, and others—became as familiar as home. Before he left the Fifth Air Force, Fitz flew a total of 340 combat hours.

He waved his hand and shrugged. "It was the usual routine," he explained as he blew another cloud of smoke into the room. "We flew most of our missions at twenty thousand, met a few Zeros, shot at each other. Once in a while, even in the big Liberator, we went in on the deck, getting a good share of small arms stuff and flak.

"But most of our missions were interesting; I mean they were different. They were single ship, no one else along, and extreme range with no escort. Sometimes it was kind of a lonesome feeling to be that far out in the old B-24, no fighters tagging along, spending as many as fourteen hours and seeing nothing but water. . . ."

In 1945 Fitz returned to the States, and began to branch out in his flying. He checked out in several other bomber types, went into transports and liaison planes, and then fell in love with fighters. He instructed in L-5 liaison and T-6 training airplanes, in C-45 and C-47 transports, B-25 bombers, and in the sleek North American P-51 Mustang fighter.

After a year of instructing Fitz was assigned to Mitchel Field on Long Island, and here he ran into Bill Fenton, who shunted his flying career into a new direction. Fenton was then a civilian after being discharged as a fighter pilot, but flew every weekend at Mitchel in the Air Reserve. One day they decided to go up together, each flying a T-6 trainer. Fenton and Fitzgerald became fast friends, on the ground and in the air.

Their dual flying quickly developed into the routine of a competitive rat race. It was a friendly but needling "I bet you can't do *this!*" that was followed with a blur of wings and an earth spinning crazily before the pilot. They were like kids; each tried to outdo the other, and each in his own right was a brilliant, gifted pilot.

There was no conscious effort to this wonderful blending of skill. They never tried, knowingly, to create anything in the way of team flying, or to perform spectacular feats. It was flying for the sheer love and joy of flight; two young men in powerful airplanes, rich in a love for the air that was fulfilled once again every time their wheels left the runway. They became a team without an appreciation of the fact. They discovered a reward from flying together they had never known when alone in the air, for each whetted the other's skill, demanded of his best.

They never realized the fact, but they had become the talk of Mitchel Field. Fenton and Fitzgerald flew for fun, but what was fun to them was incredible performance and co-ordination to onlookers. In their North American T-6 Texans—which were to them stock trainers, used and tried, with no special gimmicks or gadgets—they flew as few experienced pilots had even seen their contemporaries fly.

Their commanding officer approved; this was what flying should be. And as hair raising as the maneuvers of the two young pilots seemed to be, neither man was a daredevil. Neither tried to outfly his partner to the extent that safety was compromised. What they did appeared dangerous—but only to the man who was not himself experienced and skilled in the air. Fenton and Fitzgerald pushed their airplanes to the limit, but never beyond. And this was the mark of the pro.

Mitchel Field was scheduled for an open house—tens of thousands of visitors as well as base personnel and the families. Would Fenton and Fitzgerald perform as a team? The two pilots thought it over—they never once regarded their flying as exhibition material, but why not?

To say that the team of Fenton and Fitzgerald was an immediate, howling success would be a grand understatement. They stunned the crowd; the public had never seen anything quite like it. Oh sure, there had been air shows around for a long time, and the barnstormers were pilots of a different breed. But these two young lieutenants were flying stock military trainers that had been around for years—and they just weren't designed for the kind of precision aerobatics that you expect to find in an air show.

Right from the moment they thundered down the runway the two men had the onlookers gasping. Spectacular is hardly the word for their takeoff. They reached flying speed, held the nose down and then snapped the gear up. The moment the wheels thudded into their wells, feet stamped down on the rudder pedals and the control sticks slammed over. Almost scraping the runway both trainers whirled crazily through formation snap rolls—which is like doing a tight spin, but going straight ahead. Later, if they used a runway at least 5,000 feet in length, Fenton and Fitzgerald would do *two* snap rolls before reaching the end of the field!

They racked the Texans around tightly as they crossed the field, flew back with their wingtips almost hugging each other, and then slow-rolled beautifully down the runway. Coming out of the roll, both pilots fed power to the engines and soared upward, higher and higher. The airplanes slid across the field inverted, coming down in a clean, tight loop, faster this time and . . . at the top of the loop, a precise, co-ordinated snap roll. At the sight of this maneuver the pilots in the audience went wild.

They raced back to the field, pulled up tight. Engines screaming in a high, waspish sound, the two T-6's burst away from the audience, going straight up, higher and higher. The engines took on a new sound, a labored, gasping groan. In formation, making every move together as though one hand were on the stick, the trainers shuddered, stalled, and whipped into spins. Fitz and his partner let the T-6's whirl

44

through two spins, snapped into a recovery, and came out clean in pullouts away from the crowd.

They broke formation, each flying to opposite ends of the field, then came back, faster and faster. Rushing toward each other, they held their positions. A flaming collision seemed inevitable, and just as the crowd rose to its feet, fearful of the next instant, both pilots barely eased back on the sticks and snap-rolled away from each other. Men gasped and women screamed at that one, because the two airplanes were seemingly out of control, spinning crazily a split second before smashing into the ground.

They flew pylon eights, flew inverted in formation, did reverse Cuban eights. This maneuver calls for both planes to fly straight and level in tight formation. The nose comes up sixty degrees, then they flipped over on their backs, and fell through into a split-S; the moment they recovered they repeated the maneuver. The final pullout brought them low on the deck, passing in front of the crowd. Then, full of power, hard back on the sticks, and a wild, soaring loop. As they came out of the plunge, they chopped power, flattened out, dropped their gear and flaps, and eased down to a perfect formation landing.

Every show they ever flew ended with the crowd on its feet, cheering madly—and the pilots in the audience shaking their heads.

Two wonderful years of flying went by. Fenton had been recalled to active duty, and in their official duties both men graduated to the jet fighter, with assignment as P-80 jet pilots with the 4th Fighter Group at Andrews Air Force Base. It was life as Fitz had always dreamed it might be. But then there was a nightmare. . . .

The Pentagon scheduled the now-famous team of Fenton and Fitzgerald to perform at an air show in Miami, Florida. The men flew to Mitchel Field, borrowed two T-6 trainers and flew them down to Miami where they did the show. After the return ferry flight Fitz returned to Andrews. Fenton remained an extra day at Mitchel to visit with his girl, then hitched a ride in a C-45 transport heading back to Andrews. It was that ride as a passenger that nearly snuffed out Fenton's life.

He called Fitz, asking that he be met at Bolling Air Force Base, and Fitz drove to the airport to wait. Fate turned its wheels, the weather closed in and the C-45 pilot diverted to Andrews. Something went wrong. In a heavy fog and rain the pilot tried a radar-controlled landing. There were seven people abroad, the two pilots, four passengers, and Fenton, who was curled up in the rear of the transport, sound asleep.

No one will ever know the exact sequence of events, but the airplane fell off on one wing during the landing attempt, crashed and exploded. Both pilots died instantly and all five passengers were seriously injured. Fenton was, literally, mangled. He was more dead than alive when the crash crews pulled his torn body from the wreckage.

Operations called Fitz at Bolling. In his frantic race to the hospital, Fitz wrecked his car on the icy road, grabbed a taxi and actually beat the ambulance to the hospital.

"The only reason Fenton didn't die, actually, was that I owed him five dollars," Fitz explained, "and he was too cheap to go without it. Well, we can laugh about it now, I suppose, but it wasn't anything but utter hell then. Fenton hovered between life and death; by all rights he should have died. Two things pulled him through. His own tremendous fighting spirit, and a brilliant surgeon, Colonel Howard A. Lawrence. He took one look at Fenton's smashed body, and performed an emergency operation—right there and then—while Fenton was in his bed. Lawrence said he would have died on the way to the operating room. . . .

"He was in bed for a year, and in and out of hospitals for the next three years. But the ending to the story is what's best of all—Fenton's an instructor today in jet fighters."

Despite his continuing service, Fitzgerald's Air Force status for awhile became the stormy petrel of his flying career. In December, 1949, the Air Force notified Fitz that he was to be grounded! The astonished pilot was never told specifically why, only that many pilots were to be grounded for austerity reasons.

With the necessary provocation, Fitzgerald's Irish temper shows. His jaw juts out and his eyes seem to snap, and he boils into a nice, seething anger. Fitz refused to be grounded. He requested a court martial, tried to appear before an inquiry board. He offered to fly without pay—just to stay in the Air Force and in the air.

"I'd been in uniform since the beginning of the war," Fitz recalled. "I had done two years of demonstration aerobatics on top of my regular duty, and I felt it was one lousy way to treat someone—specifically, me. Unless I could keep flying in the Air Force, I told them flatly I didn't want to stay in. Flying came first; if they wouldn't let me fly, I'd fly on the outside. There was a lot of commotion, and in February of 1950 I took off the uniform I'd been wearing for almost eight years."

Fitz kept flying, albeit in a somewhat haphazard way. He was the Defense Contract Co-ordinator for American Airmotive Corporation in Florida, did some test flying, and even put on air shows with a civilian T-6 trainer. Here he was approached by a close friend of mine—Tommy Walker, then known in the air show trade as Brickwall Walker. The name was deserved. Walker was a stunt pilot, a wingwalker, parachute jumper, a wild-flying, incredible daredevil in the air. He had flown with the International Squadron for Chennault in China in 1937, he was a P-38 pilot in World War II. His specialty was slamming an airplane at full speed into a brick wall, and jumping out of the shattered wreckage to wave happily at the crowd.

Walker asked Fitz if he would be interested in teaming up to do air shows. That alone—from this writer's viewpoint—makes Fitz stand out as one of the great aerobatic pilots of the world. I know Walker well; he taught me to fly, and we have put many hours in the air together. He is a miracle on wings, and he speaks of Fitz as "one of the best who ever flew."

Air shows? Aerobatics? Another team? The idea tugged appealingly at Fitz, and he told Walker he would give the matter serious thought. But Fitz never let his thinking interfere with his flying. He left American Airmotive and flew C-46 cargo planes for Pan American's Latin America division; on free weekends as a member of the Miami Air Reserve he instructed in C-45 and C-46 transports.

Then came another war—not so big this time, but with a recall to duty. Fitz donned his uniform again, went to France with an F-84 fighter wing. At his own request he was assigned to Korea, where he flew F-84G fighters on more than twenty close-support fighter-bomber missions.

Back to France, and Lady Luck smiled broadly on Fitz. There was an aerobatic team in Europe—the Skyblazers— who flew jet precision maneuvers with Republic F-84G Thunderjets. Fitz volunteered, and they snapped him up. From 1953 to 1954 he was back in his element, flying in Right Wing position.

During his assignment to Mitchel Field in 1946 and 1947, Fitz fell in love with a slight, quiet girl, Carol Webber. There wasn't any need to explain flying to Carol, because she worked in the field's control tower, and more than once had given Fitzgerald clearance to take off. They married, and the couple have three beautiful children, Robert, Patricia, and Kathleen.

Fitz was flying with the Skyblazers over Chaumont, France, when the tower operator broke in on their radio conversation. The words were chilling: "Land immediately and report to the dispensary." Fitz came out of the sky in a hurry. He dashed into the dispensary to be met with the news that his daughter Patty had been stricken with polio.

The Air Force left nothing undone that day. Emergency treatment—major hospital treatment—was imperative. The local dispensary lacked the facilities to treat Patty, to arrest the polio. But even as Fitz picked up his daughter in his arms, his Wing Commander, Colonel Chesley G. Peterson, had a C-47 transport ready and waiting with engines running. Fitz ran to the airplane; within a few hours Patty was under the best medical care in Europe.

Because his daughter required treatment every day, Fitz left the Skyblazers and transferred to Weisbaden to remain close to his family. I've come to know Patty well; she is a beautiful child. She still requires daily treatment, but she is well along the hard road of overcoming the effects of polio. She's determined, with the help of her parents, to be just like her sister and brother. She's almost there now, and with Fitz and Carol determined to help her in every way, the issue is no longer in doubt.

This is a family matter, of course, but I feel that there

exists a similarity between Fitz's flying and his relationship with his daughter. The parental tendency in many cases of this nature, obviously, is subjective. To be assured of a life completely normal in every way, Patty had to travel a long and difficult road. The way to assure recovery was not only through love, but discipline. Patty's treatments, in a hospital, but especially at home, meant a consistent, unbroken pattern. Both Fitz and Carol have refused to allow anything to stand in the way of Patty's recovery. But the greatest thing they have done is to give that beautiful young girl the *will* to triumph over a disease that could have crippled her for life. Patty has never doubted that one day her polio would be just a memory of growing up.

Robert S. Fitzgerald is a man with a fierce pride, and it is this characteristic, among others, that has fitted him so well into the position of leadership with the Thunderbirds.

As we talked in his office, the hours passed almost without notice. Fitz had flown two full practice shows that day, and in between he managed to struggle through his greatest problem with the team—the ever-climbing stacks of paperwork that only he, as Commanding Officer, could attend to. He had been working for twelve hours and faced another day just like it in the morning.

But we were talking about flying, and the Thunderbirds, and we hardly noticed the darkness that swept down from the mountains. The team is everything to Fitz; it *must* be. Anything less than the utmost in performance, a dedicated performance, was unthinkable.

Dick Crane brought in some coffee. Everyone else had left the building. We discussed the book, specifically the problem of what this team and its mission means to the men who fly those powerful jet fighters through their punishing maneuvers. Fitz said it in words I could never improve on.

"Everyone will agree, Marty, that the team recognizes that it has a tremendous mission. After all, we represent the entire Air Force. Now this"—he warmed to the subject—"sets the theme. The very demanding mission requires just about the utmost in dedication, in self-sacrifice. That's another way, I suppose, of saying devotion to duty. It also engenders in each individual a tremendous amount of pride in being associated with such an endeavor. You've lived with us for a while now, you can see it in the men. I don't have to explain to you how they feel—Janc, Neil, Chuck, Herman, even old man Crane"—he grimaced—"who makes the *lousiest* cup of coffee . . ."

Dick grinned, smiled at Fitz, and happily blew a cloud of cigar smoke in our direction. "What the bossman says is true," he added. "We recognized a long time ago that this unit goes even further than representing just the Air Force. We're a showpiece for the entire national defense establishment; our goal is to help support the best interests of the country, not only at home, but around the world. . . ."

And all of this is true. Living with these men, it is easy to recognize that to them the utmost is a normal way of living. Every pilot on the team, every one of the men on the line and in the hangars who support the pilots in the air, every one of these people is completely and wholly dedicated to the Thunderbird mission. It is a zeal that burns at its brightest day and night, that never wanes.

You hear about such organizations, and in terms of combat groups you can understand and appreciate an *esprit* that welds them into a great fighting outfit. But you would never know the Thunderbirds were not at war. *Every* man wears his pride right on his arm; it is a tangible, real, vitally important thing, this belief that their pilots are the greatest, their team the best, their mission of critical importance to the nation. If you could take the entire organization, all the men from the lowest rank to the highest, there is to be found— always—the same theme: In the air or on the ground, this team always presents for the Air Force, and the country, its best foot forward.

Militarily, personally, professionally, the Thunderbird pilots strive for what will always be elusive, but must always be sought—perfection. And it goes deeper than this, for they have established for themselves a mode of conduct that is irreproachable morally and socially. The team lives, whether or not it prefers this position, under a brilliant magnifying glass. The only time that any of these men can relax is when they are in their homes; even then they often manage to spend their evenings discussing with one another the many aspects of their work, their flying, their mission.

The fiction writer would hesitate to create this situation for his characters; with the Thunderbirds it is normal, everyday, prosaic. And all of it can only be, of course, a reflection of the man who leads all the rest. The responsibilities of leadership carried by Fitzgerald are only in part in the air; his qualities in the cockpit and on the ground are the guiding line, the level toward which his men must aspire. Thus Fitzgerald is driven by himself—he must try, always, to improve what may already be as good as a man can achieve.

"Take these trips of ours," he continued; "when you recognize the fact that this team has *never* failed to appear where it has promised to appear, why . . . the responsibility attendant upon this performance is tremendous. We have problems of weather, support, personnel, maintenance, logistics, navigation, we must co-ordinate with military, federal, and civilian groups—and many of these operate on a basis that clashes directly with our interests and authority. Our job is to be right smack in the middle of all this; sometimes we feel we're in the center ring of a three-ring circus. This is no kick, but it's really a burden of responsibility that is without relief.

"The way I look at it, there's no excuse for not getting there—wherever we are assigned, once DOD* has accepted, has promised, the appearance of this team. Our purpose, no matter what, is to fulfill that promise, to accomplish our mission. So far as I'm concerned, the integrity of the service is at stake, and it will suffer accordingly on the basis of any failures which are created from our own shortcomings.

"There is a simple standard by which we live: there is the mission to be performed. We perform that mission with no compromise—period."

The Thunderbirds have been flying as a team for almost eight years. Their record so far in terms of meeting a scheduled appearance is nothing less than perfect. This is eloquence sufficient unto itself.

Now, leadership is a word with many meanings. We can

* Department of Defense.

understand its intent well enough in the normal sense of the word, as a commanding officer, the head of a group, and so forth. But being the leader of a jet precision team endows the word with a different connotation.

Every move the Thunderbirds make in the air demands precision timing and a co-ordination that is measured literally in fractions of a second. It is not enough to know the routine of maneuvers for the airshow; every pilot must be so familiar with every last detail of each maneuver that he can—and does—anticipate the actions of another man before he makes his move.

From the ground the observer may see a full show that to him is perfection itself. But he's not up in that cockpit, and what looks like glass-smooth sliding of four planes through the air is anything but that nice, flowing motion.

The sky is full of holes and ruts and bumps. The four-plane diamond is like a car forced to rush at breakneck speed over a rutted, potholed road. The turbulence in the air— in clear air—during some shows can only be described as wicked. It shakes, pounds, and hammers at those airplanes that slide so gracefully, with such seeming ease, through their maneuvers. It's hell on wheels when Super Sabres are on their backs, right at stall speed, falling—and I mean *falling* —in diamond formation out of the sky until their speed picks up and the wings snatch lift out of the air!

When these men come down after a siege of twenty-three minutes of hair-trigger precision flying in turbulence, their flying suits are soaked with perspiration. They are, physically, very tired. They have been flying a fifteen-ton fighter during a period of intense, sustained concentration—flying it not only with slide-rule precision, but fighting that monster fighter. Every man trims his Super Sabre to a nose-down attitude. When he flies, he *always,* every second, fights stick pressure. It squirts nervous energy through his body like jet fuel spraying under pressure into that volcano of an engine. That's why the newcomers to the team spend all their spare time in their first few weeks massaging sore arm muscles.

They do all this with the knowledge that they must fly from stall speed right to the edge of the sonic wall. One slip, one error, and a sleek fighter becomes a rampaging bomb.

You hear all sorts of comments about how the Thunderbirds achieve their marvelous precision. One man wrote an indignant letter to the Air Force after seeing the team in action, and protested bitterly that he didn't take kindly to fakes. He *knew* for certain that "One man flies one plane, and his electronic stuff flies all them other planes!"

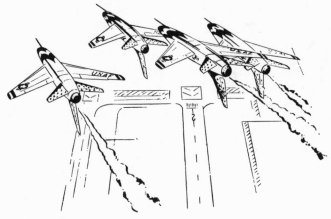

Over the top ...

Before every show, the pilots assemble for some stiff "Monday-morning quarterbacking." The men never fly a demonstration in a new area without first flying a practice show. They note every feature of the local terrain. They criticize—freely—the mistakes of any other man, and the "boss" is not exempt. They look for every possible means to forestall errors, to smooth out rough spots.

Fitz doesn't run these sessions. He's one of the four pilots involved. Actually, the wingmen consider Fitz's position as the toughest in the diamond. They at least have someone to watch, to follow, to judge by. There's always that frame of reference. Fitz can't follow, he leads in the air, and he *must* fly a perfect show, because if he doesn't and swoops through a long, wrong curve in the sky—why the whole team is going to be right there with him.

One of the most amazing aspects of flying that tight diamond formation, however, is that Fitz knows when the other fighters are tucked in close, without seeing them or talking to the other pilots by radio, because he can *feel* the Super Sabres. Actually, he feels the effect in the air of the racing airplanes. Each plane flings off its own invisible shock wave, and Fitz, skilled and experienced to every motion of his own jet, can look straight ahead and tell just how far out the other planes may be.

Every show is different, in that local conditions will almost always differ. Then, the wind conditions at the exact moment of the show must be considered. There may be a surface wind blowing from the east at twenty knots. But at 3,000 feet the wind is moving from the southeast at forty knots. And at 6,000 or 7,000 feet, it will blow from the west at sixty knots.

I've seen the smoke trails of the fighters bent sharply by the different winds at different altitudes. These men must plan exactly how this wind will effect their airplanes in a maneuver like the Bomb Burst. Who gets what drift, and how much? Remember—the Bomb Burst crossover is the climax of a maneuver that takes each airplane from ground level to many thousands of feet, over a distance measured in miles, from slow speed at the breakout to more than 700 miles per hour. And they must arrive at the crossover point, considering the effects of varying winds at different altitudes, as well as terrain problems, within a split second of one another!

Even as flat an area as Daytona Beach presents its own sticky problems. Florida is flat, all right, but just where the Thunderbirds would pass low over the ground there was a tower that stuck a hundred feet higher into the air than the altitude at which the team made its crossover. The gullies and ravines and mountains of Easley Range weren't exclusive as a problem. At Salt Lake City one of the men had to virtually fly down a mountainside as he plunged through his split-S maneuver before racing in for the Bomb Burst crossover. The team flew once at Caracas, Venezuela, where a mountain reared 7,000 feet high right on the edge of the maneuvering area. One man came down in a dive much steeper than usual; he *had* to, since he flew right down the mountain before flattening out in a punishing six-g pullout.

In the air, precision sometimes passes from Fitz's control to one of the other three men in the diamond—and knowing when to pass the ball to another pilot is yet another test of the smooth, uninterrupted flow of motion the demonstration demands. This can be a man who has to start a maneuver by speeding up, dropping back, or shifting position before the rest of the team can break their place in the diamond.

"Let's use the whifferdill as an example," Fitz explained. "Here, take these models, and we'll run through the maneuver. The whifferdill is actually a giant, vertical U-turn. The formation climbs steeply, rolls to the left, swoops in a high arch upside down and levels off right side up, going down in the opposite direction.

"Now, this is a simple, graceful way of turning around. But it's tough when we use it to change from diamond to trail formation. The slot man must back off first so the wingmen can slip back behind me in proper order, so in this case Neil is the man on whom the maneuver depends.

"I'll call the maneuver out as we do the shift. First, everyone moves the throttle to afterburner range, and then I call for AB's in. Then I announce that this will be a change-over whifferdill, and I pass the ball to Neil to call the change.

"Everyone is in full AB as the diamond rolls into the arch and Neil takes over. He calls the signals. He'll say, 'Roger . . . Thunderbirds, go trail, *now.*' Neil eases off on the throttle, Maultsby's right wing lifts as he slides back on me, and Janc's left wing rises as he slides in behind Chuck. In just about two seconds we're pulling out of the whifferdill in a single file, making about seven hundred per.

"Now, I want to stress that on most maneuvers it's the Wingmen—Bob Janca and Chuck Maultsby—who work the hardest. To put that diamond formation through all our rolls and turns, and stay together as a diamond, Janc and Chuck have got to continually play the throttle. They've got to follow the movement of my wingtips—and maintain a constant position beneath them. All the time they're doing this they're hauling back on that stick against constant nose-down trim. The *g*-pressures get pretty rough. When we pull the three-hundred-and-sixty degree turn, with the diamond standing on its wingtips, and swing into the rollout, it's Janc who has the toughest position. As the outside Wingman he's like the last guy on a string of skaters cracking the whip. He has to swing wider and faster than anyone else to stay in position."

The intrinsic secret of the Thunderbirds' precision formation flying, of course, is that Fitz knows his men can—and do —anticipate his every move. That's why the constant practice, the de-briefings where each man lays the cards on the table. And there's always Dick Crane, himself an F-100 pilot with many hundreds of hours, who has flown with the team, and who watches them from the ground with a critical gaze that misses nothing.

Timing is the lubricant on which the diamond formation glides so smoothly, and what brings it back together again when a maneuver sends the four sweptwing fighters breaking away from one another. The ultimate in timing is the cross-over from the Bomb Burst, but no one ever wants to achieve the duplicate of a show flown over Bolling Field several years back. The Wingmen on that day were Burt Spalding and Bill Creech.

Spalding shot to 20,000 feet on the burst. Plunging down from four miles high, he flattened out only three feet above ground as he streaked south with afterburner howling at the crossover point. Roaring north was Creech, who shot past his wingman at only *four* feet of altitude. Every photographer on the field that day was spreadeagled flat on the ground, and trying frantically to dig a hole!

4 Come to the Air Show!

The desert can be bitterly cold early in March, and on the morning of the day that the Thunderbirds were scheduled to fly a demonstration at Salt Lake City, it was about as cold as any of the pilots had ever remembered it. Nellis Air Force Base is a flat stretch of desert with roads plastered onto its surface and buildings shoved with frantic haste into their positions. The ground is bare and bleak and empty, and it seems to make the cold bite a little deeper.

Dick Crane dragged me out of the sack at four in the

morning; today we would fly to Salt Lake City in the team's Lockheed T-33 Shooting Star. The big F-100F was in the hangar for maintenance work, and Dick and I were resigned to being the slowpokes in the sky.

On the flight line the wind managed to howl convincingly at thirty miles per hour. By the time we arrived, wearing our parachutes and carrying our helmets, 1st Lieutenant Chester Golka had already taken off in one of the team's two C-123 transports, carrying the field servicing crew on ahead to Salt Lake City's municipal airport. The engines of the C-54 transport were just turning over, and Captain John C. Donohoe waved as the pilots walked to their big Super Sabres. And Crane and I to the T-33, a bit dinky in comparison to the sleek F-100D fighters.

We climbed into the cockpit, and ran quickly through the checklist. Dick wanted to be in the air before the team leaped off. He explained that he was going to give me a bird's-eye view of the formation takeoff from Nellis. We went through the runup, the tower announced that "Thunderbird Seven is clear to roll," and we were off, easing away from the long runway in a gentle climbout.

Dick circled the field at 8,000 feet. The six F-100D fighters taxiing nose-to-tail looked like ridiculous toys on the Nellis taxiway. We listened in to Fitz and the team on the common channel; just as Fitz in his quiet voice called out, "Thunderbirds—rolling, now," Dick swung hard around to the south of the field.

"Keep your eye on the hundreds, Marty," Dick said. "We'll pick them up just as the formation leaves the runway." And with that pleasant conversation the bottom dropped clear out of the sky.

The stick and the throttle went forward, Crane stood the T-33 almost on its wing, and we went downstairs like a bullet. A mile from the runway Dick was flattening out the screaming drop toward the earth and heading for a spot about twenty feet to the right of the runway. A cloud of greasy smoke boiled up from the field; four pilots pouring the coal to their Super Sabres. In seconds we were closer and I could see clearly the bright tongues of orange flame lashing the air behind the fighters.

I didn't think we could fly any lower, but Dick found another twenty feet of empty space beneath our wings, and decided this was too much. The T-33 bumped gently in turbulence a couple of times and then we were flying at the great height of no more than five or six feet. I looked down and to the side for a moment; it was wasted motion. Everything was a flying blur. Besides, you get dizzy looking at the world smeared into fuzziness.

Glancing up and forward to watch the rapidly accelerating Super Sabres was like putting the brakes on time. Everything changed to slow motion. We rocketed along the runway at better than 500 miles per hour, the Thunderbirds were already pulling up the gear, and Neil Eddins was starting to slide out of his right wing position into the slot.

Dick couldn't resist it. He jammed the throttle forward its final last notch, and nudged the rudder. In a second we were almost up to the climbing formation, and then skidding cleanly beneath the team. Dick's head came back. I looked upward and saw four giant sweptwing shadows that seemed to stand still as we flashed ahead. And then we were past them, using our momentary speed advantage to soar way up on one wing, swooping around in a giant barrel roll.

A happy chuckle came over the earphones, because Dick knew that this was the first and the last time this day that he would ever have the advantage of speed. As he leveled out and climbed, our speed dropped. Four big airplanes blasting flame behind them soared past us effortlessly, riding an invisible elevator into the sky. And just as the chuckle was dying out, two gleaming shapes exploded into view and then came into focus as they shot away from us. Griffin and Cass, catching up with the team.

"Hey, you characters, wait for us!" Dick called on the radio. A jumble of voices came back.

"You hear somebody calling, Janc?" That was Maultsby to Janca.

"Nah, it can't be a pilot. Sounds too much like that guy Crane."

"Crane? Who's that?"

"Ahhh, you know, that fellow we saw standing back there on the field, like he didn't know what day it was."

"Oh. You mean *him.*"

"Yeah. Poor man. Thinks he can fly, or something. . . ."

"Very funny, very funny," Dick said. "Bossman, would you mind slowing down a bit, just so we can catch up? This isn't an F-100 we got back here, you know."

The six fighters in the sky before us had dwindled to dots. Now, as the pilots eased off on the power, they grew slowly in size. The chatter went on. . . .

" *'We'*? You hear that, Major? Crane's got somebody in that flying machine with him."

"You must be wrong," Fitz replied. I could almost see him grinning. "Who would ever fly with Old Pappy Crane?"

"I suppose so, Boss. But you never can tell. You know Richard, he's liable to do *anything.*"

Griff's southern drawl syruped over the radio. "Majuh, I heahs rumors that he's got a writer-type back theah."

Everybody got into the act.

"A *writer?*"

"What's *that?*"

"Oh, you know . . ."

"No! Tell me, I never met one of those."

"Well, now, a writer-type is . . . Nope, it's too hard. It makes books, I think."

"A bookie?"

"Yeah! Sure, that's it. Crane's got his own private book-maker with him."

"Maybe they're taking bets on whether Dick will get them down in one piece."

"Hey, Marty!" I recognized Maultsby. "Is all this I hear about you true?"

"Yeah, sure, sure," I mumbled. "Just call me the Thunder-birds' own private bookie. That'll do fine, just fine."

Raucous laughter. Fitzgerald's voice broke in quietly, all business now. "Okay, troops. Let's clean up the cockpit." In that instant the team became efficiency and purpose, and I listened carefully as the Thunderbirds went back to work. Dick slid the T-33 off on one wing, and the six big fighters began to climb up and away from us. With their superior speed they could reach the Salt Lake City area well ahead of the T-33, and this would give them the opportunity to do a complete practice show over the lake, before landing at the airport. The airplanes would be too heavy with fuel on their arrival in the Salt Lake area to land, and Fitz never wasted the chance to practice, to drill the team in their intricate maneuvers.

Watching the formation take off from the T-33 as I did is an impressive sight, for the four airplanes rush down the runway with the same fabulous precision that the pilots maintain in the air. In fact, the Thunderbirds always fly as a close-knit team. It's a standing rule that everything that is done with the airplanes, on the ground or in the air, will be done on the premise that all four of the fighters are as one, that the men are always putting on their most important show before an audience of millions. This is a rule that is never willingly broken, and it is one reason, among many others, that precision is second nature to these pilots. They know, always, what their flying mates will be doing at any one moment.

The diamond doesn't form up until the airplanes are several feet in the air, and this is one of the few times that the formation changes its familiar shape. Neil Eddins moves from his Slot position to the far right, actually, as Chuck Maultsby's Wingman. At takeoff the formation is a Vee; Fitz in the lead, Janca back on the left wing, Maultsby back to the right of Fitz, and Neil to his right. Griff and Bob Cass take off together after the four airplanes before them are well down the runway. They then join up in formation for cross-country flying.

All four pilots line up in formation on the runway and go through their final cockpit check. Every man follows an identical procedure. This assures that they will be ready to move at just about the same time, and there will be no unnecessary waiting for any one man. Then Fitz calls for full power, and all four throttles move up to the maximum position—full bore.

Fitz calls, "Thunderbirds . . . rolling now." Simultaneously each man releases pressure on the toe brakes, operated with the rudder pedals. Chuck Maultsby always puts the heels of his feet on the rudder pedals to get the full strength of his feet for breaking. Pilots have their own patterns for doing different things in their airplanes.

For several seconds before Fitz calls for the release of brakes, each airplane hurls back a swirling cloud of greasy black smoke from its jet engine. With all four airplanes blasting away under full power the cloud soars upward for several hundred feet. It's an unmistakable marker that the Thunderbirds are about to leap off.

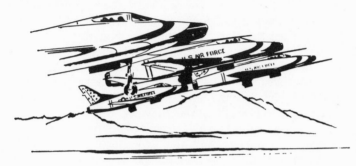

Thunderbirds' formation take-off.

They roll, the big fighters moving slowly, ponderously. Four seconds after the first movement, the next command crackles over the radio. "AB in, now," Fitz says. Each pilot has his hand on the throttle, and at the word "now" pushes the throttle slightly to the left, and forward. Flame explodes out of the tailpipe and everyone "hangs on" as an additional 6,000 pounds thrust kicks each Super Sabre forward.

The fighters roll faster and faster, accelerating very rapidly now, almost flying on the ground. The team is in precision formation, with the same separation between each airplane that they hold in the air, wingtips overlapping about three feet.

Every movement hangs on Fitzgerald's quiet, authoritative voice. "Nose coming up . . ." And four powerful hands ease back on the sticks, exactly fifteen seconds after beginning the takeoff roll. "We usually watch Fitz's nose gear strut," explains Bob Janca, "to determine the rate of rotation of the nose. We try to match his rate so that our gear comes up and leaves the ground exactly at the same time.

"Immediately after we are airborne, we pull up the gear. There's no call or signal from the leader for this."

The airplanes boom into the sky, riding that invisible sheet of glass, glued together as one big airplane. At a speed of 250 knots, and usually 150 to 200 feet above the ground, Fitz calls, "AB's out, *now!*" And four throttles move back. The orange flame disappears suddenly from four tailpipes.

But one airplane has changed its position. The moment that the gear snaps into the wheel wells, Neil makes his move to change from his right Wingman position to "home"—in the Slot. This is a maneuver that leaves experienced pilots shaking their heads in wonder, for Neil doesn't fly to the Slot position—he sort of slides over in what looks like a nice lazy wallow through the air—so low that his afterburner flame is just about washing the runway.

Like the other pilots, Neil is also on the nose-down trim. He relaxes his fingers, and this is enough to change the pressure on the stick. Responding to the trim the F-100 eases forward and down, just enough to satisfy Neil. He keeps his eyes glued to Chuck's airplane; Neil never watches anything else but the big fighter at this point. He has to slide beneath Chuck in order to move into the Slot.

With the precision built up of long practice, his left foot eases down on the rudder pedal. The Super Sabre skids to the left. It is completely a skid, for Neil is absolutely sure to stay away from any side stick movement. He wants no aileron pressure at this critical point that would provide a lateral, or roll, action. So he slides sideways through the air, watching the airplane above him. Then another wing comes into view, and the moment that Neil picks up Fitz's airplane, he works smoothly into the Slot. The diamond is now complete, still in takeoff, but climbing out in the familiar Thunderbird pattern.

I asked Neil if he—and the other pilots—always flew with the nose-down trim. "Any time we're in close formation, we do," he said. "You see, if we fly with the bird trimmed for straight and level—you know, so that she can fly hands off—it's like having a loose wheel in your grip. You get a bobbling motion. The nose-down trim gives us the positive stick pressure at *all times;* it dampens out any bobbling due to rough air. The advantage of this is twofold . . . it provides the positive stick pressure for close formation work, and yet it doesn't take away the sensitivity of the airplane when needed. Far as I'm concerned, it actually increases the control sensitivity, lets you fly with the best precision."

With Neil in the Slot, the formation climbs rapidly. In seconds they reach a thousand feet and 280 knots indicated. Fitz calls the shots again: "Thunderbirds . . . let's go to Channel Two." This is a Tactical Air Command frequency, and the Thunderbirds stay on this wavelength for their air work and communications. Then everyone checks in. For the check, however, the Number Two man—Janca—initiates the call.

Their voices now snap out. "Thunderbird Two—" Then Chuck as Number Three, and so on down the line—Neil Eddins, Herman Griffin, Bob Cass, and, for the month I flew with the team, Crane would call out "Thunderbirds Seven and Eight, right with you, Bossman."

With each pilot checked in, Fitz says, "Okay, troops. Let's clean up the cockpit."

Each man flips a switch to activate the yaw damper of his fighter. Specifically, this dampens out the normal yaw oscillation of the high-speed jet, its tendency to move from side to side. "It's like power steering," Chuck explained. "You can fly a good show without it, but it's better all the way around for us when the yaw damper is on."

As Fitz calls out the items, each man follows the same procedure in his cockpit. On the ground the oxygen regulator is always switched to a mixture of 100 per-cent pure oxygen, providing a safety factor in the case of carbon monoxide or other fumes getting into the cockpit. During the checkout to "clean up the cockpit," oxygen is switched back to "normal."

The pilots also adjust their automatic parachute equipment to a setting for normal operation at altitude. The call for this is: "Zero lanyard—off." Within one second of the pilot separating from his ejection seat, in event of an emergency, an automatic device would pull the chute pack open to release the canopy. Near the ground, however, when a split second can mean life or death, the small hook is moved to the "zero lanyard" position. In this case, in the event of ejection, the instant that the seat is away from the pilot the canopy will spill into the air.

On cross-country flights the three remaining airplanes—Griff, Cass, and Crane and myself in the F-100F—followed the same procedure. Under these conditions the team formation consisted of all seven Thunderbird airplanes.

With everyone checked in and the cockpit check completed, Fitz accelerates to 400 knots indicated, the team glued to their positions. At this point he calls: "Okay, troops—trim 'em up." On the Salt Lake City flight Dick and I listened to the call, and watched the six airplanes ease away—spread out—from one another. Normally, any radio call for a change with the airplanes initiates this move without comment. It's SOP—a standard operating procedure.

The "trim 'em up" signal means that each pilot adjusts hair-trigger trim controls of the fighter. The idea is to have the needle-and-ball flight instrument reading perfectly; the ball, which shows slips and skids, and is extraordinarily sensitive, must be exactly in the center of its tube. The speed of 400 knots is used also to check the exact position of the nose-down trim. Each man makes his final adjustments at this speed, so that all the airplanes will be flown with virtually identical stick control forces.

"Okay, gang, move it in. . . ." The diamond Wingmen during the trim check are usually about a hundred feet out from Fitz, and the other pilots—Neil, Griff, and Bob Cass—maintain a similar separation. Now it's time for the familiar tight formation, everybody neatly in the groove.

The diamond assembles in what looks like a formation shrinking into itself. The Wingmen slide in from the sides and Neil moves in from behind and slightly below. Neil, however, delays squeezing in tight until he makes a visual check of the three airplanes before him. It's his job to position the Wingmen to assure that they are in perfect formation.

"Chuck, you're out one stripe," he calls to Maultsby. Neil is asking for a formation so precise that the closely-painted stripes on the wingtips are used as markers. As he

Republic F-84F Thunderstreaks **(above)**, second fighter used by **Thunderbirds**, moving into top of high, soaring loop, rolling over on their backs. **(Left below)** First of the **Thunderbirds** was Republic's F-84E Thunderjet, with the diamond performing at the 1954 National Aircraft Show.

(Left) Author Caidin, back to camera, receiving last-minute instructions from Major R. S. Fitzgerald, Leader, before take-off for a practice show. (Right) **Thunderbirds** maintenance crewmen work in close co-ordination with visiting tech reps from North American Aviation. (Below) The **Thunderbirds** boom into the sky in their famed diamond-formation take-off.

(Above) Bomb Burst! Team explodes into internationally famous maneuver. (Below) Fitzgerald and his pilots in final preflight check on Okinawa, before Isely Range show.

(Above) Overwhelming reception is given **Thunderbirds** by Japanese at Yokota Air Base after flying their 503rd show. **(Left)** Faces of these Japanese adults and children **(lower left)** testify to sight and fury of performing **Thunderbirds**. **(Right) Thunderbirds** performing for Marines, 1959, on Okinawa.

Diamond formation rolls over top of a loop **(above)**, as **Thunderbirds** perform over Nellis AFB; end of runways are visible. **(Left)** In another show flown at Nellis AFB, the team is in trail, starting up for a high, position-changing maneuver. **(Below)** Racked in "real tight," the diamond sweeps around in a tight 360-degree circle during 1959 show in Okinawa.

(Opposite Page—top to bottom) Some **Thunderbirds** of the late 1950's and early 1960's. **Left column:** Bob Janca—Left Wing, Herman Griffin—Solo, Bob Cass —Spare (now in Right Wing), "Robby" Robinson—former Leader. **Right column:** Neil Eddins—Slot, "Chuck" Maultsby—Right Wing, Dick Crane—Narrator, "Fish" Salmon—died, 1958.

(**Above right**) "Fitz" Fitzgerald—Former Leader. (**Below**) These are the **Thunderbirds** with whom I flew more than 10,000 miles. Just before a cross-country flight, from left to right: Dick Crane, "Boss-man" Fitzgerald, Martin Caidin, Herman Griffin (back to camera), Bob Janca (hiding behind Herman), "Chuck" Maultsby, Neil Eddins, Bob Cass—the greatest bunch of pilots I have ever known.

Tomorrow's pilots . . .

receives this call, Maultsby squeezes in closer, adjusts his position, until Neil signals that he's right in the groove.

With both Wingmen where they belong, Neil begins to close in, jockeying carefully into his critical position. On several occasions Dick and I came in close behind Neil to get the feeling of the full diamond. It's incredible from this position. Neil's Super Sabre looks as if it were trying to wriggle down a tube—an invisible tube in space. Almost always he has that "bobbling" motion to contend with. The slightest turbulence makes the diamond quiver throughout its length and breadth. Shock waves stream back from the other three airplanes, and Neil is poking the nose of his Super Sabre almost into the tailpipe of Fitz's airplane.

Neil must keep a vertical separation of at least three feet between the intake of his fighter and the jet blast pouring back from the leader. He judges his position by watching Fitz's airplane, and as he makes his fine positioning adjustments, the Wingmen watch him like hawks, calling out to him his position. You watch it, you hear them talking to one another, but it's still hard to believe it when you hear Janc or Chuck politely asking Neil to "bring it over to the right a couple of inches, Neil. Ahh, that's it. Right in the groove . . ."

It's fortunate that Neil doesn't mind a feeling of being crowded in the sky, because when he flies in the diamond formation all he can see is other airplanes filling up the air. To each side and slightly above him looms the hulk of a Super Sabre fuselage. Directly ahead and barely above his own plane is the full body and wings of Fitz's F-100. With Crane, I flew in this position for a while—it's busy! I also had Dick bring me up real tight in the T-33, so that we could sit just below and partially behind Neil's own airplane. This is the way truly to appreciate the amazing *lack* of space between these big fighters.

Neil tucks it in so tight that the leading edge of his vertical fin actually juts more than three feet into the jet blast of the leading Thunderbird. For this reason his is the only Super Sabre that has undergone any major rework. To combat the effects of heat in its critical areas, the F-100 fighter uses titanium in liberal quantities. But for the Slot airplane, the entire vertical fin had to be made of a honey-comb construction of a special stainless steel. In normal cruising, the stream of air pouring back from the lead fighter maintains a temperature of 1,238 degrees F.! In afterburn-ing, when the aft section of the tailpipe has raw fuel squirted into the chamber and then exploded, the temperature soars even higher. Without that honeycombed stainless steel, the vertical fin of Neil's airplane would actually soften and begin to melt.

There is another reason why Neil's Slot position is so critical. He can't ever make the mistake of allowing his plexiglas canopy to move into that superheated torrent of air—it wouldn't take long for the plexiglas to soften and, quite possibly, to fail completely.

We watched the Thunderbirds disappearing into the dis-tance, six fighters now with Griff and Cass tucked in tight. Then they were lost to sight as dots that just faded out.

But suddenly we saw them again. Not as airplanes—this time their presence was revealed as a rapidly growing plume of white in the sky. Climbing steadily the six air-planes had reached 35,000 feet as they continued their as-cent to the planned cruising altitude of 40,000 feet. At 35,000 feet each jet began to stream a contrail, a white sliver of con-densation that hung in the sky like a marvelously straight brush stroke of some giant but invisible artist.

All this had taken but a few minutes, and Dick and I soon had the sky all to ourselves and a jet airplane in which to just fly. "Martin, want to go upstairs, or shall we do some sightseeing?" Dick asked.

I preferred to cruise just above the mountains and the hills. A haze filled the sky, and there wouldn't be much to see from 30,000 feet or above. We took up a course of 021 degrees, and Dick passed the controls to me. It looked like a wonderful day.

On this heading, holding about 12,000 feet altitude, we cruised comfortably on that magic carpet of the small jet airplane. We were well ahead of our schedule for landing at Salt Lake City; we had time to kill, and just the airplane in which to do it.

The VOR (radio direction) needle flickered as we passed

the ground station at Mormon Mesa. To our right the thin ribbon of Virgin River veered away; behind us it flowed into Lake Mead, the beautiful body of water created by Hoover Dam. Far ahead of us the earth merged into a blend of gentle browns and tans, speckled with the white of the higher mountains. The clouds were scattered, but there were still major buildings, and miles away we could see the blur in the sky that marked a localized but blinding snowfall.

It was just flying the way it should be—smooth, unhurried (cruising at 430 miles per hour) and with a feeling of limitless power. The T-33 was rock steady in the smooth air, almost flying itself. It took no more than the gentlest pressure every now and then on the rudder pedals to keep us exactly on course.

Just beyond the Mormon Mesa VOR station we flew across the border into Utah. At this point we were almost at the triangle of three state borders—Utah, Nevada, and Arizona. To each side of us loomed mountain peaks and ridges, rearing to more than 11,000 feet. We stayed on our 021 degree heading, homing in on the Milford VOR station, where we would shift slightly on our course.

The VOR needle flickered as we crossed over Milford. To our right a peak loomed above 12,000 feet, and off our left wing was Sevier Lake. A lake in name only 4,500 feet above sea level, and as dry as the bones that are scattered throughout the desert.

We homed in on the Delta Station, and I eased the T-33 to its new course of 007 degrees. Delta passed beneath us quickly. Our next checkpoint was the Provo Station. But from this point on we didn't need our charts or the electronic grid of the omni stations. Dead ahead of the airplane's nose lay Utah Lake; beyond and slightly to the west sprawled Great Salt Lake.

Dick took the controls. We still had time, and there was the chance to do some sightseeing. Thick snow lay firmly on the mountain slopes to the east of Salt Lake City, and the skiers were out in droves. The Wasatch Range is spectacular country for skiing and mountain lodges, and on this day, with clouds just brushing the level of 10,000 feet, it was perfect for all those with a yen for the outdoors.

For Dick Crane this was home country, and he delighted in pointing out to me every detail on the ground that brought memories flooding back. Dick was born in Murray, Utah, about six miles south of Salt Lake City, and we flashed over his home town, slowed down to a crawl at 300 miles per hour, but still just a bit too fast to point out many of the local sights.

We swung around in a great turn, descending slightly over Provo, then picked up a highway and railroad line that ran northeast into Heber Valley. A brilliant lake nestled in the depression between the mountains, and the high

T-33—chariot for Crane and Caidin.

peak just north of Provo, at 11,750 feet, was well above us as we sailed on our magic carpet through the valley. There was a glint of sun off brilliant red wings; far below, a private airplane banked into its final approach to a small airport near the lake. Over the town of Heber, and then we added more throttle and applied back pressure on the stick for more altitude as we threaded our way north. Then Dick lifted the T-33 up onto her left wing, and we hauled around tightly, dropping quickly again.

We were below the peaks as a highway winding through the valley below came into sight. Just over a final ridge, as we descended in a long, flat run, stretched Salt Lake City and the sprawling plains to the west of the city. And beyond that, Great Salt Lake with its islands and the salt beds along the shoreline gleaming in the sun.

We were tracing the actual route of the Mormons who had fought their way through and over the Wasatch Range, and then stood on the final slopes to see the land stretching away before them, and the expanse of the lake beyond. It is a truly beautiful sight, for from the flatlands the mountains loom as guardians to the outside world. What had required weeks and months of bitter struggle, we accomplished in a period of time measured in seconds of flawless flight!

We shot over the city, turned steeply to the right and climbed out to the northwest. I searched for the Thunderbirds. We came on the team just as the diamond soared vertically over the water, south of Promontory Point. It was dazzling, perfect beauty . . . all the adjectives rolled into a stunning exhibition of precision flight. Again the Super Sabres were tiny pinpoints of shining light, writing their fine script in the sky with their trailing smoke.

The breakaway for the Bomb Burst was perfect; unhappily, the crossover was not. We listened to Fitz and the pilots discussing what went wrong. "I think you were a little slow coming out, Neil," Fitz called to his Slot Man. Neil acknowledged, explained that he failed to get a light on his afterburner as he flattened out of his tremendous split-S maneuver to make his approach for the crossover.

Dick throttled back and we circled in a wide turn to watch another full Bomb Burst. Griffin spotted us as we came around and we were treated to what was becoming a familiar sight—two powerful jet fighters blazing past us, and flashing away in a series of exuberant aileron rolls. I swear I could hear Griff laughing every time he sneaked up on us.

The diamond came back, trailing smoke, Fitz calling out the changes in power and the maneuvers. Again the climb and breakaway were perfect. Neil half-rolled in his vertical climb, changed 180 degrees in his track, and boomed up and over on his back, streaking toward the mountains to the east. All four airplanes came around perfectly. Dick came on the intercom. "Neil's a bit slow again; he must have picked up a stiff headwind. Watch his airplane for the AB; it will come on just about now."

No sooner said than done. Flame spit from the Super Sabre. Far ahead of the Slot fighter, Fitz peered ahead, judged distance with a skill born of years of practice and quietly said, "You are slow, Neil."

Eddins answered calmly, already aware of the effects of the wind. "Pouring on the coal, Boss."

Bob Janca and Chuck Maultsby checked each other's position; right in the groove. "Looks like the lineup's perfect," Fitz called, and then the four airplanes drew magically toward one another, there was a blur of splashing light and a flash of silver and impossibly the four Super Sabres met at one point in the sky and then were gone, streaking up and around in afterburner-pushed climbs.

Dick squeezed the radio switch on the throttle. "Not bad, you guys, not bad at all for a bunch of people who only got out of flying school last week." He chuckled happily.

"Hey, look who's here!" someone snapped right back. "Enjoy the walk, Richard?"

"Yeah, that's no way to treat a dis-tin-guished author, Crane."

"Look, Boss, is that really an airioplane up there?"

"I never thought he'd make it. Can you imagine it, fellas? Old Crane actually managed to find his way up here after all!"

"Okay, Janc, you win that fifty cents. I thought I had a sure thing. How *did* he make it all the way up here, anyway?"

"Awright, you clowns," Dick growled. "Just wait'll we're on the ground . . ."

"Cut it, Richard. You'll never get down in one piece. You don't think you can land that thing, do you?"

"Man, what a good narrator must suffer to show these jokers off as hoomin bein's . . . C'mon, Marty, let's get some coffee."

Dick Crane had one nasty habit with me. Dick has introduced a great many people to the world of jet flight, and he does so with a gentle touch on the controls that is the mark of the master pilot with his machine. But with me . . . I suppose it wasn't Dick's fault. After all, I am a pilot, I had flown in quite a few jets before flying with Dick. It was natural for him just to relax in the airplane with me.

I must confess, however, that what is relaxation to Dick is like two big fists thudding simultaneously into the back of my neck and into my stomach. Dick came around to approach the Salt Lake City airport runway. It was nice and gentle and very pretty. But that pitchout!

To land a fast jet airplane is to enter into a different concept of how to get on the ground. Over the runway Dick blithely stood the T-33 on it's left wing and then sucked the stick all the way back. About two hundred people jumped on me and did their best to shove me right through the bottom of my seat. I sat on two sharp knives and my arms were two bars of lead on my knees, and suddenly I didn't have any neck because my head was pushing it out of sight. I could feel my jaw trying to reach my seat belt and guns were going off right beside my ears and the sun seemed to fall out of the sky, because everything turned gray and began to turn black.

Then the pressure lifted and the lights came back on to full bright again. The throttle was back, the gear and flaps down. Dick must have looked back through the mirror above and to his right, and maybe it was because my eyes were suddenly beady looking that prompted him to solicit my feelings. "You awright, Marty?" he asked kindly.

I said something that sounded like *"Barrff,"* and maybe it was in the form of a low groan, because Dick chortled. The ground flashed beneath us and the runway mushroomed in size. I swear I'll never know how he does it, but when Dick Crane landed that T-33, and the F-100F, he always "painted it on" the runway. The nose came up as we sailed along, the wings seemed to tremble just a bit, and there came the barest tremor below us. The T-33 kissed the runway with a touch that was nothing harder than a painter dragging another stripe on a wall.

"How we doing, Marty?" Dick's voice boomed happily in my ears.

Frankly, I wasn't quite sure. The pinwheels and comets still glittering in front of me wouldn't let the horizon steady down, and I was reminded painfully of the fact that

71

the average adult male has thirty-two feet of intestines packed neatly behind his seat belt. At that moment all thirty-two feet were quivering unpleasantly, and threatening to eject the remains of the morning's breakfast.

"Get the damned canopy up . . ." I didn't wait for any comments, but unhooked the chin strap, disconnected the mask catches, shoved the visor back up onto the helmet, and dragged the whole weighty assembly from my head and face. At that moment the oxygen mask smelled as though it had been stored for a month in a barrel of fish, and I knew I couldn't last another sixty seconds. Dick raised the canopy as we taxied off the runway, and I breathed deeply of that wonderfully clean, cold air.

I didn't quite reach the point of going *"Barrff!"* and the thirty-two feet quieted. But it was close! On too many occasions in the air I went through the bright-lights-before-the-eyes-and-Oh-my-God!-my-stomach! routine, but somehow I always managed to preserve the dignity of whatever union there happens to be for authors.

The ground crew directed us to our parking place alongside the C-123 and C-54 transports. As we climbed down from the airplane—I was grateful for the solid feel of that good Utah ground, I must admit—the six Super Sabres moaned low above us as the boys racked them around in their pitchouts for landing.

The occasion for the air demonstration was enough to bring out half of Salt Lake City. It was cold and windy and bitter, but that day was an annual event for the Utah National Guard and Air National Guard that was always carried out, rain, snow, or even a nice screaming blizzard. The ranks of blue and olive-drab were all assembled for their "annual muster." The troops were being sworn in for another year of duty.

Now this may not seem to be at all important, but the occasion called for a full-dress review. A parade, of all things, on a day when everyone was better off inside before a crackling fireplace. A great deal is said about the romance of flying with the Thunderbirds, of the jolly time that is always had by all. I wish the adherents to *that* theory could have been with us on this day.

There were plenty of generals and colonels and high brass around, and what appeared to be a few thousand other men in uniform, the latter finally assembled in precision ranks along the taxiway. In front of the hangers and along the flight line were many thousands of people, for despite the cold and the wind, the promise of the Thunderbirds' performance had brought out a full house to watch the demonstration.

After their fighters were parked, the team met in the Air National Guard operations office to work out details of the show. They had to operate on a time shedule that was maintained down to the second. For several minutes before and after the demonstration, the field was closed to all other air traffic. The commercial airlines at times take a very dim view of this Federal Aviation Agency requirement, since it does disrupt their scheduling. There were problems of buildings, the mountains looming to the east, altitudes to be flown —ad infinitum. The weather began to close in, the tops of the mountain ridges faded from view and were replaced by heavy clouds that wafted down a steady shower of snow on the slopes.

Would there be enough of a ceiling to do the High Show, or would it have to be the Flat Show? The team leader— Fitzgerald—makes this decision. When the sky is clear and the clouds don't get in the way of the airplanes, the demonstration takes exactly twenty-three minutes. There's no problem in maneuvering, because the whole sky is available. But when the clouds come down, then things get sticky. The team cannot exceed a certain altitude, they must remain below the clouds, and the pilots suddenly gain a new interest in any mountains that might just happen to be in the vicinity. Today there were plenty of them.

The problem due to changing weather conditions—and the Thunderbirds ran into it at Salt Lake City—is that many times the pilots don't know until minutes before they open their demonstration just what show they will be flying! At Salt Lake City and several other sites, the team had to evaluate their requirements while they were in the air, circling around, while Herman Griffin counted off the seconds before making his solo entry to introduce the Thunderbirds.

While Fitz worked with the FAA representative and the field commander of the Air National Guard, the other pilots compared notes on terrain, wind, and other factors. As the Spare, Bob Cass participated in the planning and took detailed notes. During the demonstration he would be in the control tower of the airfield, in constant touch with Fitz, and assisting local authorities in carrying the demonstration through smoothly. When all this was done, the team met again and went through every last detail of the demonstration to be flown.

Then came two hours of—you guessed it—waiting. In the small airport restaurant the pilots had a light meal, then returned to the operations office. Finally it was time for the local ceremonies. This called for the pilots to join the local brass and city officials on the reviewing stand. Today this distinction promised to be more of an ordeal than honor, no matter what the regulations say. The reviewing stand promised to be windy, cold, miserable. It was all of those things

I tried to beg off, but Fitz and the team would have none of it. "You live with the team and fly with the team," Fitz explained as I was dragged out of operations, "so you stay with us. Besides, you'll love it up there. Think of all those parades you were in when you walked in front of the stand. Today's your day to live!"

So we all stood for about an hour, and sat for another forty-five minutes. If this is romantic and exciting, then those words have connotations I've never thought of before. Oh, yes, there is also the belief that girls throw themselves en masse at the Thunderbirds. Their field trips hold a promise of doe-eyed adulation by the fair sex.

We didn't stay overnight in Salt Lake City, but I've flown with the team on their field trips, moving from city to city. Never forget that flying those airplanes is a wearying, strength-draining task. Also, that when they are on the ground—except for retiring to the hotel rooms and bolting the doors—the Thunderbirds are on review. *All* the time. They also fly at least one or two practice missions every day. There is flight planning to be done, uniforms to keep pressed and neat, weather to be checked, a thousand and one things to bedevil a man out of any spare moment he can call his own. And on the road the team operates under a strict curfew. Midnight was the reckoning for Cinderella, and at midnight the bell tolls for the Thunderbirds as well.

Now, on the reviewing stand there *was* a beautiful girl. She was that year's "Miss National Guard." I remember that she stood on legs that were both beautiful and fascinating. Beautiful because of obvious reasons, fascinating because after about thirty minutes on that reviewing stand they were turning a remarkable shade of blue.

Finally the last rank filed past the reviewing stand, the ceremony reached its end, and everybody gratefully stamped their feet to restore the circulation. The Thunderbirds had about twenty-five minutes before starting engines, and the group lost no time in hurrying to the C-54 transport where they climbed into the cabin and slammed the door.

"Somebody gimme some coffee!" It was piping hot and waiting, a private service of the airplane crew. The pilots sipped gratefully, then left for their Super Sabres.

Crane and I returned to the reviewing stand, from which Dick would narrate the demonstration to the massed audience. For most shows the audience receives its introduction to the Thunderbirds when Griff streaks in at low altitude. Today, however, the crowd was fortunate in that the fighters would take off from the same field over which they would perform.

Dick explained the starting procedure, watched for a hand signal, and abruptly cut short his words. The upraised hand came down, and from beneath Fitz's airplane white vapor burst downward. A shrill screech blasted through the air; then another, and another, as the hands of each airplane's crew chief swept down, and the compressed air bottles of each F-100's internal starter whipped turbines into action.

Here was yet another proof of that amazing, consistent precision of the Thunderbirds in everything they do. Even starting their sleek fighters is an operation of skill and split-second timing, and it is a sight to bring tears of joy to any veteran line chief. For in this instance the precision and timing is not due to the efforts of the pilots, but rather their mechanics, who are just as cold as their individual pilots were on that reviewing stand.

Each team of men by each Super Sabre does not look down the line to assure that they are keeping pace with the other F-100 teams. Rather, it is a superb skill on their part that permits them to perform the same operations in almost the same period of time, with differences measured literally in seconds.

The Thunderbirds taxied out in tight, neat formation, the long nose of each fighter bobbing up and down on the oleo strut of its nose gear as the pilot used the brakes. At the end of the taxiway they halted, then moved out to their hold positions on the runway at the radio call from the tower. Throttles forward, and the boiling cloud of black smoke. From afar, the airplanes seemed not to be moving, but Dick's practiced eye announced the start of the takeoff roll. Then the glare of flame, and the booming explosion of four afterburners lighting simultaneously. Faster and faster they raced down the field, the audience watching in awe the flawless movement of the four big fighters in formation, their thunder swelling in volume until finally it crashed in an overpowering wave across the field.

Dick called the attention of the audience to the single airplane still on the ground, directing them to pay close attention to the takeoff of the Solo Pilot. And Griff didn't disappoint anyone in that audience. His Super Sabre streaked down the runway; without any apparent upward motion, Griff snapped up the gear and gathered speed like a boulder tearing down a steep mountainside.

The nose came up, and the audience expected the same long, flat climbout of the formation. But the nose continued to come up, higher and higher, and just before it pointed to the vertical, the wings went around and around. And then he was vertical, rolling straight up from the field on takeoff. Standing behind Dick and myself were several fighter pilots. One of them gasped, "Good Lord! I see it, but I don't believe it! Look at that thing *go!*"

During the brief periods between each maneuver as it is performed before the audience, Dick explains to his listeners exactly what is happening. The mission of the Thunderbirds, their manner of precision flight, the type of maneuver, how it is flown, brief biographies of the pilots . . . his is a narration that is vital to the mission of the team, for it is not enough for the diamond formation and the solo airplane simply to perform. There must be an explicit understanding of what is happening, of what it means. Under first consideration, it is understandable to dismiss the narrator's task as that of any public announcer.

But the more time I spent with the team, the more I learned the intricacies of their operations, the better I came to realize that without a skilled narrator—a man who is as gifted in the Super Sabre as the men who fly the show, and who understands everything that is happening in the air— the Thunderbirds would be much less effective. The narrator also must possess a certain kind of stamina not demanded of the men in the air during any demonstration.

I need not go deeply into details, but have you ever seen a man orating with flawless words before thousands of people, while a small, dirty-faced little boy—who has crawled between many chairs on the reviewing stand to reach his target—chews away with gusto at his leg? Dick Crane's endurance was remarkable that day. Perhaps it is because his own small son has very sharp teeth.

Flying at the Easley Range in Okinawa, Griff was able to open the air show with a supersonic pass at minimum altitude. But Salt Lake City is not Okinawa, and the supersonic pass would smash too many windows and frighten too many people in the town who weren't quite aware of what is happening. So the single Super Sabre comes in low, but just below the speed of sound. As Dick calls the maneuver:

"And now opening our show, low and from your right, trailing white smoke, will be our Solo Pilot, Captain Herman E. Griffin, of Sumter, South Carolina, demonstrating the use and the sound of the F-100 afterburner with a high-speed, low-level, afterburner pass."

It may not be supersonic, but the on-off operation of the flaming AB is a sensational maneuver. Griff came over no more than a dozen feet off the runway, quartering before the audience, and ramming his throttle in and out of the afterburner position. It was like a series of deafening explosions hurling the sweptwing airplane down the field. The big engine is bad enough at close range. Each time the afterburner goes on, flame spits out of the tailpipe and a blast of thunder booms outward. On this initial pass, playing his run across the field with plenty of altitude, Griff was slow —subsonic—but still impressive enough to send a crowd of Boy Scouts scurrying back from the safety ropes marking the audience's area.

The schedule for maneuvers is timed so precisely that Dick can give the audience a brief biography on Herman Griffin. He pauses then, and announces, "And now, Ladies and Gentlemen . . . The Air Force *Thunderbirds!*"

And that's all, because the diamond streaks in from the rear of the audience, all afterburners blazing; the shaking of heads and excited glances, the pointing arms and shouted exclamations always testify to the effectiveness of the maneuver. These people have never seen anything like this before; the reaction is a wonderful sight to behold. The adults are as excited and as awed as children.

From start to finish, the High Show is flown precisely through its allotted time scheduling of twenty-three minutes. Dick explains every step, every motion. Here's an example:

"Out to the front and center you will notice the Thunderbirds have changed to an Intrail or Follow the Leader formation, and are now approaching directly toward us. The Team will pull up from minimum altitude to perform a Cloverleaf Turn while changing from this trail position back into the tight diamond formation.

"A Cloverleaf Turn starts out much like a loop but adds a ninety-degree change of direction just before coming over the top. Notice how the Team breaks sharply as they approach the vertical position and return into the tight diamond as they go over on their backs, with Major Fitzgerald, the Leader, rolling the entire formation ninety degrees to the left."

And so it goes. The thousands of people with their heads back, way back, following the diamond formation that performs every maneuver within a mile radius of the demonstration area. The excitement mounts with each passing minute, and everyone strives to spot the four airplanes as

78

they finally break out of their positioning turns and begin their run-in for the next maneuver. The shouts and gesticulations, the pointing hands and the exclamations of wonder, the almost tangible feeling in the air of respect, the sense of pride that this is *their* Air Force . . . It happens every time.

When the team pitches out for its landing approach, and then drops in, one behind the other, the crowd is shouting its applause for what they have just seen. Half the audience waves frantically at the pilots as they taxi by, kids standing on tiptoe, shouting and yelling. In formation the Super Sabres taxi to their parking area, line up perfectly. At the signal from Fitz five jet engines are cut, and whine piercingly to a halt.

The day's work is far from over. There are dignitaries and VIP's to greet, hands to be shaken, kind words to be exchanged, autograph books to be signed, and pretty young schoolgirls who would "just *die!*" if the handsome pilots didn't smile back.

Then it was all over, but the crowd stayed on. No one wanted to miss that formation takeoff as the Thunderbirds left for home. The two transports would be the last to leave for Nellis, but Dick and I climbed into the T-33, fired her up, and scooted out to the taxiway as the pilots climbed into their airplanes.

As we took off and climbed in a wide circle around the field before heading to the south, the formation was just lining up on the runway. It had been a long and a tiring day, but now, back in the air, everything was fresh and clean again.

We climbed to 12,000 feet and leveled off for the flight home. And just as we expected, without warning the sky was suddenly filled with the big F-100 fighters. This time, however, I was given a rare treat.

Six Super Sabres surrounded the T-33. We had a fighter to each side, one directly ahead and barely three feet higher than our airplane, one behind the T-33, another almost sitting on top of our canopy. And about the entire formation a single F-100 whirled around and around along an invisible curving line in the sky, Griff happily cavorting in aileron rolls. It was marvelous!

We went home just above the mountains, sliding through the sky effortlessly, the radio busy with the banter of the pilots. Everybody slipped by a peak that hung above us to the northeast of Nellis, and then down we went. Janca called in to the Indian Springs control tower; the bombing and gunnery range was clear, not in use, and the message was "It's all yours, Thunderbirds."

The sky belonged to them, and the Super Sabres of the team seemed to go wild in the air. The formation just . . . burst. One second we had airplanes in our hip pocket, poking wingtips almost in our eyes, and in the next moment all we had in sight were blurs flinging themselves through the air.

"On the deck, troops," called Fitz, and the six fighters dashed earthward, a rat race of fighter pilots letting loose, tearing after one another in bone-wrenching maneuvers. They didn't even pause to razz us in that slow old T-33, but curved off toward the desert floor.

Dick kept our altitude, and ten minutes later pointed to the right. Two F-100's, right on the deck curving around the hills as they followed a gully. Dick couldn't resist the temptation. The horizon flipped and we were on our back, dropping like a bullet to bounce the two unsuspecting pilots.

I should have known better. We were dropping for the desert at more than 550 miles per hour inverted—*inverted*, mind you—when I glanced around. In perfect formation, their wings overlapping ours by at least six feet, were two big fighters, each pilot with his thumb to his nose and waggling his fingers merrily. "Don't look now, Richard, old man," sang Griff, "but you got company—again!"

Dick politely said, "Aarrgh," and rolled out. The Team reformed, and veered toward Thunderbird Lake—to fly a complete practice show. That was fine with us, we kept going lower and lower, right to the floor of the desert, and went home, singing merrily.

A range of hills appeared before us several minutes later, and we shot skyward. Beyond, the Nellis runways came into sight, and Dick called in, requesting a Thunderbird pitchout. The tower came back with permission.

"How you feeling back there?" Dick asked

"Wonderful! Just wonderful!" I said. "It couldn't be better." And it couldn't. I was flying; we were on top of the world.

"Okay, Marty, we'll come in to land with the Thunderbird pitchout. You feel up to it?"

"Anything, Richard, anything you say. Just go right at it."

He did. He took me at my word. I should have expected, of course, that there *is* a difference between a pitchout and a Thunderbird pitchout.

Dick started down at least a mile above the field. He pointed the T-33 at the runway, and dove. Steeply. A few hundred feet out we were flat above the ground, the T-33 booming along with every last ounce of speed Dick could squeeze out of the jet. The field leaped toward us, a black streak shot under the nose. We were over the runway, at least three feet over it, anyway. Dick brought the nose up, gained clearance for the wingtip, snapped over to a vertical bank, and it happened again.

The two hundred people called in all their relatives, and I went down beneath a storm of weight. My eyeballs just sagged until, I'm sure, only the whites showed. I was pinned helplessly into that seat. The roaring in my ears got louder and louder, the sky got blacker and blacker, and that was all.

I went out like a light. When the pressure eased off several seconds later, we were drifting toward the runway. From a hundred miles away I heard Dick's happy voice. "You still there?"

Where did he think I was? That I had ejected?

Through a daze I recognized that we were on the ground. The canopy came up and, weakly, I pulled off the helmet and mask. I slumped in the seat like a wet dishrag; when we stopped, it was with honest gratitude that I slipped out of the parachute harness and climbed down to the ground.

We walked to the office, where I collapsed into the chair behind my desk. Beverly Cassel, the Thunderbirds' secretary, confidante, and guardian angel, shook her head in sympathy.

"Coffee?" she said.

"Barrff," I said.

5 The Beast

The North American F-100C Super Sabre is a single-place, supersonic airplane with a primary mission of carrying out combat strikes as a fighter-bomber. It is also an airplane designed for maximum climb, ruggedness, versatility; it functions in a secondary role as an air superiority fighter to contest enemy aircraft.

To fulfill its missions, the F-100C is a beast. It is a monster of an airplane that even resting quietly on the ground seems to be spoiling for a fight.

When you think of the fine, whirling precision that marks the aerobatic airplane, the F-100C is not the first thing to pop into your mind. Representative of aerobatics is the Bucker *Jungmeister* that famed Bevo Howard flies at airshows to leave the crowds gasping with disbelief. Since it was designed to perform as a dervish, it is unbelievably sensitive to the controls. Its construction is simple but rugged. It enjoys a superfine balance in flight. It almost thinks for the pilot. Then, too, there are very few things that can go wrong with the Jungmeister. If the engine runs as it should, some 99 per cent of all operational problems are solved.

This is why the F-100C, in terms of aerobatics, has earned its name of beast, or more disrespectfully by less skilled pilots as a lead sled. It is *not* a whirling dervish, and it weighs more than a few pounds. Indeed, in the configuration in which the Thunderbirds fly the F-100C, the airplane weighs exactly 28,800 pounds.

Stated bluntly, this is a hell of a lot of machine in which to fly precision aerobatic air shows. It was never intended for this purpose. The F-100C is a heavy, powerful, fighter-bomber, and in that respect it is a superb weapon that knows no superiors. That it performs with its amazing team agility, that in this airplane Herman Griffin—as well as the other pilots who flew the Solo position with the team—make pilots shake their heads in disbelieving wonder, is all to the credit of this amazing powerhouse and airframe.

Any airplane that is designed from the outset for aerobatics is obviously well suited to its task. Any airplane that is designed to function as a weapon system crammed with heavy equipment, to withstand the stress of supersonic flight, to fly for many hours at extreme altitude, to carry cannon and bombs and rockets and external fuel tanks, ad infinitum, is just as obviously not well suited to the task of aerobatics. Or it shouldn't be, anyway.

The F-100C is a paradox to these conditions. Even an airplane that is heavy by aerobatic standards, if it is intended to be strictly a fighter airplane designed to combat other fighters, is better suited to aerobatics. I asked Fitz what he thought of the advantages enjoyed by the Blue Angels, the Navy precision team, that flew the light Grumman F11F Tiger.

"Right from the start, the F11F weighs much less than the F-100C," Fitz said. "It's a carrier fighter, designed for air superiority work. It's powerful, it's light, it has better acceleration than the F-100C. It's an airplane that is better suited to putting on an aerobatic show—no doubt about that."

And this is what makes the Thunderbirds' performance all the more outstanding. They are flying an airplane that is not essentially a fighter. Frankly, the F-100C, and its successor F-100D model, is in every sense of the word a warhorse. It fights from treetop heights to better than ten miles high. With air refueling it flies and fights to any part of the world. It is a close-support tactical airplane, and a long-range fighter-bomber that carries a greater load in weight than a four-engine bomber of World War II, yet can strike at supersonic speed with a hydrogen bomb slung beneath a wing. It is a deadly, versatile weapon—but it just wasn't intended for air show work!

According to the book, then, the Super Sabre is not suitable for precision airshows. The trouble here is that the Thunderbirds have never read that book. They've never considered the F-100C as an airplane that might restrict them in their performance. Indeed, quite the opposite is true. The reliability of this machine despite its complexity of internal equipment delights them. There's never any doubt of the supreme stability of the Super Sabre. It responds to the controls as flawlessly as can any jet airplane. So the Thunderbirds just never think about the Super Sabre as not being suited to their flying, and to them nothing counts better than performance. The record stands for itself—no one who has ever seen this airplane in the diamond or in solo passes would ever believe that its designers from the outset didn't have precision aerobatic work in mind.

I had good opportunity to become well acquainted with the big Super Sabre when I flew with the Thunderbirds, and the paradox of complexity with reliability never fails to amaze me. First, this is the airplane that made the Air Force supersonic. The *first* airplane that was a mass-production, operational weapon, and capable of supersonic speeds. In 1953 an F-100A model brought the world's speed record safely home for the Air Force, with a run of 755.149 miles per hour, flown at minimum altitude over California's Salton Sea. Then on August 20th, 1955, Colonel Horace A. Hanes raced a production-model F-100C across the Mojave Desert at an official 822.135 miles per hour—and gave the Air Force its first supersonic *weapon.*

Now, first of all, the Super Sabre is *big.* You think of a fighter as a light, small airplane. With its pitot boom extended in front of the nose, beneath the air intake, the F-100C isn't at all dainty. It stretches fifty-three feet eleven inches from the boom to the tail. Swept back at a rakish angle of forty-five degrees, the wings span a distance from tip to tip of thirty-eight feet nine inches. And even just standing still, the bird is impressive in size—fifteen feet six inches in height.

In the leading edges of the wings are special automatic slats. At the "slow" speeds of takeoff and landing, the wing leading edge actually slides forward and down, changing the flow of air across the wing to give the airplane greater lift and controllability. On the ground you can push the slat in and out of its positions. The pilot doesn't operate this control; it's automatic and its movement is determined entirely by speed and the angle of attack of the wing in flight.

All control systems in the Super Sabre are power-boosted —"hydraulically-actuated," if you want a quote from the Tech Manual. But power boost by itself isn't the answer to controlling the big jet fighter. To give the pilot the sensitivity he requires, an "artificial-feel" system is built into the control linkage, and the pilot actually "feels" the airplane responding to his control maneuvers. Essentially, this allows the pilot to fly the 15-ton fighter with the strength of a dozen men, yet it doesn't handicap him with the bluntness of overcontrol.

The refueling probe—called a single-point probe—is a long tube of metal that is mounted close to the fuselage, and extends out from the right wing. We'll see more of this probe in a later chapter, but let me explain that the probe doesn't at all fit an impression of supersonic flight. At the very high speeds of the Super Sabre, an airplane flies through an atmosphere that becomes filled with invisible reefs and barriers in the sky.

At 800 miles per hour, for example, if an airplane gets away from its pilot and skids too sharply, the effect is much the same as if the fighter simply slammed into a stone wall. At this speed the air is compressed to the density of brick, and any excess of imbalance can tear a powerful fighter to pieces. Not only can, it has done so, and on too many occasions.

That's why this refueling probe left me shaking my head. First, it doesn't have the extraordinary rigid strength that you associate with the Super Sabre. The horizontal tail of this beast, for example, is simply a big slab of metal. You can cut sawteeth into its leading edge and it will slice through logs like butter. It's *strong*. It's rigid. You can beat on it with a hammer. It has a nice satisfying feel of being able to take the brutal punishment of supersonic shock wave flying.

But that long probe . . . uh uh. On the ground you can push it with one finger, and it responds with a spasmodic quiver. Hit it harder, and the whole thing shakes and dances in its mounting as though it were imbedded in a bowl of jelly. How can it stay together in flight? It's impossible! Remember those Thunderbird maneuvers . . . the g-forces, the sudden maneuvers, the turbulence? These conditions should tear the probe right off the airplane, but they don't.

In the F-100F with Dick, I've stared in complete fascination at the probe as it went through a snake dance. Unless the air is twice as smooth as glass, that probe is never still. I know that flexibility can be built into metal components to an extraordinary degree, but I wasn't quite ready to equate structural strength with spaghetti flexibility. I am now.

I've done most of my flying in airplanes where I can easily recognize the controls. There's either a stick—a nice, easy-to-hold grip—or a wheel. And the throttle. If it's on the dash, it's a knob that fits easily into my hand and slides in and out of its groove. In a ship like the Cub, the knob is atop a metal handle that bends into a groove. That, too, is easy to grasp and to use.

But the controls in the Super Sabre defy the requirements of simplicity; most airplanes are intended to fly, but this thing has been designed to fight a war all by itself. The throttle and the stick aren't at all what would be expected in an airplane that slices through the air with such deft precision and control.

The throttle sits to the left of the pilot. It is a thick, tubular gadget with ridges running around the tube. The only familiar thing I found with this throttle is that it moves forward to increase power, and moves back to ease off on all those horses in that jet engine. There's the added requirement of afterburning, of course.

With the throttle all the way forward in maximum power position, the big Pratt & Whitney J-57-21 engine pours out a static thrust of 10,200 pounds. When the pilot pushes the throttle slightly to the left and forward again, the afterburner kicks in. Suddenly the static thrust is up to 16,000 pounds. Pounds thrust is a term for jets and rockets. What this means in our language is that when the F-100C booms along at 850 miles per hour under full afterburner, that engine is putting out to the howl of some 37,000 horsepower!

Instead of being just a plain, ordinary throttle, in the F-100C this control contains several subcontrol systems. Atop the throttle is the speed-brake switch with three positions. In the center is neutral; when the pilot thumbs the switch back, a big slab of a door is rammed out into the airstream from the belly. In a split second a smooth, swift flight turns into the rumbling and roaring of going straight down on a roller coaster; deceleration is rapid and effective.

To retract the brake, the switch is flicked forward.

On the side of the throttle is the microphone switch; the pilot presses in with his thumb to position the radio for calls to other aircraft or to ground stations. And finally there is the sighting and caging switch for the multiple armament

Details of smoke gear by tailpipe.

systems of the F-100C; in the Thunderbirds' Super Sabres this has been replaced with a small button for smoke control. To create the smoke trail the team uses during maneuvers, the pilot presses the switch down—and the smoke pours out. Release the switch—and smoke is off.

The Thunderbirds' F-100C's have had their big ammunition cans for twenty-mm. cannon shells removed from the fuselage. In their place the mechanics installed special tanks that hold fifty gallons of 10-10 engine oil; these provide a total of some fifteen minutes' smoke. A tube leads from the tanks to the aft section, and juts out beyond the tailpipe, just above but pointing down into the jet blast. The oil sprays down into the flaming exhaust and presto!—we have smoke.

Now for that control stick. Years ago a common term for this control was the joystick. Probably the expression was coined by a barnstorming pilot who found happiness only when cavorting in the high blue. But whatever its origin, joystick does not apply to the F-100C control. That thing has more gimmicks on it than some light planes have in the entire cabin.

The grip is curved to fit the pilot's hand; it's like holding the grip of a target pistol that has been fashioned with exquisite attention to providing maximum flex and use of the fingers. The best way to describe the F-100C stick is to say simply that it is a complete control system in itself. In addition to manipulating the basic controls of flight—the ailerons and the slab tail—the grip also contains the trim switch, which faces the pilot. By thumbing the switch to the left or right, he trims the airplane for lateral (rolling) flight; moving the switch forward and backward attends to longitudinal (pitch, up and down) trim.

To the left of the trim switch is a bomb-release and rocket-release button. In front of the grip is the cannon trigger; this is grasped by the forefinger in time-honored tradition. Below the bomb-rocket release switch is a radar-reject button (to "erase" radar gunsight locks), and there is still another button that actuates nose-wheel steering on the ground. Flying the F-100 sometimes feels like the pilot has to manipulate his fingers as though he has a flute in each hand and he's required to play—expertly—two different tunes simultaneously. And while this goes on his feet are working the rudder pedals and he is maintaining that hair-trigger formation and fighting the effects of turbulence and shock waves and about fifty other things.

It's *work!*

The Hollywood picture of the handsome young jet pilot dashing to his airplane, climbing quickly into the cockpit, starting the engine, waving good-by to his crew chief and blowing a kiss to the beautiful young thing sobbing behind the wire fence, all in about thirty-eight seconds flat, is a burlesque of reality.

Before the Thunderbirds leap off from a runway with

their bodacious afterburners spitting flame, each man must first complete a checklist of *152 separate items* on the exterior of the airplane, within the fighter, and in the cockpit. When a pilot makes his walk around the Super Sabre and comes to the nose-wheel well, for example, he has seventeen separate items here to examine. Then he works his way along the forward fuselage. After this he comes to the right wing. Just a wing, you say, but here is what he must inspect—carefully:

Air-refueling probe; slats and rollers; main wheel brake, where he looks for loose or broken drive keys and broken hydraulic lines; main wheel tire for condition of the tire, slippage, and inflation; main gear door uplocks, and microswitch (actuating switch); main gear ground safety locks; pip pin (this is the quick disconnect for fairing doors); main gear-wheel well (and the maze of lines and wires inside); antiskid sensing unit; external load installation and mounting, and the ground safety lock; wingtip and position lights; and, finally, the ailerons.

The F-100F cockpit is a duplicate of the F-100D, and I received firsthand instruction in the incredible complexity and diversity of controls, switches, triggers, buttons, and so on. When I climbed in, I first had to check the ejection seat and the canopy. The word *pin* has different meanings. To the doting mother, handling a pin requires care, because in the event of misuse baby is likely to get jabbed in his posterior. But baby gets over it; misuse of a pin in the cockpit can—literally—kill a pilot.

Here the safety pin is a device that prevents explosive charges from going *whoom!* when they shouldn't. The jet fighter has explosive charges to blast the canopy free of the cockpit in an emergency. The pilot always sits on a small volcano, because his ejection seat is armed with an explosive cartridge that, when fired, blasts him up and away from his airplane.

There's a checklist for reference; it's not safe or good practice to trust to memory, and no pilot in his right mind runs through his cockpit check without a flip-page booklet before him. In the cockpit, the pilot checks all handgrips and triggers. Then, the safety pins, to be sure they are installed. He checks the seat disconnects, the tubing and hose (oxygen, communications, g-suit, etc.) to his suit, and then the switch for the standby external release (for the canopy).

Before he can even prepare to begin to start the engine, the pilot moves through a maze in the cockpit requiring his meticulous attention. He checks *everything,* and this includes such items as circuit breakers, speed brake controls, g-suit pressure settings, throttle friction, pitch and yaw dampers, radio and navigational equipment, lights, flight instruments, engine instruments and controls, electrical supply equipment and inverters, oxygen, anti-icing, emergency systems, and many more.

After he has individually checked off eighty-five separate items, the pilot is now ready to start his big jet engine. He puts his self-starter switch to ON, turns the master switch to ON. Then he presses down on the starter and the ignition. The throttle goes forward to the Idle position at a setting between twelve per cent and sixteen per cent of maximum possible revolutions per minute. As the engine "catches" and comes to life, he checks the exhaust temperature gauges. Then at forty-five to fifty-five per cent rpm, the DC generator cuts in, ending the power drain from his battery, and he carefully checks all engine instruments, the hydraulic system and the trim system.

With the Super Sabre fired up, the pilot still isn't ready to move so much as an inch. He runs through his hydraulic flight control check, rechecks all his personal equipment, puts his UHF radio equipment to ON. Then a check of all flight instruments, radio navigation aids, IFF (identification: friend or foe) system to ON, a complete recheck of the oxygen and g-suit pressure systems. The ground crewman removes the nose-gear safety lock, the pilot removes all safety pins. He checks his emergency fuel system, switches oxygen to 100 per cent, sets and checks the engine pressure gauge, and sets his altimeter. The line crew hauls away the wheel chocks, and pilot now has permission to move out.

The canopy is partially lowered, and the nose wheel steering system engaged. Again, because it is better to be down here and wishing you were up there, than to be up there and wishing you were down here, the pilot rechecks his flight and engine instruments. He switches to ON his antiskid system, works all the flight controls, puts the hydraulic gauge on Utility. Moves the speed brake switch to ON, then to OFF. The canopy is closed, sealed, and locked. Yaw and Pitch dampers on Standby. Takeoff trim, checked and okay. Then, with permission from the tower, the pilot taxis into takeoff position, and holds.

He's still got work to do, and in this order he checks the tachometer; sees that exhaust temperature is at least 320 degrees Centigrade; that the oil pressure reads in the green; the throttle is moved to Military Position; heat and vent systems are okay; engine pressure gauge and all engine instruments read in the green. Then, and only then, can he move the throttle to Full Military Power, and release the brakes.

All this is from the pilot's viewpoint. One afternoon, Chief Warrant Officer Myron D. France, the Maintenance Officer for the Team, and James M. Stuart of North American Aviation, spent several hours with me poking through the recesses of a partly disassembled F-100C. What these two men don't know about the F-100C isn't worth bothering with.

I wanted to bring to this chapter something entirely different for the reader. What happens *inside* that fifteen-ton fighter during just *one* stage of operations? It's all well and good to discuss what happens in general terms when the pilot flicks this and that switch, punches buttons, pulls and pushes controls, and so on. I wanted to slow time itself down to a crawl, to illustrate the fantastic internal activity that takes place during just several seconds. Nothing seemed better suited than just starting the Super Sabre, and we set ourselves to the task.

Now, the F-100C as assigned to the Thunderbirds has an equipment change that is quite important in carrying out the Team's role of precision movement—on the ground. To start the modern jet fighter is an operation requiring external power equipment; this isn't compatible with Thunderbird operations. The fighters are often at fields where power equipment for military aircraft isn't available. Then, the idea is to have all six fighters standing on the flight line with only the pilots and line men present—the hands come down, a sudden high-pitched whine blasts the air, and suddenly all the Super Sabres are alive, booming with energy. To do all this, the starting system had to be placed entirely within the airplane.

The F-100C fighters of the Thunderbirds, therefore, have an Internal Turbine Combustion Starter. This is a fuel-air combustion starting system that makes the airplane completely self-sustaining, for, instead of external power, there is available the energy of four 800-cubic-inch storage bottles of air compressed to 3,000 pounds per square inch.

The starter itself is actually a miniature jet engine that uses air from the high-pressure source to support combustion—to light the fire that makes the Super Sabre go. Geared to the engine, the starter spins the jet compressor turbine, then the entire engine, to a speed of thirty-two per cent of maximum revolutions per minute. At that moment the bird is alive; the fire is on.

A sidelight to this installation in the F-100C airplanes is the outstanding effort and skill of the maintenance team that supports Thunderbirds operations. The mechanics of the team installed the internal starter units for all seven F-100 airplanes in a flat three days.

The accomplishment may be judged in a better light when you consider that this operation, normally performed by a maintenance and modification depot that does only such work, estimated that the job would require a minimum of three weeks, and more likely about six weeks. The team couldn't afford to have the Super Sabres tied up for this period of time, so the pilots flew the fighters to the Sacramento Air Materiel Area at McClellan Air Force Base, and sixteen men of the maintenance team went along in a transport to attend to their precious birds.

"They had to remove the aft section of the airplane," France explained. "Then the men removed the paneling within this section—took out the inner skin in order to install the four air bottles in each airplane. These are made of steel, about a foot in diameter for each—" We poked among several spare bottles on the hangar floor.

"To start the job," France continued, "the men had to remove the old turbine starter, which was a low-pressure system that tied in to a ground cart. Then they installed the new starter, the whole system of plumbing from the bottles to the starter, tying in the air and fuel lines. I know they're *good,* but three days . . ." He shook his head. "It was really a fantastic job."

Jim Stuart dragged over a powerful light, and we studied the complex interior of the Super Sabre. "Now, the pilot puts on his master switch," Jim explained, as his finger pointed along the power leads, "then presses down on the starter and the ignition. He moves the throttle forward to the Idle position at fourteen per cent rpm. . . .

"This applies electrical power to the system. Oops, forgot—he turns the battery switch to ON, and turns the inverters to ON. This system converts the twenty-eight volts DC to 115 AC—"

"Why?" I interrupted.

"Well, DC is a powerful jolt. It's a low-voltage, high-amperage that requires heavy wiring, more heat, heavier equipment. Weight is too important just to throw any system in here. AC allows the precision control of equipment and even precision instruments, notably the gyros. The inverters convert DC current to the kind of electricity in the home, tame it down.

"Once the pilot has all his switches turned on, he punches the starter button. This is a red button, on the right instrument console."

It's an intricate procedure, and here I am slowing down the passage of time, stretching out considerably what requires only seconds. When the starter button goes down, energizing the system by drawing power from the battery, air and fuel are brought immediately together. The potential for firing up the bird is always in the airplane. The battery operates a boost pump, and the fuel flows from the low-pressure fuel system, along the line between the aircraft and engine fuel systems. Punching the starter button pushes the fuel through the line into a combustion chamber within the starter unit. The air is sucked in through a solenoid, an electromagnetically operated valve.

The valve opens, and the fuel and air rush together into the starter combustion chamber. Here a sparking plug, a regular aircraft spark plug, has already been activated, creating an electric arc.

The fuel flows through its line at 18 pounds per square inch pressure, the air as it leaves the bottle under 3,000 pounds per square inch. But this is too high, and as the air flows toward the combustion chamber, its pressure is reduced to exactly the best level—300 psi—required to initiate combustion.

The mixed fuel and air spray into the chamber, and meet the electrical arc. The reaction is instantaneous; the mixture ignites, there is tremendous compression, and heat is created. Now there is available for further energy a flow of superheated gases.

These burst against the wheel of the starter turbine; the turbine is of steel construction, with a line of small buckets that face in the same direction. The blazing gases pound across the turbine wheel, ram into the buckets, and send the wheel explosively into action. Within seconds the turbine wheel is spinning at more than 35,000 revolutions per minute—*585 revolutions every second!*

The spinning of this turbine feeds power through a linkage into the gears of a shaft drive system, what the mechanics call a Bull Gear. This in turn forces a high-speed rotor of the jet engine to spin. The movement of this rotor (known as N2, or high-speed rotor) shows up on the pilot's instrument panel where he reads the N2 rotor rpm.

Now the airplane is coming to full life. As the N2 rotor spins, it passes energy to the No. 1 turbine in the aft section of the big jet engine. As the compressor spins, it begins to suck air into the engine through the front intake. The result of this inward air flow is to build up pressure in what is known as the Hot Section, or burner can. "This is the heart of the engine," explains Stuart, "where the combustion process goes on."

As pressure builds up, the N1 compressor in the forward part of the engine begins to spin; simultaneously, the No. 2 and No. 3 turbines, in the rear part of the engine, also come to life and begin their spinning motion. The air that is being sucked in to the high-speed rotor is now turning the N1 compressor. The latter system has no gear linkage to any of the

94

other equipment; only the flow of air sustains its motion.

The engine is now turning, rotating with increasing speed. There is a definite flow of air. There is still the same electrical power being drawn from the battery. The main source of power now is fed from the internal starter unit itself.

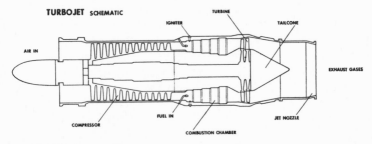

F-100 jet engine.

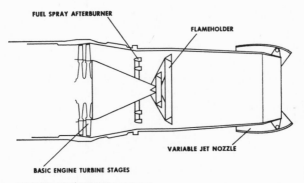

When the engine spins at between twelve and sixteen percent of its maximum rpm, it is time to introduce fuel, and to ignite this fuel. At this moment the pilot is ready to actually start his engine. He has engine rotation, but not sustaining power. He still has to light the fire within the engine itself.

With the rpm at the desired level, the pilot moves his throttle forward to the Idle position. This initiates a new sequence of events.

As the throttle goes forward to Idle, it opens the shutoff valve from the fuel control to the engine. This forces fuel under pressure toward the engine. The pressure comes from the engine-driven fuel pump; the starter unit, as a result of beginning rotation of the jet engine itself, has also started all accessory equipment in the gear box and engine compartments. Even though it does not yet have its own fire started, the big engine is "alive" and functioning.

The fuel rushes through its lines, and sprays through a nozzle into burner cans. There are eight of these burner cans, mounted as though they were ringed along the inside of a giant stovepipe (which, essentially, the jet engine is). Each burner can is hollow in the sprayer-bar nozzle end; it is here that the fuel is injected, and then sprayed into a cone-shaped deflector inside the can.

Now air pours in, and this is the result of a separate but major operation of the system. Air is sucked in from the intake, and is being compressed through sixteen individual stages, through sixteen separate compressor wheels. By the time it bursts into each burner can it has been heavily compressed.

At this point we've got the fuel spraying in, and a flow of compressed air around the fuel. At the same instant that the fuel is introduced through the spray bars into the burner cans, the engine system electrically excites two spark plugs.

In each of the eight burner cans these plugs create an arc that exceeds 4,000 degrees F.! Under this lash of fire the fuel-air mixture disappears; it flames, expands with enormous pressure as intensely hot gases. These are flung back through the engine by their own expansion, and they race across the three main turbine wheels. The result is immediate acceleration, which in turn speeds up the front compressors, and the entire engine.

At this point the Super Sabre is fully alive; the big engine is entirely on its own. The moment the fire is lit, and becomes self-sustaining within the engine, the starter unit automatically cuts out. Combustion is now into its full cycle.

On the flight line, the sounds of this procedure have been distinct, and *loud*. Seconds after the pilot energized the system by pressing down on the starter button, a blast of compressed air shot in a spray directly beneath the plane, accompanied by a startling, ear-wracking hiss. Then, as the

96

engine gained momentum, there came a whine, gradually increasing in pitch and volume.

Finally—the fire was lit, combustion was achieved and became self-sustaining. And then the sound was familiar, the tremendous shriek, a deep-throated cry of power—the song of the Super Sabre.

Once the engine is started, crew chiefs go to work atop the airplane. Directly behind the canopy on the fuselage is a removable panel; working in this area between engine start and when the airplane moves out is known as "pulling a saddleback check." The crew chiefs visually check the hydraulic flight-control system. Since the F-100C flies entirely on the basis of power-boosted controls, standard procedure is to be absolutely certain that the system functions properly.

The crew chiefs check for proper working pressures and to assure that air has not been trapped in the hydraulic fluid. They watch a compensating pin as the pilot operates the rudder and stick controls from the cockpit to move the external surfaces. Not until then do they seal the panel—and they do this literally in seconds.

The men then check the Super Sabre in its entirety for any fluid leaks. There are no flaps on the F-100C, but before the pilot so much as moves an inch he lowers the speed brake, then retracts the broad surface, in order for the mechanics visually to note its proper operation. A man pulls the gear downlock pins, someone else snatches away the wheel chocks. The crew chief checks the canopy to assure perfect closure, climbs down from the wing, and signals the pilot that all *he* has to do now is to fly the bird!

6 How to Fly like a Thunderbird

Taking off in pairs, a swarm of F-80 Shooting Star fighter-bombers lift sluggishly from the runway of the Fifth Air Force's K-13 advanced airfield at Sumon, Korea. The airplanes are from the 35th Squadron of the 8th Fighter-Bomber Group, an outfit that has seen rugged, constant service in the thick of the Korean War. The missions are the "dirty" kind—shooting up trains, roads, and canals; hitting enemy troops with napalm, rockets, guns, and bombs on close-support missions. And anything else that might be necessary in the grim ground-support tactical missions of the Korean air fighting.

The mission today promises to be mean, and costly. The strike is against a concentration of armored vehicles, tanks, supply trucks, and troop reinforcements at Kunri in North Korea, a rail and road center of critical importance to the Communists. It will be well defended; every pilot expects that.

Each plane carries a 1,000-pound bomb beneath each wing. Takeoff in the F-80 with a full load of fuel, ammunition, and the ton of bombs is a long, dragging affair. The airplane responds poorly to the controls. To ease the problem of takeoff, the pilots roll in a lot of nose-up trim. Immediately after becoming airborne, they roll the trim back to hold the nose down and accelerate to a safe maneuvering speed.

In one of the weary fighters, Lieutenant Charles W. Maultsby starts to curse. Quietly, but vehemently. As he rolls the trim back for a nose-down pressure, a circuit breaker pops out suddenly. The trim at that moment is inoperative. Chuck Maultsby makes an immediate decision. To fly to Kunri, he will have to push hard on that stick all the way to the target and in his glide-bomb runs, and twice as hard on the way back to K-13 when the fighter has dropped much of its weight. Maultsby doesn't turn back, although he would be blameless if he did.

This is his seventeenth mission. The previous sixteen taught him the value to our ground-pounders of the deadly load he carries in bombs and his machine-gun bullets. What the hell; fighting the trim is a lot better than lying in a foxhole. He stays in formation.

He cannot anticipate what will happen this day, of course, and so he does not know that Kunri is a trap. The Chinese have brought in dozens of light and heavy guns, including several batteries of deadly, accurate 88-mm. flak guns. They realize the Kunri target is too lucrative to pass by, and that the fighter-bombers will be coming. So they augment the bait with a bristling wall of flak guns.

Chuck Maultsby doesn't know this, and neither does he know that that circuit breaker that has popped out so annoyingly will, literally, mean the difference between life and death. Or that the very trap the Chinese have set up at Kunri will also save his life. Fate takes strange turns with pilots, and few men will know so bizarre a chain of circumstances which allowed Maultsby to suffer impossible odds . . . but to survive.

The fighter-bombers circle the target, and the pilots are stunned at the fury and volume of the antiaircraft pouring up from the ground. Great clouds of oily black smoke, their centers marked with blotches of angry red, erupt everywhere in the sky. Tracers hose in broken lines from the hidden guns. "We'll never get through that stuff with glide-bombing!" a pilot shouts. The squadron leader agrees, and orders the pilots to change their attack to dive-bombing. And at this point the series of miraculous incidents begins. Death tries hard, several times, to snatch at Maultsby, but fortunately, miraculously, without success.

Chuck rolls over almost on his back, and shoves the F-80 into a steep dive. At an angle of sixty degrees a heavy shell crashes into the side of the airplane, and the world blows up in his face. At the moment of the explosion Chuck is concentrating all his attention on the rail lines with their freight cars packed with supplies. All hell breaks loose, and a fantastic shock smashes through the airplane, slaps Chuck with a giant hand against the side of the canopy.

The shell has exploded just about seven feet behind the pilot. The blast rips forward into the throttle quadrant, dissolves the instrument panel, and transforms the windscreen into a blur of cracked glass. Sharp thuds slam into the back of the seat; the armor plating saves Maultsby's life, stopping a barrage of jagged shards of metal.

At the same instant a flash fire whips through the cockpit, and Chuck stares down at his left arm, wrapped completely in flames. He sticks his left arm straight out into the air and the windblast snuffs out the fire.

And that is when he realizes through the numbing shock

99

of the explosion what he has done. He has extended his arm to the side *into the air*.

This is where the first intervention of fate pays its dividend. In the glide-bombing attack Chuck would have flown with his hand on the throttle, on the left side of the cockpit.

"The decision to dive bomb is the only reason I have a left arm today," he explained. "When the shell hit the bird it blew out the whole side of the airplane, throttle quadrant and all. Because of the dive mission, my hand was at that moment on the gunsight, right up forward, just above the instrument panel. I was changing the depression of the sight. In glide-bombing you need more depression on the sight to predict the bomb fall; dive-bombing however, is virtually line of sight. . . ."

Several things happen almost simultaneously. When Chuck sticks his arm out in to the airstream—extinguishing the fire on his blazing arm—the move is not made intentionally because of the fire. The blast knocked out the F-80 control system, and immediately Chuck knows that he cannot control the aircraft. The stick is useless, it moves about without response from the fighter.

Chuck is diving straight in to the earth, helpless, out of control. He has just seconds to live.

But remember that circuit breaker that popped out? The trim controls are inoperative, and Chuck has been flying with a stiff forward pressure on the stick all the time. Because of that jammed trim—a steep nose-up position—the moment the elevator controls are knocked out, the airplane responds to the trim and pitches up with a violent jerk.

Chuck's hand goes out into the airstream because he has reached for the throttle. He knows at once that he must get out of the airplane. "I was going to tell the guys that my controls were shot out, that I had no elevator response," he recalled. "I reached out for the throttle quadrant to press the radio switch—and, of course, nothing was there, just a tremendous hole. The whole side of the airplane had been blown away. . . ."

After a period of time, training becomes instinct, as does training specifically for emergency situations. When the stick fails to respond, without even thinking of the motion Chuck

100

squeezes the bomb release, and a ton of metal and high explosives falls away from the airplane toward the target. It is this sudden release of weight combined with the nose-high trim that causes the tremendous pitchup of the F-80.

All this happens within seconds. The jammed trim control has saved Chuck's life by preventing the wild dive into the ground, but the succor is only temporary. The Shooting Star pitches up, and unless Chuck gets out—*fast*—the airplane will continue in its wild zoom and then tumble crazily out of control. He may not be able to get out then.

A fleeting thought comes to him. "No use sitting here any longer. . . ." Later, he is amazed at the calmness of that thought, because at the same moment he is in critical danger. The pitchup is so severe that violent *g*-forces ram Chuck's head down between his knees. His legs are straight out. He cannot lift his head, he has no throttle with which to chop the speed of the fighter. His hands grasp the ejection handles, and yank back, hard. As he pulls to actuate the explosive charge, he remembers that this is the way a pilot loses both legs, chopped crudely off at the knees, by their being smashed into the front of the upper canopy. It is not a pleasant thought, but he has no choice.

Call it what you will, another miracle perhaps, but as the seat explodes with ramrod force out of the airplane, it tumbles, and it tumbles forward. It is impossible, it cannot happen, but the tumble causes Chuck's legs to miss the sharp canopy edge, perhaps by no more than a thousandth of an inch!

A terrific roar, the airstream, strikes his ears. The sky and horizon tumble crazily before his eyes. He has no automatic separation device from the seat. He is at low altitude. He threshes his legs—the legs he should have had severed—and kicks the seat away from his tumbling body. The pilot chute snaps away, drags the canopy out in a long streamer, and then *CRAA-CK!* In that moment the tumbling flight ends, and Chuck is suspended beneath the blossomed silk.

It should be quiet; other pilots have described the sensation of drifting earthward beneath the silk. It is no more than a quiet sighing of the wind.

But not now. There is a terrifying din, a "tremendous,

constant crackling roar in the sky." Three squadrons of jet fighters scream earthward, engines howling. A forest of heavy antiaircraft guns and the smaller machine guns and cannon blast away in an upward hail of fire. Bombs smash into the earth, the concussion waves rippling out and slapping at his body.

The earth is covered with heavy white snow. Chuck floats down beneath a chute that is all white; if it were red and white the other pilots could see him, know that he had ejected safely. But parachute canopy and snow blend into one, and he is invisible.

He floats gently to earth—directly into the center of the target. At the same moment a half-dozen thousand-pound bombs strike the ground, and Chuck is in the middle of a violent, blazing hell of explosions and waves of concussion.

"I hate to say it, but it's a good thing those guys couldn't hit what they were aiming at," he mused in recollection, "because they sure as hell would have killed me. On the way down I thought the Chinese were shooting at me. The chute was riddled with holes, and I could even hear the bullets passing right by my ears. But they weren't; they were just firing madly with every gun they had at the planes."

On the ground, he slips out of the parachute harness, and dashes madly away from the target center. A knoll is in sight, and this is his objective. Get behind the knoll, away from the firing. Disappear from sight, and run for it while the Chinese are focusing all their attention on the sky.

Chuck makes it away from dead center of the target, but he fails to get very far. He is much closer to the knoll when two thousand-pound bombs that explode less than a hundred yards away churn the earth into a vibrating, maddened volcano of flame, shock, and thunder. A fist slams him against the ground.

Dazed, he climbs to his feet, and starts to run again. But there are twelve airplanes in their dives, and the bombs continue to smash into the earth. Every time he gets to his feet and runs the shock waves hurl him heavily against the ground.

He has been knocked down a half-dozen times in his attempts to escape capture. But he manages to cover only a

102

few hundred yards when suddenly he faces a ring of rifle muzzles pointing unerringly at him.

He is listed as "Missing in Action." Not one of the F-80 pilots saw him parachute to earth. They did see, however, the blazing fighter whip crazily through the air, then explode as it hit. No one believes that he is alive.

It is difficult for anyone else to decide what is worse: the harrowing experiences of Chuck Maultsby in the air and his incredible brush with death, or what he endured for the next twenty-two months as a prisoner of the Communists. When the Chinese captured Chuck, he did not see a friendly face for many weeks afterward. His captors kept him isolated from any American or other Allied prisoners, and not until he was brought to an interrogation room at Anju did he meet another POW. This was a B-26 pilot shot down on a low-level attack; his presence was a great joy to Maultsby.

They stayed together for the next several months, living in a prison cave dug in the side of a hill. The cave was not quite high enough for the men to stand, or to lie down with feet outstretched. They slept and lived on filthy straw, passed their body wastes almost like animals, and endured all the discomfort—and sometimes the horror—of living in a stinking hole in the ground infested with all manner of insect life and rodents. It was bitter cold, and for all those months the two men subsisted on rice and some water—and nothing else.

Yet, during those trying months, the two pilots never relented in their attempts to escape. Atop the cave was a strong but crude structure of boards, and Maultsby and his fellow prisoner tried every way imaginable to dig, scrape, or gouge their way out of their hole. Their efforts were intense and unremitting, but success was not to be had.

The remaining time at the hands of the Chinese, and sometimes with the North Koreans, began to melt into a blur of unreality. There was pain, intense pain. The months filled more and more with hunger and privation, with cold, and with interrogations that went on endlessly.

It is impossible, really, to describe what took place day after day, week after week, month after month. I cannot —and neither can any other writer—condense into the pages

103

of an entire book the terrible psychological impact of those two years. It is impossible to assimilate, there are too many aspects to digest, there are no bridges of eloquence to convey utter loneliness at times, the sharp, penetrating scalpel of the Chinese methods of psychological torture.

"Pain and torture is an everyday occurrence to these people," Chuck told me quietly. "To us it is horrible, starkly horrible. Yet much of that same torture—torture of everyday living, sometimes—is intense only by the contrast of comparison. They treated their own people the same way many times. You come to understand this, you *must* understand the enormous, yawning gulf that creats the variance of thinking, of psychology, or you begin to bend. And you can bend only so far; you must have resilience, belief in yourself, in your country, in what you are doing over there in those stinking caves and prisons. If you believe, you can stand *anything*."

Exactly what happened to Chuck Maultsby is a story that must stay locked within his own memories. Suffice to say that he was dragged and shoved and prodded from place to place, rarely knowing where he or fellow prisoners were.

There was solitary confinement. He did not co-operate with the Chinese; they resorted to beatings. He resisted interrogation, he proved himself to be an enemy of the People's Republic—solitary, beatings, starvation. He tried to escape, and this was unthinkable to the Chinese, and because they did not care very much for the lives of their own fellows, he came very close to being shot or skewered by irate Chinese guards with long bayonets.

Never once did he yield. He bent only so far, but that was all. To yield, to break, was more than to receive the assurance of an end to the maddening physical and psychological treatment. To yield, even to claims so ridiculous as to be impossible to believe, was to be false to everything that he believed in, that he loved. To Chuck Maultsby there were never two choices. It was as simple as that.

One bright moment came in the darkness of the twenty-two months. Beginning an interrogation in a closed room, a Chinese officer spoke to Chuck in perfect, crisp English.

He noted the prisoner's raised eyebrows, waved his hand casually.

"Relax, Lieutenant Maultsby," he said, "this will not be the interrogation you expected." He offered a cigarette. Chuck accepted, breathed deeply, gratefully of the smoke. The Chinese officer explained his command of the language —he had received his education at the City College of New York.

The Chinese did not press Chuck with questions. He explained that he had left the United States only to visit with his family still in China, and was then trapped by the outbreak of war in Korea, and the commitment of Chinese forces to the battle.

Chuck spoke frankly. "You're an educated man. You've lived in the States, obviously you know us well. My God, do you really believe all this Communist nonsense?"

The Chinese smiled and shook his head. "Of course not— you have answered the question yourself." Suddenly his hand slapped the table. "But what can I do?" he almost shouted. "My family is in China. Nothing would be more satisfying than to walk over to your lines, to return to the States. But no, that is impossible. If I were to make that mistake they would wipe out my entire family to the last person; my immediate family, and every relative they could identify . . ."

He fell silent, and pushed the cigarettes across the desk. An hour later he informed Chuck he would have to return to the prisoner compound. But before Maultsby left, the Chinese rose to his feet, and said quietly, "Good luck."

He needed every bit of that luck. There were more interrogators, and a repetition of everything he would like to wipe from his mind. But time passed, the guns were stilled. On September 1st, 1953, Chuck Maultsby was in an exchange of prisoners.

Despite the privations of the two years as a prisoner, he was in surprisingly good physical shape. "Your physical shape depended a lot on your mental shape," he recalled. "If you wanted to be convinced that you were in a bad way, that's just how a man usually ended up. Too many men, good men in all other respects, wallowed in self-pity, or gave up hope altogether.

105

"And that broke them. If you believe in what you have been taught are the important things in life, in honor and morality and country, if you believe in these things with all your soul"—he looked directly at me—"then they can never get through to you. You can take anything."

Chuck Maultsby came home, and went back to his first love—flying. He checked out in the swift F-86 Sabres, and then moved into the supersonic F-100's. In September of 1953, the same month that he left the Chinese prison camp, he received assignment to Nellis Air Force Base. In 1958 he joined the outstanding Air Training Command Gunnery Team, and Chuck was a member of that Team when it won every phase of the Air Force's 1958 World-Wide Fighter Weapons Meet!

In October of 1958 he achieved what he considers the high water mark of his flying career—he joined the Thunderbirds.

Chuck Maultsby's thoughts of airplanes and of flying go back as far as he can remember. He was born in Greensboro, North Carolina, and remembers to this day that he was four years old when his folks introduced him to the world of flight. It was a Sunday, and the family drove along the Carolina roads for a relaxing afternoon. The car rolled past a cornfield, but the excited screams of the young boy quickly forced its return.

Young Maultsby stared with rapt attention. On the field was a Ford Tri-Motor transport flown by a barnstorming pilot who worked the small town circuit and sold sightseeing flights. Chuck looked up at the monster airplane, dancing around his father and begging for a flight. "I don't think my mother appreciated it"—Chuck grinned—"but the old man just couldn't resist. He paid the man and I dashed across the grass to climb into the airplane. . . ."

The Ford was a giant to the boy, and fascinating in every line. It had a strange corrugated skin, three roaring engines, and smelled strongly of gasoline and oil. Chuck drank it all in, and it was heady wine.

He stared out the window, hypnotized, as the engines ground over slowly and abruptly burst into a clattering roar. The Ford shook and rumbled and vibrated, then bounced heavily as the pilot trundled over the ground to the end of the cornfield. The clatter became thunder, the airplane shook down to its last rivet, and there came a sudden and rapid movement as the pilot released the brakes.

It's not likely, of course, that a boy of this age would remember details, but the rough field, the fumes of gasoline, the strange metal touch of the airplane, remain strongly to the brilliant pilot of today. "I remember the motions in the air, the marvelous sensation of floating above the earth." Chuck sighed happily. "It was all so wonderful. I savored every minute of the descent, the wind whistling past the wings and the fuselage, the rumble as the wheels touched down, taxiing back to the starting point. I remember leaving the airplane reluctantly . . . but what I remember most of all is that from that day forward, all I wanted out of life was to fly."

Four years later, when Chuck was eight, his mother died. He went to Norfolk, Virginia, and the remaining years of growing up were spent with his foster parents, Mr. and Mrs. L. W. Griswold.

Directly across the river from his house was an old dirt airfield, a cow pasture that had become an airport by the simple expedient of using it for airplanes. Whenever he had a spare moment, Chuck pedaled furiously on his bicycle to the airport, ready to do *anything* that would get him a ride. He worked every weekend at the field, rolling planes out of the hangars, carrying buckets of water, sweeping trash, painting, fueling planes, cleaning out the office— anything that could get him into the air.

"I was a beggar," he laughed. "I used to look at pilots with a hangdog expression of complete woe, until out of sheer exasperation they would take me up. I wheedled flights, I begged flights, I worked for them. One man had a Stinson Reliant at the field, a beautiful high-wing monoplane. I used to wax the airplane for him in return—if I did a good job—for a ride when the man flew to another airport a hundred miles away. I polished and buffed that thing until it shone so bright that it hurt your eyes. It was worth it, too, I got a lot of flying in that Reliant."

Chuck scrimped and saved and worked, and when he was

thirteen years old, he proudly showered crumpled dollar bills and change on the office desk to purchase his first flight lesson. He took to the air as a new pilot just as he had always dreamed it would be. But when he began to attain proficiency, the field closed down.

Undaunted, Chuck rode fifteen miles on his bike to another field. Flying cost a lot more than a boy his age could normally afford, but that didn't keep him on the ground. He begged jobs all over town; he carried trash barrels, mowed lawns, chopped firewood, anything that would allow him to accumulate his nickels and dimes and quarters so that he could fly. And fly he did, in an old J-3 Cub and a Fleet biplane.

Flying was an obsession that drove his folks crazy. Money came dearly to the Griswolds, and Chuck worked during his summer vacation in order to buy clothes for school. But at the end of the summer he hadn't any money or any new clothes—it had all gone for more lessons. The hours piled up in his logbook, and on his sixteenth birthday *the* day arrived. Chuck had forty hours logged by this time, but the regulations required a student to be sixteen years old before he could solo.

At the crack of dawn on his birthday, he was waiting impatiently at the airport. He soloed, with music ringing in his ears. "I'd been ready for a long time," he said, "and it was a thorough and satisfying experience. I got drunk that day—on flying."

World War II began while Chuck was still in high school. He tried everything to join the aviation cadet program, but he was not yet old enough. Then the Army Air Forces announced it would accept as cadets students in their last year of high school, and Chuck nearly broke down the door to sign the necessary papers. He passed all his tests, and was sworn in as a cadet in March of 1944. Three months later, with his diploma safely in the record books, he went on active duty.

It was a forlorn Cadet Maultsby who passed the next several months, for Chuck never made it to flight training. At Keesler Field he went through preflight training, and in special tests drew his instructors' attention by qualifying at the top of the list for pilot, navigator, and bombardier. He underlined *Pilot* heavily on the assignment forms, but by then the cadet program had been sharply cut back. With no flying in sight, Chuck left the Air Force to attend Northrop Aeronautical Institute at Hawthorne, California.

He found it impossible to stop trying; after his graduation in late 1948 from the Institute, he left nothing undone to regain his aviation cadet status. In April of 1949 he was back in uniform; two years later the long struggle paid off. Chuck received his commission and his wings as a fighter pilot.

Then came Korea and combat, the long, gruelling months as a prisoner, and finally his return to Nellis and, in 1958, the coveted assignment to the Thunderbirds.

I spent a long and particularly rewarding evening at home with Chuck and his family during my stay with the team. We had flown for several hours that day, and I looked forward to dinner with the Maultsby family. Besides Chuck there's Jeanne, much too pretty and young to be the mother of two husky boys, Chuckie and Shawn. After dinner, we discussed at length the particular problems of flying the Right Wing position with the Thunderbirds. I'd already done considerable flying with Crane, I had moved in with Dick to the Right Wing position when Chuck skidded away, and, through the years with former team members and the men now flying, I had seen more than sixty full air shows in practice and before the massed crowds. But no one can ever know exactly what it's like to fly the Thunderbirds' Right Wing except the guy who's in that cockpit, riding the position.

"Well, you've got to be realistic about this," Chuck began. "First of all, any fighter pilot worth his salt believes absolutely that he can whip anybody else in an air fight. If he didn't think that, he wouldn't be a fighter pilot. But no matter how great his skill, he needs a lot of practice and training before he can fly precision formation aerobatics.

"The amount of practice is a variable; it depends upon the pilot's own skill, his receptiveness to learning, his *willingness* to be taught. Attitude is everything in this game.

"The glamor of formation flying is all on the outside,

when you're looking in. Formation flying is mostly just plain work, and the ability to have the sense of anticipating what happens next. Flying formation with the Thunderbirds is merely harder work and more anticipation, and the ability to blend all your thinking into the concept of the team. You *are* the team, or a part of the whole."

"From what I've learned so far," I said, "it's necessary that every man know, at all times, what the other three are doing, and that he can anticipate at any one time what that man not only will do, but *may* do."

"Don't make us out as having two heads," Chuck protested. "Sure, we're good. If we weren't, we wouldn't be here. But insight isn't so much the answer as practice, practice, and more practice."

"I know," I replied. "Good old Fitz and his 'Everybody up at four in the morning for the first dance!' "

They laughed. "It's true; there's no other way to gain proficiency except by constant practice," Chuck said. "Remember what Robby told you when we were at Daytona? That even a few days out of the air shows up quickly. We get rusty. All of us. To stay sharp at this business you've got to stay in there and work, all the time.

"Everything is a natural progression. When a new pilot comes on the team, he begins with the two-ship formation. Primarily, this is because of safety; then, the new pilot has the chance to learn quickly. He devotes *all* his attention to staying in formation, and he doesn't have to concern himself with three airplanes—only one. In the beginning, just staying on the wing of the leader takes about a hundred and fifty per cent of all his energy."

"Yeah, I know," I said. "I've watched Griff leading Cass all over the sky like there wasn't going to be any tomorrow, that they just *had* to get all their flying in today."

Chuck smiled. "Yes, Griff does like to fly, all right. Any pilot like Cass is good, really good, before he comes on the team. Running all over the sky with Griff is excellent training. And as the new pilot becomes more experienced, he also becomes more proficient, and before long he's right there in the full diamond.

"The key to success here is for the new pilot not to be

overly concerned with being smooth. If the guy tries to fly the best possible formation in all respects right from the start, he may get into trouble. It's too much. We tell a new man to 'just stay in position. Everything else will come by itself; don't worry about the bobbling up and down.' "

There are several basic and important differences in formation flying as practiced by the Thunderbirds. First and foremost is that the pilot undergoes a constant high g-force conditioning. This can't be ignored; I've already mentioned the new men massaging those sore arm muscles for weeks from fighting the nose-down trim. The g-forces make it worse.

You have to see these men after flying not only a full show, but perhaps a complete practice mission before the show, after flying to the show area. The rat-racing in the tight formation wears them out. Their flying suits are soaked through with sweat. They sit around the debriefing table, and either slump back in their chairs, or lean their elbows on the table. They are physically very tired, and if you look closely you can spot the eye glaze which comes from intense sustained concentration.

Except for the initial pass and the Bomb Burst, the aircraft are constantly under stress. And if this weren't bad enough, there are some other things to put a pilot to the test. In all combat flying, the position of the sun is uppermost in the pilot's mind. Flying into the sun, he's blinded, and he compromises his position. Diving out of the sun, he uses the glare as a weapon to cloak his movements.

But the Thunderbirds never consider the sun in positioning the flight. There is a definite flight line for the formation and it is adhered to rigidly with no alterations because the sun stabs the pilots smack in the eyes. This means that every man must fly under a high-g condition, possibly in turbulence, and while looking into the sun.

"Each pilot is trained not to make any corrections of his position while the flight is in front of the crowd," Chuck continued. "Traveling at the speed we do, the crowd can't see if one airplane is out of position a few inches, and we do measure everything in inches. They can, however, spot any movement within the formation, so everybody stays put until we pass by the reviewing area.

111

"And we can't let the other planes in the flight distract us. You've been in the diamond with us, Marty, you've seen that sometimes we bounce and bobble. But this can't affect our own flying or position, because if we started to worry about the other guys, the formation would get sloppy.

"There's another thing—other ships in the air. We encounter them, like that light plane that sailed right through the demonstration in Daytona. If anyone spots a bogie, he calls it out and then forgets it. If we worried about those planes, we'd be too erratic. That's why we have the Spare Pilot in the field tower. Then, when we're going through our maneuvers, Griff flies as top cover and keeps a sharp lookout. We do the same when he's down on the deck running through his maneuvers."

He handed his glass to Jeanne for a refill. "We like to loosen up, if we can, before any show. Like we did at Salt Lake. It was a good thing that we had the chance to get in that workout over the Lake before putting on the show." He shook his head in distaste. "Those winds at altitude that day . . . they were enough to drive you crazy. They were all over the place, but the practice session gave us the chance to figure out what compensation we would need later.

"Usually we loosen up with some rolls and whifferdills, and possibly some loops and a changeover cloverleaf. The maneuvers don't really matter. The important thing in the warmup is for each pilot to get the feel of Fitz that day, and to be sure that his airplane is properly trimmed. The warmup session is perfect for this. You can tell with a pretty high degree of accuracy just what type of show the leader will fly on that day, and then everyone is prepared for it. From the audience's point of view, there isn't any difference in the shows. But upstairs, the slightest change, no matter how small, means something. Being able to recognize this difference—so that you can anticipate properly—is also the difference between being a wing man who's right there in the groove, or just another throttle jock."

Bedtime was long ago, but Chuckie sneaked in quietly behind his Dad and joined his mother on the couch. The old man was talking shop—in *detail*—and who wanted to be in that old bed, anyway?

112

"On the initial pass to open the show," Chuck explained, "I always keep in quite a bit of nose-down trim. This helps me keep the airplane from bouncing when we cut in the AB's. And here I have to be carefully aligned with the rest of the diamond. If I'm in too close, and we all don't get our AB lights at pretty much the same time, then I may have to get out of the way. At that point we're all accelerating, and it's too easy to overcontrol.

"Also"—he used his hands to demonstrate positions—"as soon as we pass over the crowd on the go-away, Fitz is going to be turning into me. We break to the right after passing over; if I'm in too close, it means I may have some trouble with Fitz coming in. This is a good example of anticipating —the smoothness of our turn is pretty well decided by what happens even before we reach the crowd.

"But now, as we pull up into the whifferdill, I start easing some of that nose-down trim out. And as Fitz begins to roll away, I've got to be right on my toes, ready to use left rudder to stay exactly in position. The faster Fitz rolls, the more left rudder I need.

"The changeover is one of the most unnatural maneuvers in the show, and it takes a while when you're new to get accustomed to it. When Fitz gives the word to begin"—his hands were all over the place now, simulating the flight— "I drop down into trail behind and below the leader. In fact, as soon as I start to break out of position, I fly completely off the leader. When I drop down I'm almost directly beneath him, and as we continue to pull through, I look out of the top of the canopy; after I'm in position, however, I change my view and I look through the windscreen.

"Right in here, I've got to watch carefully that I don't fall behind. And if I do, it means the AB for that extra kick. My responsibility in this maneuver is to get into position just as quickly as I can. If I wait on the afterburner and light up at the wrong moment, there's the chance that I may overshoot slightly. Then, too, the faster I get into position, the easier I make it for Janca and Neil, who are number three and four.

"As soon as I'm sliding into the trail position, I stack down more than enough to clear the jet exhaust in front of me. In

113

fact, this even helps my flying; it gives me a damper layer, so to speak. If Lead bounces, I'm not greatly affected—that is, if he doesn't bounce severely—and I can damp out the oscillations. Whenever I go into trail, I usually fly with more nose-down trim than for any other part of the show. Except, of course, for the initial pass."

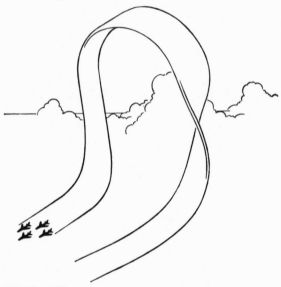

Whifferdill.

Chuck's son gazed in rapt fascination at his father, hanging on every word. And something else that doesn't happen very often was a true pleasure. Jeanne was as interested, as concerned, in the *details* of her husband's flying just as much as would be another pilot. Major Robinson described in an earlier chapter the value he places on the wife's role in the Thunderbirds. And here was a graphic example (if Jeanne will forgive my describing her in that term!) of the "Thunderbrides," as the team wives are known.

To her, Chuck's flying isn't merely his means of earning a livelihood, and the reader might well be astonished at how many pilots' wives regard their husband's activities on the same basis as the man sitting behind a desk from nine to five, and experiencing no more excitement in his life than the annual two weeks at the seashore. To Chuck, flying *is* life.

Jeanne's response to this is simplicity itself; she takes a position, perhaps, slightly behind her husband's flying. Without that flight, life would to a definite extent pall on Chuck Maultsby. With the sky before him, Chuck is *alive*, and the heavens are his in which to roam. Jeanne as a wife will always live with tough competition for her husband's affections —but all she need do is to lift her eyes to the sky and, wonderful woman that she is, she can understand what stirs inside Chuck.

Not only Jeanne, of course. It's difficult for a woman who must attend to the daily, incessant chores of life and the upbringing of children to gain so intrinsic an appreciation of what the heavens mean to her husband. The wives of the Thunderbirds are remarkable persons.

Having known what it is to feel the icy fingers of death so close, perhaps Chuck's approach to life is different than that of most of us. He appreciates the gift of life, of his family, his home, of doing what he wants to do more than anything else, of continuing to serve his country in the best, most effective way he can.

Chuck and Jeanne Maultsby, the Fitzgeralds, Dick and Helene Crane, all of the pilots, and their wives; I think that what these people *are*, what they represent . . . well, I think the world needs much more of what they have to give.

But I'm getting away from that Right Wing position. "Chuck, what's the most difficult part of the show?" I asked. "What maneuver would you say gives you the most trouble?"

He leaned forward, rubbing his chin. "The roll," he said. "I would say that the formation roll is the trickiest to get down pat. The roll is the basic maneuver of the formation, and it's also the hardest. To be completely successful—and I think that this is representative of all the positions in the diamond—I've got to give the roll maneuver my constant attention and effort at all times. . . ."

His hands began to weave a simulated flight through the air again. "Here . . . this is Fitz just as he pulls up for the

115

roll. Now, right here there is practically no change in power. As the roll begins, however, I've got to apply a good back pressure on the stick and also feed in power. I've found that that if I end up below Fitz, then I've goofed. I didn't have enough back pressure on the stick.

"There's a tendency, common enough, I suppose, for a pilot to use more aileron if this happens. But this isn't the cure; I just get more of that back pressure in with the stick. If I stray from the right wing, too far in or even too far out, I've got to stay off the ailerons if I want to keep it smooth. Using the rudder solves the problem. Ailerons will do it too, but then there's too much bouncing and flapping around.

"Now, when the roll reaches the top of its arch, I—" He broke off and turned to his son. "Chuckie, get me two of those models in your room, please." With these in hand, he held them inverted, simulating the top of the roll.

"Here—we were just at the top of the arch. This is where I've got to be especially careful with the power. I've got to match Fitz right down to small fractions. Also, as the roll comes back into me, I'm ready to use some left rudder. This keeps the centrifugal force from slinging me out of formation, like a rock tied at the end of a string and whirled around. Then, as the formation bottoms, I push the power right back up and start pulling back on the stick. It all fits in fine."

"Sure, sure, nothing to it," I said. "All you have to do is to be a magician at the controls, have the endurance of a weightlifter, ignore the sun all the time, disregard the g's ... it all fits in fine. Nothing to it." I shook my head and Chuck laughed.

"Well, it's practice, Marty," he said. "Practice, and conditioning yourself in all respects. Any fighter pilot can do it with the training and the practice."

"When you're cavorting around the sky," I asked, "who calls the shots? I know that Fitz announces entry into maneuvers, the breakaways and so forth, but are there any specific moments when one of the other pilots takes over?"

" 'Taking over' wouldn't be the best way to describe it. We can use the change into trail as an example. Usually it's either myself or Neil in the Slot who'll call the command of

116

execution for change in trail. I call it out just as the formation is approaching the perpendicular to its original flight path. Sounds real confusing, but in the air everything is reduced to simplicity for this move.

"I'm referring to Right Wing now . . . on the *'now'* of the command, I simply move down, and slip below Fitz who's flying Lead. In this move I never use the throttle, unless I'm entering into or leaving a correction; generally, however, I stay away from power in here.

"The trick is that I don't wait for the Slot Man to move out of the way. Neil is watching Janca and he will watch Fitz. I worry about my position and I let the others fly the way they're supposed to; we all know what's going on. As I initiate the change, I'm under Fitz's aircraft, looking at him through the top of the canopy.

"Then, as the turn and the roll continues, since I'm below Fitz, I drop farther back"—the two models slid around an invisible line as Chuck demonstrated—"and then, as I roll out on track, I'm in the proper trail position.

"Now, some time before I reach this position, or even while I'm rolling out, I have to shift my view. Instead of looking out through the top of the canopy I change back to looking through the windscreen. When I come out I like to fly just a bit low in trail, so that I can absorb some of the movement of the aircraft before me.

"Experience teaches well enough that if you fly right on the edge of the jet blast, then the pilot can't make smooth minor corrections. This, of course, is being a 'dirty bird.' It works a double hardship on the Slot Man, and it presents a very unprofessional, rough formation for the crowd that's watching us.

"Getting back to the working part of it . . . the smoke comes on, the roll starts, and as the number two man in trail I call the breakout with *'now!'* As Fitz moves out, he may unconsciously relax just a bit on the back pressure—we all do sometimes—and this can bring me too high and force me to correct at once. And because we are pulling, the nose-down correction sends number four careening wildly around.

"I don't think Neil likes that too much! Again, as in the changeover cloverleaf, I move directly up into position. I watch Janc carefully here as it's easy for me to slide in too close to his right wingtip. Also, I've got to be sure I do not go to the outside, since this extends the time of the join-up. To do it smoothly, I've got to move directly up into position. The thing I have to remember through all of this is that at the beginning of the roll, Fitz is going away from me, and as we rejoin, he is sliding back. Here, to keep my position just where it's supposed to be, I use the speed brake freely, and jiggle power only for minor adjustments."

The doorbell rang, and there was Dick Crane, come "to rescue the Maultsbys from that writer-type." We coldly directed him to a seat and threw some pillows at him, because he had inconveniently forgotten to bring his wife. And Helene is much too pretty—either for Crane, or to leave at home. Dick bared his teeth at Jeanne; apparently he had done this enough times to make it a signal, for Jeanne sighed and went into the kitchen to prepare coffee.

"Do you have any problems in the three-sixty, Chuck? I mean in particular to hanging up there with everyone going around in the squirrel-cage, especially if there's any turbulence . . ."

The 360-degree turn, a wide, sweeping complete circle made directly before the audience, appears to the onlookers as the easiest of all the Thunderbird maneuvers. The airplanes sweep around in a perfect giant turn that finally closes in on itself. They are rock-steady, aligned perfectly, a turn that's as smooth as silk.

The *apparent* simplicity of the maneuver belies its punishment, and a requirement for instant reflex actions on the part of the four pilots in the diamond. As the Super Sabres sweep around the field, each pilot is subjected to a force of five times that of gravity, and this is ten times as mean as in a pullout, because the *g*'s are *sustained*. It's bad enough to suffer the morass of weight when going through a maneuver, but to be rammed down into the seat from the start of the turn, and all the way through, well . . . I don't like that kind of flying, I never have, and I never will.

What looks easy is often dangerous, and this turn fits right into that category. The pilot has to hold that stick back real tight, it means a lot of pressure all the way, and the re-

118

quirement for strength is aggravated severely because of those *g*'s. The airplanes are near the ground in almost a vertical bank, and this is the kind of flying where years of training and instinct scream *"Stall! Danger!"* at the pilot.

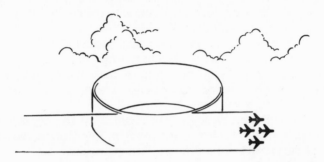

Vertical 360° Turn.

Holding that precise altitude all the way through the turn demands a lot of Fitz, who has to lead everyone. This seems to be easier on the other pilots, but they've got to juggle and adjust position on the basis of inches when they're undergoing all the unpleasant things about the turn—the *g*'s, the horizon jutting straight up and down, and so on.

It looks beautiful, it looks easy, but it's rough as it can get. Chuck doesn't describe it in these terms as Right Wing; he's a lot more clinical about the matter. "As we level off prior to beginning the three-sixty," he said, "I push forward slightly on the stick and then we roll in and begin the pull. And I mean pulling back hard and without wasting a second, because no one wants to get behind on this thing. Rudder keeps me in or out, and most often I'll use a little left rudder to stay up in position. You get used to the *g*'s, but that sun . . . ! You sweat, cry, and cuss at the whole damn thing, but you stay with it. And about two or three hours later it's time to roll out, light the AB and go back to something really simple and relaxing like a nice, precision high loop.

"I'd say that one of the more deceptive of all our maneuvers is the cloverleaf to the right. It's easier for me since the team rolls into me, and this gives me every opportunity

119

to correct. The usual technique in this is to add power and pull back on the stick; however, the opposite is true from where I sit, and at first I found this a bit difficult to master. When the roll part of the maneuver begins, I ease off on power and relax stick pressure. This puts me into the maneuver easily. Once the roll is established, I continue pulling and then play it along like the back side of a loop."

I wanted some specific information on the Bomb Burst, that sensational climax to the show when the crashing noise, speed, and nearness of the airplanes have the crowd almost convinced that they're about to see a spectacular splashing of Super Sabres all over the sky.

"This will surprise you," Dick said, "but the Bomb Burst is actually the first chance the pilots in the diamond have to *relax* during the demonstration."

Chuck nodded assent. "I know it's hard to accept, Marty, but Pappy Crane is right. But this is in the physical sense only. The *g*-forces are finally off our necks, and we get a physical break. But as you know from sitting over us when we come around to cross, the pilot who fails to stay absolutely alert is liable to make a sloppy crossover and rejoin.

"Coming back in prior to the pullup for the Bomb Burst, I anticipate some forward stick pressures at times; Fitz is playing his position carefully so that the formation is directly above the runway or the crossover point just at the moment that the diamond breaks outward to the four compass directions. As Fitz calls out '*now*' I break sharply ninety degrees to the right. At the same moment I shove the throttle forward and go into the last part of an Immelmann.

"As I break away, I keep my eye glued to Fitz's airplane to assure that I'm moving out at ninety degrees to him. Then, before I roll out, I can look down and see the runway; this gives me a reference to line up on as I roll out.

"During this time I can also tell if the formation is to one side or the other of the intended point. Now, if the distance is great enough to make a correction necessary on Neil's part or by Fitz, I may call out: 'On Neil's side slightly,' or whatever my particular position may be.

"This gives everyone else, on the basis of this call, an idea of exactly where they are. I roll out with the nose above,

120

or level with, the horizon. This permits me to maintain my altitude as I continue away from the burst. I retard power to ninety per cent, and right here my concentration is on holding altitude and heading.

"If I'm off track to the left as I roll out, I make my corrections immediately. Rolling out on Fitz's call, I roll in the direction that it's necessary for my correction to get back on track.

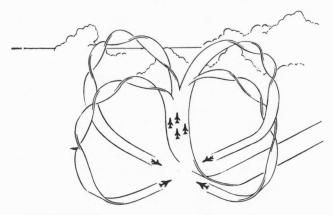

Bomb Burst!

"The critical requirement here is to maintain my *attitude* in the roll. I'll be moving somewhere between one-fifty to two-twenty knots, and I just roll it on over and around.

"Everything depends on split-second timing. When I'm on my back in the roll, I look down to recheck the track. If more correction is necessary, I make it as I roll out. And at this time I also check on Fitz's position and also Neil. I snap out a look in the rear view mirror to check Janc's position and see how he's coming along on his track—he does the same with me, of course.

"If he's off, then I know exactly where he will be when he bottoms out of the split-S. Unless the wind is extremely strong—like it was at Salt Lake, and at Indian Springs when we flew that last practice mission—or unless I've noticed from the others that I'm the one out of position, I make no corrections on the split.

"And I split only when Fitz calls it. Right here, I roll some forward trim into the bird to help me make the flat pass without excessive forward pressure on the stick. When I come down and I can see the runway, I'm ready to make the final corrections which mean whether or not I make a perfect crossover or flub the works.

"As I come in I look to the left to pick up Fitz, and I plan to cross on him. I line up on my side of the runway, making sure I don't crowd Janc, and from here on it's a matter of playing my power and speed brakes and the AB. Whatever I need to get to the right place at the right time.

"Of all the maneuvers we do, this one demands the most practice, and that goes for all positions in the diamond. Closure rates are never the same, and no matter how many times you fly this maneuver no one ever comes back in at the same airspeed or ground speed two times in a row. The only way to gain that judgment that gives you consistently good crossovers is practice and more practice—"

"Yeah," grunted Crane. "Knowing how to fly helps a little bit, too."

"It doesn't hurt." Chuck grinned.

"Now, let's see . . . there are a couple of pointers I always keep in mind. I always make sure, if I have to use the speed brake, that I get it up before I pass in front of the crowd. When I bottom for the crossover, I make another alignment on my side. From here it's a matter of playing the altitude, either as the terrain or the Left Wing man dictates. Sometimes conditions require that Janc call the shot, and I play it on his cues.

"I always play for about ten feet above the ground for the crossover, because this is assurance for staying out of trouble. Many times, of course, we're well above ten feet because of buildings or terrain problems. What many pilots fail to realize, also, is that a man's eyesight varies from day to day in respect to his depth perception. When you're sure you're at ten feet, you may be at five on one mission, and the next day at fifteen. There's one final thing—the moment I cross I always get the nose up. This takes care of any problems with terrain that may come up, and I'm free to concentrate on re-joining Fitz as he starts up in his half of a Cuban Eight."

Chuck rose to his feet and stretched. "I guess that's it, Marty. Now you know how to fly like a Thunderbird."

"Oh, sure!"

7 Talking It Over

It was the end of a long, hard day. The flying began only minutes after the first splash of sun ran down the flanks of the mountains bordering Nellis. The team flew two full prac-tice missions in the morning, came home for lunch, thrashed out some problems and ideas, and then went out again in the afternoon to fly another complete show. Dick Crane and I were in the air during the morning sessions. In the after-noon, however, we watched from the ground—or, more ac-curately, from the control tower of Indian Springs Air Force Base, where Dick recorded on tape a significantly critical re-view of the proceedings.

It was well into the first hours of evening when the pilots collected in the conference room, and threw themselves wearily into the chairs surrounding the conference table. They were still in flight suits, stained with perspiration, and the sighs of relief were something that might be heard when a man is let loose after being strung up by the thumbs for a couple of days.

For a few moments they relaxed, dragging deeply on ciga-rettes, sipping coffee, or just stretching out, arms and legs loose. Bob Janca rubbed his arm slowly, carefully.

"What gives, Janc?" I asked.

"Trying to get this thing to come back to life a little," he groaned. "We had some turbulence on that last mission; the stick pressures were murder. We were bouncing like yo-yo's for a while."

Dick was busy unsnarling a mass of tape, but he never was one to pass up an opportunity. "I never saw so many guys do so much complaining," he said. "Hit a little puff of cloud, and right away they all come downstairs yelling for liniment, nurses, bandages." He shook his head in mock despair and rolled his eyes. "Now, if they could only take things in their stride," he said beseechingly. "Not complain, go upstairs and fly their little toys for a few minutes. But *noooo,* you'd think they were flying in formation, the way they talk."

Janc looked at Dick unhappily. "Why, oh why, Fitz, did we have to get this guy, of all people? Did we do something wrong? Does the Pentagon hate us? How come *we,* of all the organizations in the whole blessed Air Force, have to get this guy and his golden sinuses?"

Five minutes later, the jesting faded out. There had been a lot of words bandied about and mock cries of anguish, but the effect was such that in those few minutes the tension of flying so many hours right under the gun, hard, demanding flying, was being eased.

Dick, as narrator, was often the butt of the pilots' anguished cries, but when it came to flying, the other pilots listened with great care to their boy with the "golden sinuses," as Janc is prone to repeat at every worthwhile moment. Before he came to the Thunderbirds, Dick had proven himself a real authority in jet fighters, flying F-80 and F-94 fighters for several years before transferring to the Far East; here he collected several more years of intensive flying. He flew in the first squadron in the Tactical Air Command to fly the F-100C, and thus had more experience than any other man in this airplane by the time he came to the Thunderbirds. Besides all this, and his nearly 3,000 hours of military flying time, Dick was an aircraft engine mechanic, an aeronautical engineer, Flight Commander—just to mention a few. When he spoke critically on the performance of these pilots, they all listened.

Dick switched on the tape recorder, and as the tape unwound, we heard not only Dick's voice (plus some comments of my own that Fitz had requested on certain maneuvers), but the whistling roar of the airplanes, and the conversation of the pilots.

Dick was merciless, and nothing escaped his eyes. Turns I thought were absolutely perfect, the best I had ever seen, revealed major flaws to Dick. He called out "poor spacing" when the airplanes were little more than a few inches out of line. He observed the drifting of the formation before the wind, and castigated Fitz for letting the diamond ease back until it was directly over the tower on its breakouts, instead of being directly over the center of the runway. He saw everything, the bobbles and weaves, the yawing motions, the off-timing turns—off by seconds, and he counted every one of them out loud on the tape.

He didn't critique that show, he dissected it, step by step, turn by turn, move by move. When they were good, Dick was lavish with his praise. But when the team was off by so much as a hair, Dick was in there, digging and cutting and explaining exactly why.

He was, to put it bluntly, murderous in his criticism. And the pilots listened with painful attention, ignoring the criticism except for what it revealed to them as a flaw in their own flying, and making notes on the spot which would eliminate those flaws—invisible to anyone else, so far as I was concerned, except Dick Crane.

The moral was obvious; perfection is impossible, but nothing was going to stop this team from trying just as hard as they could for the impossible—or as close to it as men may reach. Never was there an unhappy reaction to Dick's words; the pilots sometimes got angry, but at themselves.

This is the heart of this method—criticism is to be wielded freely, so long as it is valid and has meaning. Every pilot *asks* for criticism, wants it, because he feels that he *needs* that critique to make himself even better. The unwritten law is that false pride can't do the Thunderbirds anything but harm.

The tape ran for twenty-three minutes, the full show the team flew. When it was over, darkness had filled the eastern horizon, and the strange quality of the desert's spear of light beneath a mantle of black swept around more than half of the western skies.

With the tape completed, the meeting was over. Ninety minutes of details, critical review, discussions, and plans for improvements. The pilots stood and stretched; some called their wives to pick them up. We were standing around when someone knocked on the conference room door.

Cass pushed it open, and a flying blur of teeth, fur, and uproarious yelps of delight shot past him and leaped through

125

the air at Fitz. Carol had driven over to take Fitz home, and the dog? This was Heidi, a whacking big German shepherd that one day is certain to be neurotic. Heidi is unaware of the fact that she is a dog, and protests any moves that might push her toward recognition of a canine status. She has the run of Thunderbirds headquarters, sits in on the conferences and critiques (under the table), where she will either sigh contentedly beneath Fitz's boots, or else nibble happily upon those of the other pilots.

Within five minutes the building was empty, except for Dick and myself. We were tired, but it had been a good, satisfying stretch of hours. We stayed on for a while, working on notes for the book, finishing the pot of coffee Bev Cassel had made for us before she left for the day.

"Richard, what got you to join the Thunderbirds?" I asked. "I'm curious. How does a pilot get picked as the narrator? I know the routine to fly in the diamond or as the solo pilot, but you have to have the same qualifications pilot-wise as anyone else . . . so how come you got this spot?"

Dick closed a desk drawer. "Funny, but you're the first guy that ever asked me that, Marty."

"What the devil, I'm the inquisitive type."

He stretched his feet out on the desk and laughed. "Well, the surprising thing about my being the narrator is that I've enjoyed it tremendously. You know what I think about being a part of the Thunderbirds, but the best part of it is that I've done so much more for the team than I could have if I'd only flown a position."

He blew a cloud of smoke in the air and thought for a few minutes. "I volunteered for the team, of course, just like everyone else. There wasn't much chance of getting in, the odds are too great. Everyone who's considered as a team member is good; it doesn't help to know that you just qualify, because so does everyone else who's kept on the list of those who may be accepted.

"A few months went by, and I didn't hear a thing. Then I received orders to report to Thunderbird headquarters here at Nellis, to see Robby. I did about three slow rolls right through the room, I was so happy. I rushed right home to tell Helene the good news, packed a bag, and I was off like a shot. The interview went real well, too. And then the world opened up beneath my feet. Robby told me that I was being considered for the position of narrator. I think my heart broke; I was dead set on flying as a part of the team. I'd almost considered it a sure thing by then.

"It took everything I had to keep a straight face. When the interview was over, Robby told me to think about it. But I did all my thinking in those few moments. No, I wouldn't say that. I'd say that everything I'd thought about for so long just passed through my mind.

"I remembered how I felt about this team—as I do even more today. They were the best, the greatest flying bunch in the world. I remembered how badly I wanted to be a part of that team, and suddenly I realized that just being a member was enough for me.

"Right then and there, I knew all this. I knew that if they wanted me to carry the water buckets, paint the airplanes, or anything else, that was good enough for me. It was a team, and as badly as I wanted to fly, I also knew that the narrator played a highly important role, that he was the one they gave the responsibility to for speaking to the millions of people. . . .

"I think that Robby sensed what I was thinking. 'Before you say anything,' he told me, 'I want you to know something. As far as we're concerned, you've got—if you accept—just about the toughest job on this whole team. Your qualifications for being narrator are from our viewpoint a lot rougher than they are for just flying. You have to be a diplomat, a pilot like the rest of us, a magician, and God knows what else. . . .' Robby went on like that for a while, and told me to give him my answer within the week.

"But I had the answer already, of course, and I told Robby that being part of the team was what I wanted, that if I could do the best job in this capacity, why, what was there to think about? Robby grinned from ear to ear; he knew all along what I was thinking. So, in January of 1958, I sewed the T-bird patches on my gear—and I've been here ever since."

Dick's position with the Thunderbirds is unique in a special way—he was the only narrator to serve more than two years with the team. Although his first two years were in the primary capacity as narrator, he found himself sinking beneath administrative requirements that began to assume mountainous proportions.

Today, as you read this, Dick Crane is no longer the Thunderbirds' narrator. Instead, he has assumed about ninety-five other jobs under the dual titles of Thunderbirds' Information Officer and Unit Historian. He no longer makes all the trips with the team, and instead travels only on those trips requiring more extensive information activity.

Now, I've explained that Dick's position as narrator has required him to be a highly-qualified F-100 pilot. In the position of narrator, flying the F-100F, Dick has had the additional assignment of flying government officials, reporters and commentators, mayors, congressmen, senators, and all manner of VIP's for their first supersonic flights.

He has also held down an unhappy position as the Show Support Requirements Officer for the team, a job that requires him to have three heads, six arms, the ability to go without sleep, and a talent for legerdemain that would sorely tax the wizardry of no less an individual than Merlin himself. In this job, Dick was personally responsible for making all the multitudinous arrangements for more than two hundred air shows.

Bad enough that he has employed—as Janca puts it, his "golden sinuses"—to talk to more than *twenty million* people, but he has also for these 200 demonstrations made all the preparations for arrival, billeting, transportation, fuel, oil, maintenance, gasoline, publicity releases, and public appearances for the forty-odd members of the team that travel on the road together. And Thunderbird schedules are so wickedly inflexible that if Dick wasn't on the ball *all* the time, sheer chaos would result.

I traveled, worked, and lived with Dick on the road— and his requirements make him the only pilot who doesn't observe the midnight curfew imposed on the six other team members. This is because we were usually up at six every morning and working until two or three in the morning, a stint that leaves very little time for anything but hacking away at the many things that *must* be accomplished if everything was to function smoothly. In three days and nights at Daytona Beach, when the team performed consecutively, Dick and I managed to put some 600 miles on a car, just dashing around from the show site, the motel, television and radio shows, newspaper offices, ad infinitum.

As team narrator, Dick flew nearly 800,000 air miles with the team—thirty-two times around the world—across several continents and oceans. And in between the flying, support arrangements, narration, he managed to write all press releases, and to work with radio, television, magazine, and newspaper representatives in preparing stories, articles, spots, television shows, and feature films. Suffice to say that the one-armed paperhanger was an individual who languished lazily through the worst of his comedy adventures in comparison with Dick Crane's weighty responsibilities with the Thunderbirds.

And like the rest of the team pilots, he came home every now and then to renew his acquaintance with his family— Helene, his two daughters, Christine and Linda Kaye, and that little boy with sharp teeth, Gary. For 302 days in 1959 the Thunderbirds were on the road.

Technical Sergeant Robert W. Bandy, who works in the Thunderbirds information office for Dick Crane (and who has served as the first enlisted narrator with the team), slipped a folder from his personal file to me. I was surprised to read the papers within, for Dick had never said a word about the fact that he was a nominee in 1959 as the U. S. Junior Chamber of Commerce's award for the Outstanding Man of the Year. It is a lengthy document, and I shall not long pursue its contents here.

The papers state, in part, that in his capacity as narrator, the "influence of this single individual is felt, not only by the adult military and civilian public, but perhaps more important, by the youthful public. It is Captain Crane's mission to explain the Thunderbird story—its meaning and significance. In keeping with this, it must follow that he explain our United States Air Force and the military establishment of which it is a part.

"Thus, he is making understandable to young America a way of life—a vitally necessary and omnipresent way of life in today's America. His contributions to the orientation and guidance of young Americans is . . . far in excess of the very considerable contributions made to the military establishment."

I'm going to bring things to a personal plane for the moment. From the day that Dick and I began to work together on Thunderbirds, we became friends. As we made our flights from the desert floor to more than 40,000 feet, we came to understand each other. Today our friendship is close, and it is strong, and I am very proud to have come to know this

Narrator.

man so well. For the story that brought Dick to the Thunderbirds is, like that of the other pilots, a story of America itself.

Dick was born in the little town of Murray, Utah, six miles south of Salt Lake City. His grandfather, William Crane, a short, stocky and powerful man, exerted a profound influence on the thinking and life of Dick's father. William Crane settled in Utah in a one-room log cabin with a dirt floor, as much a part of the history of the early west as any man ever was. Tireless, fiercely proud, he became one of the state's most successful sheep and cattle ranchers, and spread his extensive holdings to land in Utah, Nevada, Idaho, and Wyoming.

This was the story of his grandfather that Dick's father, John J. Crane, passed on to him. Not merely in words, but in sights and feeling and the vastness of the country in which they lived. William Crane died when Dick was only two years old, but to the F-100 pilot of today, his grandfather lived on in the philosophy and ideals by which his own father shaped their lives.

The boy who became a fighter pilot never forgot what he learned, what he was taught, how he lived. Dick, who today regards both his father and grandfather as "grand and dedicated old tigers," was to learn this lesson by the whiplash of life.

During his early years, after the death of his grandfather, Dick spent much of his time on his grandfather's ranch at Herman, Utah, which nestled at the foot of the Oquire Mountains. It was a magnificent setting, and the family lived according to a strict code of ethics and hard work. At this time, Dick's father was managing most of William Crane's ranches and properties.

And then the depression of 1929 struck, and in one black week after another, the vast property holdings vanished in the quagmire of shattered finances and a toppled economy. The Crane family emerged from the turmoil without land, and destitute.

From this point on, Dick received his lessons in fortitude and a grim determination to climb back to the top. John J. Crane stormed into the insurance business when it could hardly have been worse, and wove a brilliant climbing trail through his competition. Today, despite two heart attacks that would have crippled an ordinary man, he has become one of the top five men in the country in the insurance agency business and training field.

Dick Crane is fiercely proud of him.

It was at his grandfather's ranch, in the midst of the old West, that flying made its first and permanent impressions on Dick Crane.

The old mail planes and Ford Tri-Motor transports flew regularly over the ranch. Others swung in over the mountains to the south, either landing or taking off from Salt Lake City. Western Air Lines, one of the oldest systems in the country, flew this route regularly. Thus Dick had, always, the sight of wings and the drone of motors to capitivate his interest. To him, the pilots in those lumbering craft were as much heroes as the knights of King Arthur's Round Table, or the legendary figures of the Greek and Roman legends.

What was serious interest became a burning ambition. The mail pilots flying old Jenny biplanes would sometimes circle the ranch, and then swoop and soar in aerobatics while the boy watched in complete awe. These were spectacles too rich and important to forget, even in the hectic days of boyhood. "I have never forgotten those moments," Dick mused. "They kindled the love and desire to fly that has never left me to this day."

Flying is many things to different people, but I have flown long enough with Dick to recognize the intensity of his feelings toward flight. The elements of beauty and grace, "the ability to soar like a bird through the beauty of sky and clouds always seemed to me to be just one step closer to the heavens and God."

Dick Crane is one of those pilots to whom the sky has never lost its deep meanings. One night we stood on the flight line at Nellis, watching the powerful fighters booming down the runway, crying with power, afterburner flame stabbing painfully in the darkness.

"Look at them," Dick almost whispered. "This is what it means to me, I suppose. There is that something about shedding the bonds that have held man to the ground for centuries . . . and only pilots know what it is, only they have soared and wheeled, only they—we—have experienced the many and rare beauties of nature that God has let us see from the skies."

So there is the culmination in thought of the early dreams stirred by the old fabric-covered biplanes, dreams that were sustained and nourished, and brought finally in manhood to reality. From those days on the ranch Dick's future life was charted for him; it would always follow the path that led him to the air, despite the obstacles that would arise.

Dick's schooling was a hectic affair, for his father traveled

132

throughout the midwest and far west as a requirement of business, and took his family with him. As he matured, Dick voiced his desire to fly. These hopes met with no opposition —only a condition—from the family. The completion of college was mandatory; they would help Dick in every way possible to realize his most important hopes.

When he was seventeen, in 1944, Dick enlisted in the Army's Aviation Cadet Program. But pilot training for him at that time was a goal that, despite his desperate seeking, managed to elude him. He went on active duty in January, 1945; the war was then rapidly approaching its climax. Flying schools bulged with cadets, and training programs had already received the first of continuing major slashes.

When Dick sits at his desk in the Thunderbirds building along the Nellis flight line, it must be with mixed feelings. For he was in that same building eight years before the Thunderbirds ever flew. After cadet basic training, he was assigned to Las Vegas Army Air Base, Nevada, and to what he describes as "that lost legion known at the time as 'Permanent Party on the Line Trainees.' We were doomed, it seemed, to the duty of glorified hopeful cadets who would be used for every odd job that might come along. Actually, we were being held in limbo until the flight training schools could catch up on their backlog.

"But it wasn't for me. With a close friend, I talked my way through the Airplane Engine and Mechanics' School. Then we managed to get into the B-24 Flight Engineer's Course. Pretty soon we were one of the strangest breeds of cat in the Army Air Forces—an Air Cadet Flight Engineer on a B-24. We drove everyone nuts! There just isn't and never has been such a category . . . but we were it."

In that same building now used as Thunderbirds headquarters, Dick Crane once stripped airplane engines. But all his effort availed him was an excellent education as a mechanic and a flight engineer, for in October 1945 the AAF discharged all cadets not then assigned to flight training.

Before entering the cadet program, Dick had completed a year of Aeronautical Engineering at the University of Minnesota. After his discharge he enrolled in the University of Utah, and promptly joined the Air Reserve Officers Training

133

Corps; if he couldn't get into flying through the front door, there was nothing wrong with the back way.

Life had its other moments. He married Helene at the end of his sophomore year and soon discovered that he was about to begin raising a family. And this began a period of time in which the world revolved about work and study. The GI Bill covered Dick's expenses only for a short period of his college—"After that," he recalls, "I was on my own—only this time with a spouse to support and a young one on the way. So, back to work. . . ."

Dick went to school for almost two years from eight in the morning until three in the afternoon. He then dashed downtown to work as an assistant pharmacist in a drugstore for seven hours, quitting at eleven p.m. He went directly home, and studied each night until two a.m. Six hours later he was back in the classroom.

The things that a man does in his life reflect well his personal traits. During this grueling period Dick's parents were willing to provide whatever help he needed. But at times Richard is a very independent, stubborn, and unyielding cuss. Both he and Helene were willing to make it on their own merits and work—and they did just that.

"For the last two years I supported my family and paid all of my own way through college," Dick said. He didn't add —but Helene did—that in 1949 he graduated as a Distinguished Student. With graduation came the offer of a Regular Officer's Commission in the Air Force. "They asked me if I wanted it," Dick explained. "Asked me that—can you imagine it? I nearly broke the instructor's arm, I shook it so hard. And with that Regular Commission came those wonderful, wonderful orders to report to Randolph Air Force Base in Texas. I left a trail of dust all the way down there."

In the summer of 1950 his commanding officer pinned the wings of a fighter pilot on Dick's uniform, and there is little need to speak of the pride Dick felt at that moment. He flew fighters for two years, and then was assigned to school at the Air University in Alabama. From here he transferred to Okinawa, where much of his time during the next two and a half years was spent flying combat patrols in jet interceptors.

Dick assumes an air of great seriousness when he recalls

134

part of his Okinawan duty, as the aide-de-camp to Major General Fay R. Upthegrove, who was then the commanding general of the 20th Air Force. To Dick, his relationship with General Upthegrove was tremendously vital, for what Dick calls this "grand old gentleman's dedication, loyalty, beliefs, and the influence he had on my life."

"This wonderful officer," Dick explained one night, "left me with a deep and abiding respect for any man who has a star on his shoulders. I found out one thing—that by and large you don't get a star in this man's Air Force without being just about as sharp as they come. Sure we make a few mistakes—we are still human—but from my observation as an aide he made very few.

"I realized this Air Force has some mighty dedicated and competent men leading us—and I've never failed to feel just a little prouder of my service as a result of this knowledge and experience. America can thank the Lord for such men as these.

"For the two years I served under this man, he was a hard and understanding taskmaster. He gave me a job to do and expected me to do it. He gave his commanders their responsibilities and he expected them to command!

"He was a perfectionist—we soon learned that we needn't stand around after a job was well done waiting for a kind pat on the head—often as not we only heard from the 'old man' when things had not been done right or as good as they could be. Yet after I returned to the States he came five hundred miles out of his way one day—unannounced—just to drop in on my base to see me and find out how I was being treated, and how I was getting along.

"I was floored—as was my base commander—and this kindness, and the *lesson*, I've never forgotten. He was always looking out for his men, even after they left him; this to me in every sense was the mark of a true commander."

The next assignment for Dick was with the 450th Fighter Day Wing, and subsequent duty in the F-100C. And after that, the coveted acceptance as a member of the Thunderbirds.

The Cranes' son, Gary, was born during Dick's assignment as the Thunderbirds' Narrator. But here we leave the realm of the military and enter a deeply personal plane. On the day that his son was born it was difficult for Dick to rejoice. Instead there came only the inner feeling that the father knows to welcome his child to the world.

On that same day, Dick Crane buried his younger brother.

It was not an easy subject to discuss with me, and only because we had come so close to each other did he speak of it at all. We had landed from a night flight several minutes before. Somehow the conversation, a relaxed and wonderful time of talking about our favorite subject—flying—brought out the fact that Dick's brother was also a pilot.

"Was?"

Dick put an arm around my shoulder. "C'mon, Marty, let's take a walk. Down the flight line . . ."

He talked about his brother. Slowly, Dick spoke quietly about a part of his past that still remained a deep, painful wound. I've tried to remember his words as best I could, as only Dick could have said them that night, pausing every now and then as a fighter howled its defiance at the earth and shot into the skies.

"He believed that he always had to struggle to keep up with his older brother," Dick began. "And yet, in the long run, he lived his life and set an example that I must try all *my* life to live up to myself.

"His love for flying and the Air Force was as intense as mine; college was a necessary ordeal to be put up with until he could learn to fly, and be up there with his big brother."

Dick paused as two sweptwing shapes pitched out over our heads, shark-nosed shapes moaning with subdued energy as they swung around to return to earth. We looked up, then Dick went on:

"I often wonder if I would have encouraged him just a little bit less, not taken him with me on his summer vacations to let him see and taste and live the life in a fighter squadron, to meet its people and join the inner circle . . . I wonder about that sometimes . . . that things might have turned out differently and that he would be alive today, a successful young man in the business field, married, raising his own kids."

Dick shook his head and smiled. "But no—he followed

136

just as fast as he could in his older brother's footsteps through college, and then immediately into uniform.

"He was a brilliant young man, and more important to me, Marty, he was an outstanding flier. You know that gift; he had it—a kid that you wanted to help with all your life and soul. God, but he was good upstairs. You couldn't help it, you tried to pass on all your own experience and help in the knowledge that it would make him just a little bit better, bring him a bit further along because he could benefit from your own mistakes. He did all this, and went much further beyond.

"He gave his life—quietly and without any fanfare or glory, or even a comforting word from any human being— for his service and the people he had taken an oath to protect.

"I'll never forget when it happened. It was October 26, in 1958. He flew an F-86L Sabre with the 332nd, a fighter interceptor squadron at Stewart Air Force Base in New York.

"He was making a bad-weather approach to the field. Right then it happened. The airplane flamed out; he lost all power.

"He . . . he rode it down into a vacant lot. He could have gone out, ejected safely. But he didn't. He refused to turn the airplane loose over the town and the surrounding housing area. There were people down there, kids sleeping in beds. So he stayed on the stick, and pointed it at that field, and he went in with the airplane.

"Life can be very bitter in these moments. . . ." Dick was quiet for a long time before he went on.

"Self-pity can be an all-encompassing thing . . . you can't help the bitterness when someone who has so much potential and is so brilliant, so tremendously full of life, is taken away so early."

We stopped along a row of parked fighters: Super Sabres ready for the dawn training missions, loaded with rockets and bombs. "I suppose that it's a lesson few of us learn, Marty, but one day the realization comes that we fly today on the sufferance, legacy, and the sacrifice of so many brave young men like the kid I loved so much. I can think about it more clearly now, of course, and I think about things . . .

137

he and the kids like him helped make this golden age possible. To be bitter and filled with hate at the way he died would be for me to turn on the very thing he and all the others gave their lives for. If I hadn't come to understand that it would be to make a mockery of their sacrifice. . . .

"When I think of him today, I also think of my kids. He left things just a little bit better, a little safer, for them and all the others. I don't think he's sorry that he had to go."

I didn't say anything to Dick for a long time; I couldn't.

8   In the Slot

"That first show . . . it is really an experience. It's like opening night. Man, was I shook!"

Neil Eddins was describing his opening play with the Thunderbirds, at Bangor, Maine, in the summer of 1959, when he flew his first performance in the diamond's critical Slot position.

He grinned. "My hands still get sweaty whenever I think of it," he said. "The apprehension kept building up in me like it was a case of stage fright. The same things kept grinding through my brain; I kept thinking that tens of thousands of people, no matter where we were scheduled, had already seen the show.

"They *know* the Thunderbirds are terrific, and the more I thought about this audience expecting more of the same, if not better, the shakier I got! Because there's a drive going on inside you; you've just got to do everything in your power to keep up to the standards set by the men who have flown this position, this airplane, before you.

"I look back on it now and laugh a bit—weakly!—because I aged five years in those twenty-three minutes. I flew with so much intense concentration I ended up with a whopping headache.

"My arms and legs seemed to belong to someone else. When we pitched out and came in to land I was absolutely disgusted with myself. I was sure I had flubbed the whole show, that I wallowed all over the place. Every time the airplane bobbed or weaved—although it couldn't be seen from the ground at all—I was sick.

"Your real critics, Marty, are the crew chiefs and the narrator. And the support pilots—Johnny and Ray and Chester. They've watched so many shows, they know every move in the sky. They've also watched you progress all the way through your training. Everyone is always concerned about the new man in the diamond . . . he's really the object of scrutiny until he's an 'old head.' And that comes only after the first complete show; not until then, as far as I'm concerned, are you really a member of this organization.

"They acted like I surprised them a bit . . . everything seemed to go so well, they *said* it was good, real good; but I never knew whether or not they were just being polite.

"I learned that the confidence to fly that diamond like you're stuck to the other planes has got to come from within yourself. You sweat out the next show, and the next, and the one after that too, until suddenly you land one day after the demonstration, and something *happens*.

"Everything just fits into place. You see things more clearly, the clouds never looked so pretty, and then . . . you know, to yourself, that you're really *in*. And it's like a great big shout welling up inside yourself that howls with joy. You say to yourself, 'Eddins, you've done it, boy, you've really made it. You're a Thunderbird!' And you climb off that wing and you just can't stop grinning. The other guys look at you like you're crazy, but then they grin back because, you see, it's happened to all of them, too. . . .' "

We were in Neil's office, doing our best to crowd Chuck Maultsby out of the room so that we could get some notes down on paper. The trouble with having Chuck around at a moment like this is that he sits quietly until you forget all about him, and then comes out with a yuk that busts you up. We finally bribed him into making coffee for the three of us.

"Neil, the Slot gets a lot of attention as the most difficult of all the diamond positions to fly," I said. "Everyone knows that you're stuck way up in there and that the sky is full of airplanes all around you. I've watched; Crane just about stuck the nose of the F-100F right down your tailpipe. Now, what gets me is that you've got that sky full of airplanes to keep in mind. It's bad enough for Chuck and Janc, but who the blazes do you watch? You've got your wings—both wings —and the nose of the bird to keep tucked in all the time. I'd think you would get claustrophobia in there. . . ."

Neil thought it over. "Well, I know you've spent a lot of time with Fitz on this. Umm, the key—the big key, I'd say —to flying the Slot—is anticipating. Yeah, that would be it. You start anticipating the leader's movements. Before you know it, you're living in a world that's a few seconds ahead of reality.

Diamond heading for Thunderbird Lake.

"You've got to anticipate power. You've got to anticipate everything the leaders does, because all you see is his airplane. You glue your eyeballs to it. You work with power and stick forces, and it's so easy to overcontrol that power! But when it all falls into place, that great moment comes, why, then you start to see things. Suddenly you can unglue your eyeballs a bit, and you start to see Janc and Chuck up there in the diamond as well. And after a while you *fit* right into the Slot like it's where you have always belonged."

140

"What's the most difficult position to fly in the diamond? My opinion would be right where you sit, in the Slot. But that's just my opinion."

Chuck stood in the doorway with the coffee. "Watch how you answer, flyboy," he warned. "You can't trust this guy too much. Remember, he and Richard have been plotting things."

Neil laughed. "Okay, okay, I'll make him sign a waiver. Now gimme my coffee, shaddup, and siddown."

Neil sipped for a moment, going over the formation flying in his mind. "It's hard to say," he reflected. "Some pilots say the Left Wing is the toughest because the rolls are *into* him. Then others claim that it's the Right Wing, because they roll away *from* him, and he has the longest way to go around, more stick pressure to contend with—"

"Absolutely right." Chuck beamed. "You heard the man, Marty. Put it down on paper. Quote him: 'The Right Wing is the most intensively difficult position to fly; I think Chuck Maultsby is a grade-A hero-type.' "

"I'll do that little thing. Where do you want the loving cup sent?"

"Give it to Jeanne," he chortled. "I always told her . . ."

Neil buried his face in his hands and moaned. "Not again! The David Niven of the Thunderbirds is about to launch a review of his amorous voyages." He looked up. "Marty, this guy will weave a spell about you. Be careful. Besides, he's so mad about Jeanne that he'd cold-shoulder Miss Universe."

"Big man," I said.

Chuck rose to his feet. "Okay, you birds, I know when I'm not wanted. I'll go talk to some intelligent people."

We got back to work.

"Basically, in diamond work," Neil explained, "the Slot position, once you have gotten over this claustrophobia of moving in so close with all these airplanes in front of you . . . well, then you can hack it. Once you're *beyond worrying* about those ships, you've got it knocked.

"Of course, if something happens where you've got to get out of the airplane in a hurry, you can't get out that easily or that quickly. The only way to get out, that you can get out in a real emergency, is down. If you're going to eject,

141

you've got to remember that the immediate sky is full of air-planes. Airplanes all over the place. You've got to get away from them, and that means going down if you've lost power.

"I think that the Slot, very frankly, is the hardest position to fly and really do a good job. About half of our show is flown in trail, and the farther back you get, the more you're in that so-called whip position.

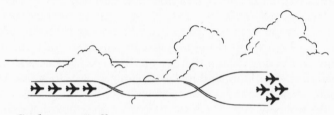

Corkscrew Roll.

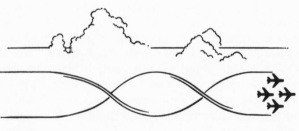

Roll.

"Whenever the team moves from trail into a diamond, the Slot Man has the longest distance to go. The move calls for more power, it calls for afterburner more often. I'm often running right close to the red line with power."

He grinned happily. "And that's why I've got the fastest bird on the team, in the entire formation. That ground crew of mine gives the airplane lots of TLC—good old tender loving care. They take care of that machine like it was a thoroughbred about to race for a million-dollar stake.

"Then there's the problem of all that bobbling up there.

Any bobbles or turbulence that the other pilots experience are just magnified as they come back to the Slot. If the leader hits a bump or turbulence, it passes through each individual airplane in the trail, and by the time it gets back to me, it's a lot worse than when it began. It ends up as a pretty good bump."

"I know. I've watched you in there, like someone was bouncing the ship on an invisible sheet of glass. Up and down, up and down. How the hell do you manage to keep it in so tight all the time?"

"You start with the basis of skill, and an absolute confidence in your other pilots. Then you add to this practice, practice, practice, and then more of the same. You can actually take any pilot who basically is good and has the knack of flying it in close, and he can be brought into this team. I like to think that I'm good, but there are an awful lot of guys who are better."

"Did you always want to fly, Neil?"

He looked sheepish. "No. And that's the funny part about it. For some time now I'd go absolutely nuts if I couldn't fly. But in the beginning, I just couldn't have cared less about it."

And it's true. Neil Eddins' background just doesn't jibe with the story of the dedicated, tremendously skilled pilot of today. Neil and his younger brother, Boyd, lived on a ranch in the Star Valley section of Wyoming. Neil's major interest was sports. He is a husky six-footer and through his teens he stood out clearly in his skill. A four-letter man at Star Valley High School, Neil starred in football, track, and boxing.

Boyd, in the meantime, cluttered up the house with model airplanes, and haunted local airports. When he was thirteen he started taking flying lessons; three years later he soloed. Fired with an ambition of flying, Boyd purchased a wrecked airplane and rebuilt it into a J-3 Cub as good as new. All this time the future Thunderbird grandly ignored the activities of his brother. At eighteen, Neil concentrated on basketball and football. He was taken for one flight that lasted thirty minutes, landed, shrugged his shoulders indifferently, and turned his back on flying.

"I liked it," he recalls, "but what the devil, it didn't seem

143

the thing for me to worry about that much, or really to pursue it further. Oh sure, it was interesting, but so were a lot of other things. Frankly, I couldn't have cared less. . . ."

Neil's biggest ambition in life was to become a doctor, and he enrolled in pre-med school at the University of Wyoming. Then came the breach of the Korean lines and the flood of troops southward; with service pending, Neil laid his plans carefully. He would meet his requirements for military duty by joining the Air Force. With his tour over, he would then return to school to complete his medical training toward becoming a doctor.

Flying seemed as good as anything else, and Neil applied for cadets. After a year of enlisted service, in April, 1952, he passed air cadet requirements and was assigned to attend the class of January, 1953. Then he refused to accept; his required military service was almost up, and he couldn't see staying in uniform. Discharge loomed invitingly on the horizon, and Neil was eager to get out to return to school.

"But a bunch of officers ringed me in one day—pilots, I should add. They talked me blue in the face, telling me that I was a fool to get out, that I didn't know what I was missing. Boy, they were persuasive. . . . They changed my mind for me, and I went into cadets. But it wasn't because I was hungry to fly. I more or less took the aviation cadet test as a challenge, just to see if I could hack it, if I could meet all those requirements."

And the amazing end to all this hesitation was that Neil took to flying as though he had wanted nothing else in life. He fitted into a cockpit like a glove; the trainers responded to his touch with a sureness and agility that drew admiration from his instructors. He became cadet commander of a group, and at Hondo, Texas, solely on the basis of merit, became the ranking cadet officer, and then the top man in his class.

Everything moved smoothly until Neil ran into his first critical obstacle. In one of those unhappy circumstances that befall some students Neil was saddled with an instructor who was a fanatical perfectionist, and this can kill the growing love for flying in the best of youngsters. The other cadets had serious trouble, for he rode his students so hard that many of them, including Neil, began to feel that perhaps flying just wasn't worth it after all. Neil was ready to call it quits.

Fate played its hand, then, in the form of assignment to a new instructor. Bad as was the former pilot, the new man was outstanding. And so were the others that followed. What had begun to grow now flourished, and then became a song of joy. Neil literally fell in love with flying, and looked back with amazement on the days when his interest just wouldn't "catch." As his rapport with the world of flight waxed, so his plans for a medical life waned and finally disappeared altogether.

Flying became the substance of Neil's life, and he attacked his work with an unquenchable determination to be the very best. He was. When they pinned the wings to his uniform, it was as a Distinguished Graduate, and one of the few new pilots to be awarded a Regular Commission.

One day Neil saw the Thunderbirds, flying the straight-winged Republic F-84G Thunderjet fighters. He stared in wonder and awe at the team moving with its famed precision through the skies. A new ambition flared. Neil *had* to get on that team. But how? He lacked the experience in the air, the time in uniform. He would have to wait, and work. Neil read everything that had ever been printed on the Thunderbirds team, and the more he read the more grimly determined he became to one day join what he considered the elite of the entire Air Force, the ultimate in flying.

Neil received assignment as a fighter pilot to the 450th Fighter Day Wing at Foster Air Force Base, Texas, where he flew F-86 and F-100 fighters. He took so naturally to the powerful jets that he soon became an instructor in the F-100C and D models.

But in May of 1955, the F-100C—which he flies today in the Slot—almost snuffed out both his flying career and his life. It was close, terribly close. The big fighter exploded on takeoff with a terrifying roar and a burst of flame that was heard and seen from all over the airbase. In fact, as Neil's airplane shot downward, blazing, he was immediately assumed to have been killed.

"It was a maintenance test flight," Neil recalls. "The airplane had just undergone extensive maintenance work and

145

modification. I went down to the line at about ten in the morning to fly the beast. Everything started out smoothly enough; I made a normal takeoff, and it was then that things very rapidly became unglued. . . .

"Just after breaking ground I heard a terrific explosion. The entire airplane shuddered like it was coming apart in the air. Immediately the fire-warning light flashed.

"Normally, on takeoff, I establish an attitude so that I can climb at once to a safe bailout altitude. The moment I'm airborne I pull up into a steep climb. This way, before I level off, I have enough altitude to get out if I have to. It's a move I cultivated until it became a habit, I suppose."

That habit saved his life. The sweptwing fighter was about 200 feet off the runway, afterburner flaming, and climbing out at 250 knots at a thirty-degree angle. The Super Sabre was still accelerating rapidly when the explosion ripped through the airplane.

There was a fuel leak about the afterburner section. The fuel was ignited, and the result was the roaring blast that shredded the AB section, blew out a large panel in the bottom of the fuselage, and then ejected the heavy drag parachute (used to slow down the airplane on landing) and all the operating gear.

This was that moment when a pilot must operate almost by instinct, by the habit he has drilled into his flying methods. This was the grand payoff for the months and months of practice, for diligent attention to details, for anticipating an emergency—*any* emergency—that might one day explode in his face. This was the day.

Neil moved swiftly, much faster than it takes to tell on these pages. Immediately he realized that the hydraulic lines leading to the elevator control had been blown out completely; both the primary and reserve lines were lost. He had no control. The big slab tail was a useless hunk of metal. The F-100C had become a potential deathtrap. Any moment it might erupt into a fiery bier.

"I moved fast in that cockpit," Neil said. "I never thought I could do so many things in so short a period of time, but man-a-live, how I moved inside that cockpit!"

The explosion and the fire-warning light were almost simultaneous. Neil's eyes scanned the instruments; hydraulic pressure was falling rapidly on the number one system.

Immediately he hit the switch to actuate the ram-air turbine to operate the emergency hydraulic pump. He switched the hydraulic selector gauge to the number two system; almost at once that dropped to a zero reading. His foot tramped down on the rudder as he slammed the stick forward to get the nose down.

"Save the airplane. . . ." The thought flashed through his mind, but almost at the same instant he realized the attempt was doomed. He had lost all his elevator control.

He flipped the radio transmitter to "guard channel"—not even looking to see that he was exactly on 243.0 megacycles on the UHF radio. Everything now was without wasted motion or time. The stakes were life itself.

The mobile control unit at the end of the runway kept this frequency open, and Neil snapped, *"This is eight six one. Am I on fire?"*

No answer.

Neil recounted the events. " 'The devil with it,' I thought. I figured for sure that I was on fire. I stop-cocked the engine; grabbed the throttle handle and yanked it back to the OFF position, locking it.

"Everything seemed to be in a blurred sort of slow motion; I knew that I was fast running out of time. I kicked my feet into the seat stirrups and wedged them in tightly. Then with both hands I grasped the armrest grips. Funny—I didn't even have time to get worried. The alarm bells were clanging in my head. I just grabbed those grips and yanked. Didn't even have time to put my head back against the headrest. I just hauled back as hard as I could. . . ."

The shoulder harness locked automatically, pinning Neil's shoulders back against the seat. The instant that he yanked back on the grips an explosion blasted in the cockpit and everything was blotted from sight by swirling vapor. As the grips came back the canopy was blown free; it twisted up and backward as it flashed away. The vapor was condensation from the sudden change in pressure.

There wasn't even time for this to make its impression on Neil's brain, for even as the roar struck his ears there came another explosion—the ejection cartridge firing. A terrific blow from beneath the seat smashed at his spine and in the next instant he was hurtling up and away from the airplane.

To underestimate the expression, luck rode with Neil as he fired out of the burning fighter. When he jerked the handgrip triggers, the force of the blowout slammed his head down between his legs. So severe were the *g*-forces that he instantly blacked out.

That same motion is the reason he is flying today. Neil's sun visor was still up on his helmet. He had no time in which to push the visor down over his eyes, or to uncouple the hoses and wires connecting him to the airplane. The explosive force of the ejection slammed the visor down . . . but at the same moment one of the hoses that was torn free stretched far out, and then crashed back with terrible force directly at his face. So hard was the blow—stopped by the visor which in that same split second had snapped down—that the hose coupling cracked the thick plexiglas. Had not the visor come down, the coupling would have torn the eye from his face.

Unconscious, Neil soared up and away from the airplane in a great arc. And again luck played its part on his side. In his entire squadron, only two pilots wore the B-5 type parachute. This was equipped with an automatic seat release and an automatic chute release. Neil was one of those pilots! He was still unconscious as the seat pulled away from him and the canopy yanked free, and opened. Had he worn the regular parachute, he would have smashed into the ground still in the seat without regaining consciousness.

He came to, spinning wildly in the air. For a moment everything was dark, until he realized that air pressure through the cracked visor had twisted his helmet around his face to cover his eyes. He yanked it around and looked up—and his heart just about stopped.

The shroud lines were tangled into a twisted mass, causing the chute to spin rapidly. But before he had time to reflect on this the earth rushed upward at him. Neil hit on his feet, moving backward, and twisted his body as he fell, taking the impact on his right shoulder, rolling with the fall.

Exactly fourteen seconds had elapsed from the moment he yanked the armgrip triggers.

As he ejected, the blazing F-100 arced over toward the ground, dove, and expoded with a tremendous roar on impact. No one saw Neil get out—the news was flashed that the pilot had been killed in the crash and explosion.

Neil's speed had taken him more than three miles off the end of the runway. Several jets passed overhead, but the pilots didn't even look for him—why look for a dead man? Then a helicopter sped low over the ground, headed for the burning wreck. Neil whipped a signal mirror out of his survival kit and flashed his position. The chopper bounced to the ground and Neil's group commander jumped out— staring at Neil with bulging eyes and sagging jaw.

"He sure thought I had bought the farm," Neil grinned. "He took a good long look at me, let out a roar, and threw his arms around me. I thought he was going to break my ribs, he was so happy. But then, so was I!"

Neil flew with the 450th Day Fighter Wing for two years, then went overseas to Morocco where he flew on combat status as a fighter and fighter-bomber pilot. In September of 1957 he was reassigned to the 405th Fighter-Bomber Wing, flying F-100D's from Langley Air Force Base in Virginia.

Then the Air Force announced that the Fighter Weapons School at Nellis was being reorganized, and that pilots were to be selected for the elite of all pilot schools in the country. Neil wanted this, and wanted it bad. In April of 1958 he had it, and transferred to Nellis in the Training, Research and Development Section of the school. For the next year he flew to his heart's content.

"There was only one problem—I was so close to the Thunderbirds that it hurt," he said. "I'd made up my mind at Langley that one day, somehow, I was going to get on that team. I flew with the School for about a year, and really, I had the world on a silver platter. The two best areas in the Air Force were the Fighter Weapons School and the Thunderbirds, and there I was, right in the middle of both. I liked the School, but I just couldn't get the Thunderbirds out of my system. I filled out my application and began the wait."

In December of 1958 he was asked to ferry one of the Thunderbird airplanes as a spare pilot, and he snatched at the chance. He flew Robby's wing on a flight to Sacramento and lost no time in personally badgering the team leader for a position. Robby said he would keep it in mind, but when the next position was available, Chuck Maultsby had the door opened for him.

"I knew about Chuck's flying record," Neil reflected, "and he sure could fly. So I hitched up my belt and started campaigning all over again. But then in an unexpected—and tragic—way, the door opened for me. Robby was still flying with the team, but Fitz had just taken over as the new leader. And then one of the greatest pilots who ever lived—Fish Salmon—was killed.

"Fitz called me in for an interview. It didn't last very long, because there's only one way to find out about the way a man flies—and that's upstairs.

"I flew the Right Wing with Fitzgerald for an hour. Did he give me a *workout!* He ran me ragged. When I landed my arm was just a pincushion of aches and pains; I hurt so much and I was so tired that I almost had the crew chief fill out my postflight forms.

"We started out first in moderate chandelles, and then did lazy eights. But steadily Fitz was working into the steeper maneuvers. He went into rolls, loops, whifferdills, cloverleafs, everything—and I was eyeball-deep in stick and rudder trying to stay with him. He felt me out carefully every inch of the way, learning what he needed to know.

"When we landed, he didn't say too much. You know Fitz; the world can go through some tremendous cataclysm, and he remarks on it in his own offhanded manner. He told me that I had done a good job, but he said it so casually that I didn't expect very much.

"I went back in to talk to Robby, dragging my rear. Robby shrugged off my concern, and said that I'd likely get into the Slot. The position was set up for Herman Griffin, but that madman was doing so well and liked being Solo Pilot so much that he preferred to stay right where he was."

Captain Homer Whitlow, who joined the team in December of 1957, and was getting ready for his next assignment, returned to the Slot position at the request of Fitzgerald. Neil tacked on to Homer and was given an accelerated course in the fine points of flying the hole between the other three airplanes. He had much less training than the position called for, but he fitted so beautifully into the routine that the other pilots all felt he was as good as he would ever be—only experience could further sharpen his touch. On May 17th, only six weeks after joining the team, Neil flew his first show.

For the next year Neil spent only several weeks at the Thunderbirds' home base, and saw precious little of his wife, June, and their daughter, Patti Ann. "I'd been married only three months when I moved into the Thunderbirds," Neil laughed, "and June had to learn the hard way what it was to become an Air Force wife—and especially one of the Thunderbirds. It was rotten of me, I suppose, but June wouldn't have it any other way. For the next couple of years, though, I think I'd better stick pretty close to home!"

There's one further episode with Neil that brought him into a rather exclusive fraternity of pilots within the Air Force—a select group of men who have *twice* ejected from supersonic fighters. This time the ejection was not at all frantic. . . .

The team was practicing various types of close formation maneuvers, flying at Thunderbird Lake. The diamond had shifted to trail, and raced low over the deck at 400 knots prior to starting a changeover cloverleaf turn.

Fifty feet off the ground, nose still coming up, Neil's engine flamed out. For a moment he had no indication of the complete loss of power—but he knew quickly enough what had happened when the other airplanes accelerated away from him. A glance at the instruments confirmed it—the fire was out.

Neil horsed the stick back and moved the plane slightly to the right, chandelling upward in a climbing right turn. He had more than enough speed to reach an indicated altitude of 6,000 feet, at least 3,000 feet over the immediate terrain. At this height, with his airspeed falling to 220 knots, the recommended deadstick gliding speed, he nosed over to maintain his speed.

As soon as he began his climb, he called in his emergency. "Lead . . . Number Four just flamed out."

It was all very calm and, seemingly, unhurried. "Roger, Four. The dry lake is just off to your right."

One of the Wingmen dove for the ground, sweeping low over the dry lake bed to see if it could be used for a wheels-down landing. By swinging into the climbing chandelle Neil was automatically moving into a position from which he could land. In the emergency situation, of course, many things were going on at the same time, and Neil couldn't push aside the thought, "I swear I've gone through this routine before!"

His immediate concern was a restart, to light the fire in the bird so that he could regain power and head for Nellis. If this proved impossible, he would try to save the airplane by landing with his gear down on the dry lake bed.

He flipped on the airstart switch—and suddenly all radio calls blanked out. The switch automatically cuts the radio and all other electrical items not necessary to sustain the airplane in flight. Four times Neil tried to restart the engine, but without success. He flipped on the secondary bus tie-in, got the radio working, and acknowledged Fitz's repeated calls to him.

"I'm getting rpm and ignition, but no fuel," he said. "I'm going to deadstick her in. How does the lake look?"

One of the fighters streaked upward. "It doesn't look very good, Four."

"Well, I'm going to have to get out of this thing, then. . . ."

One of the boys rode off Neil's wing. *"Whuuy not!"*

"Yeah, Neil, if she won't fly, might as well walk!"

He had time to disconnect the hoses, check the chute for the zero lanyard position, wedge his feet in place. He pushed his helmet back against the headrest, took a deep breath, and yanked on the grips. It was a lot better than the first time. The seat shot up and over, tumbling forward.

Until this moment everything had worked fine, but then things got sticky. The chute deployed almost immediately— just *before* Neil could get away from the seat. There was a terrific jolt as the canopy cracked open to its full position; Neil had a twenty-eight-foot canopy which opens faster than the standard parachute, and is ideally suited to low-altitude ejections.

Neil stared unbelievingly as the seat sailed upward within

the shroud line and pushed into the canopy. In that moment—several hundred feet up—the canopy collapsed.

"I figured right then and there that I'd had it—finis, end of the story," Neil said. "But a second or two later the chute reopened, slowly, and blossomed out full again! That blasted seat was still there, however, and it drifted down slowly in the risers, entangled in the shroud lines. I didn't have much time in the air, since I'd gone out only nine hundred feet over the ground.

"I grabbed the seat and pushed like mad to throw it clear, but I didn't have a ghost of a chance of doing that. Then the ground came up at me and I started paying attention to business. . . ."

Just before he touched the ground, Neil pushed the seat away from him with his right hand, shoving with all his strength to keep the heavy seat from crashing into his head and shoulders. The sudden motion spun him around, and, off balance, he hit the ground with a sickening jolt, landing full on his right leg.

Neil doesn't remember if he heard the snap, but there was no question that he had broken at least one bone in his leg (it was two; both leg bones just above the ankle). Even as he hit, Janc and Chuck streaked low overhead and Neil waved at his teammates; both had circled his descending chute all the way to the ground.

As he collapsed on the ground, Neil heard the booming explosion of an afterburner cutting in. That was Fitz, boring upward to 25,000 feet where he rolled over and flipped on his IFF switch to emergency position. Radar observers at Indian Springs and Nellis almost went out of their seats as the crazy emergency blip flickered on the scopes. The moment Fitz got word that the rescue choppers were near by, he peeled off, turned on his smoke, and dove directly toward where Neil had landed, a great finger in the sky pointing to his downed pilot.

Sprawled on the ground, Neil wriggled free of his parachute harness and gingerly pulled off his boot. Janc and Chuck continued their circling, and every now and then Neil waved to let them know he was all right, while Fitz maintained his higher cover. As the choppers closed in,

Neil had that signal mirror out again, flashing his position. A flight surgeon helped the crew load him aboard, and Neil was on his way to the hospital. "It wasn't bad at all," he said. "The doc put my foot into a splint, and they sent me home. I was back in the air in sixty days—besides, June didn't mind at all. I was really home for a while!"

9 The Upside-Down Pilot

Six gleaming Super Sabres rushed over Nellis Air Force Base in tight pitchouts, swung around the southern approaches to the field, and settled neatly down to the long runway. They taxied to the flight line, jockeyed into position, and then the pilots cut the engines at the hand signals of crew chiefs. The airplanes sparkled in the sun; they had just been flown back from McClellan Air Force Base by the team after a thorough overhaul and modification program.

Dick Crane, Chuck Maultsby, and I were in a group to greet the pilots. Chuck had remained home to help Jeanne move into their new house, and a fighter pilot from the weapons school went along to fly his airplane back to Nellis.

The pilot—we'll just call him by his first name, Rick—walked up to us, dragging deeply on a cigarette. His hair was matted and sweaty from his helmet, and he appeared to be almost exhausted. Herman Griffin stood beside Rick, grinning as though enjoying some secret joke. On the return flight from McCellan, it had been Rick's assignment to fly Griff's wing position.

Suddenly Rick thrust out an arm. "Cripes!" he exclaimed, half in jest and half seriously. "Flying with you characters is worse than flying combat!"

Chuck Maultsby walked up. "Why, what happened?" he asked innocently. He knew the answer beforehand; Rick wasn't the first pilot to have been given "the treatment" by Griff.

"Well, this guy"—he jerked a thumb at Griff—"he starts to make a turn to the right. I see his wing drop, so I follow. You know, flying. In an airplane. At least, I *thought* I was following. Every other time I followed this way everything

154

went right. But then the cotton pickin' airplane disappeared! When I looked around, Herman was a couple of hundred yards off to the *left*."

He blew out a cloud of smoke and sighed. "I still don't know what happened, or how he got over there. And from then on it was strictly a matter of self-defense. He was like a snake. I said to heck with the wing and I dropped back into combat trail formation. Stayed there all the way home, too."

He glared at Herman, who smiled and bowed from the waist. Rick snorted. "Nuts to you characters," he muttered, and walked off, shaking his head.

Herman Griffin, a pilot with incredible talent in a fighter, just about had to kick the door off its hinges to join the Thunderbirds. The first time he applied for admission to the team, his application never reached Robby, who was then the leader. It seems that Griff was then an instructor at the Fighter Weapons School, and his commanding officer wasn't about to release one of his best pilots. Griff fretted for a month, and doggedly sent in his second application.

His CO recognized the inevitable, and bucked on the papers to Robby. The Thunderbird leader checked over Griff's background and his flying record, and took him up for a checkout. For forty minutes Griff did his best to hang on to Robby's right wing while the team leader whirled through the sky in rolls, loops, and some maneuvers Griff hadn't heard of. Robby is a master at this sort of thing, and he put Griff through the wringer.

On the ground, Robby told Griff, "You're a bit rough on the controls, but you can fly. I can't promise you anything, but I want you to come along on the next trip when we do a show." That trip was to Foster Air Force Base in Texas. From here Griff flew the spare Super Sabre to Knoxville, Tennessee. Still nothing but dragging the airplane from base to base. On the next flight, to Tinker Air Force Base, the airplanes arrived at their destination with sufficient fuel remaining to practice a bit before landing.

Robby called Griff to take up his wing position, and again they went through the intensive checkout Robby kept for team applicants. This time, however, Griff knew what to expect, and he hung like a leech to the other fighter plane. When they landed, Robby walked over to Griff's F-100, stuck out his hand and grinned. "Okay, Griff," he said, when can you come to work for us?"

"Right *now!*"

On their return to Nellis, Griff became the 28th Thunderbird to receive assignment to the team. For the next three months he flew as spare, and chafed at the bit as the weeks wore on without specific assignment to the solo pilot slot. The normal progression within the team was from spare to solo to the diamond. While Griff flew his spare airplane, Fish Salmon held down the solo job; Fish moved to the diamond slot when Sam Johnson received assignment for overseas duty. The long-awaited solo was open, and Herman joyously greeted his new responsibility.

It seems that this was the moment for him truly to come into his own, and all the pilots recall the intense fervor with which Griff threw himself into his flying as the Solo Pilot. Every man who had ever flown solo was a lot better than merely good, but Griff was determined to make the solo position just a little more distinctive than it had ever been before. In this he has certainly succeeded, at least from the viewpoint of this writer, and I've watched many pilots in the teams going through their paces.

Griff flies his Super Sabre with a combination of precision, skill, and with what *appears* to be a dash of deliberate madness. By now the reader has learned, of course, that nothing is ever done with the Thunderbirds that hasn't first been thrashed out in a meeting, and then flown repeatedly, time and time again, in the practice area of Thunderbird Lake. For this is the secret of the Thunderbirds' success—that incessant practice and infinitely cautious appraisal of every move they make in the air. The idea is to demonstrate the awesome power and performance of the Super Sabre, and you don't exactly accomplish this goal with rocking-chair quiet or speed. The point is that the Solo Pilot, because of his flashing maneuvers—the minimum-altitude passes, vertical aileron rolls, four-and eight-point hesitation rolls, and so on—just seems at times to be flying with untrammeled joy. But then, Griff is happiest when in the air.

156

The skill and airmanship of Griff make it almost impossible to believe that this young man is a former high school teacher in the rather quiet subjects of Business Law and Accounting. Nor does the average person think of the tremendously competent fighter pilot, which Herman Griffin certainly is, as a man who came out of an orphanage, and then worked and fought his way up the ladder of life through college.

It's impossible not to be personal here, for Griff and I have been calling each other "Cuzzin" for many months now. When I began to assemble my notes on this supersonic flyboy, we discovered that there existed some remarkable similarities in our lives. For one thing, we were born on the same day—September 14th. We both lost one of our parents, and we both went into an orphanage. We worked at the same types of jobs, knocked around the same way, and we both ended up in flying—and finally meeting each other and flying together.

There were three brothers in the Griffin family; Herman was in the middle. He was five years old when his father died. Herman's mother tried desperately to maintain a home for the three boys, but it proved impossible to provide the necessary food and clothing, and still take care of her children. The youngest of the family was then only several months old.

Reluctantly, Mrs. Griffin brought her two older sons to the Crosswell Home orphanage in Sumter, South Carolina. Herman was then six, his older brother, nine.

This is a change from the familiar story of a boy raised in an orphanage, for the pilot of today has only pleasant memories of the ten years he spent in the Crosswell Home. Griff and I talked at length on this subject; we had some notes we could compare. There is no question but that the people who ran the Crosswell Home did their best so that the school's work, training, and discipline would make a man out of each boy who came there to live.

"My mother for a long time could never get over the fact that she was forced to bring us to Crosswell," Herman explained one night, "and she has suffered from a conscience that just wouldn't let her alone. You know what I mean,

Marty, she felt that perhaps we missed the things in life that are so necessary to kids who are growing up. I think that she finally understands that there was nothing ever to regret. I saw how she worked just to keep my kid brother, how she just about slaved to take care of him.

"You see, Mom never really 'left' us. We knew how much she loved us, how she wanted more than anything else in the world for us to be with her. But it just couldn't be done. There was still the depression that kept salaries down, and . . . well, it wasn't in the cards. But Mom never quit trying."

The authorities at the Home did their best to give the boys in their care as much affection as was possible, but they left nothing wanting in respect to work and discipline. Griff worked with the other boys on the Home's dairy and truck farm during his stay, and knuckled down to a strict scholastic routine during which he consistently remained in the top group of his classes.

Once, Griff answered the growing tug of wanderlust, and ran away from the orphanage. To his surprise, after he was caught and returned, there were no scenes of outrage and no special punishment. The people who ran the school understood their boys well. They would have been disappointed in the spirit of the youngsters had they not tried, at least once, to try and disappear into the world around them. "It was almost a mark of graduation," Griff recalls. "Once you took off, you were at least showing that you had the spirit to try and shake authority. They were wonderful and understanding people in that place, the nearest thing to a real home that any kid could ever hope for."

When Griff was thirteen, his brother left him for the first time in seven years. He had finished high school, and went into the Navy. Three years later, Herman reached his sixteenth birthday, and was awarded his high school diploma.

In 1945, after spending several months with his mother, Griff entered Athens College in Alabama. It was the beginning of four hard, grueling years for the teen-ager, for money was still scarce, and college could be sustained only by working.

Griff worked every day in the college dining hall as a waiter, but this failed to provide the necessary minimum income. In the late afternoon he worked four hours in a textile mill owned by the college. And after all this, he did other odd jobs such as collecting laundry in the dormitories. He had yet another job, working as a janitor in a church in the town of Athens; this brought him an additional five dollars a week.

There was precious little time in which to study, but Griff took advantage of every spare moment to cram. His is the classic story of the boy coming up from behind, of slugging his way through obstacles in a private "operation bootstrap" to climb to the top. Griff held down four separate jobs, was forced to do his studying on the run. Nevertheless, he accepted being in college as deserving of his most intensive energy, and in this respect he left nothing undone. So outstanding were his efforts that he was elected to "Who's Who Among Students in American Universities and Colleges," in 1948-1949.

In May of 1949, Griff received his Bachelor of Science Degree in Commercial Education. He remained in Athens for the next two years, teaching Business Law and Accounting in the Athens High School.

Griff's future in education was assured; his ability as a teacher and his driving energy promised much more than his contemporaries could foresee in the future. Yet he chafed and found little satisfaction in his gains. Perhaps they sufficed for the men around him, but Griff could not long remain in front of a classroom.

A year after the Korean War broke out, Griff signed the papers that put his name on the list for aviation cadets. There wasn't any question on the part of the Air Force, and in September 1952 it was Lieutenant Herman E. Griffin who graduated with new silver wings as a fighter pilot from Webb Air Force Base in Texas.

Griff transferred to Moody Air Force Base in Georgia for all-weather combat crew training. From the outset he fitted hand-in-glove in the routine of the Air Force pilot. College had occupied almost all his waking time and energy. His two years as a high school teacher, although more than successful, seemed empty of purpose to someone who had fought so long and hard to make the climb.

But there no longer existed the search for that purpose—

Griff found it in the cockpits of jet fighters. He fell in love with the sky, he exulted in the marvelous freedom of the air. He cavorted at supersonic speed, flashed through clouds, drank in the sparkling life of the airman's realm. Whatever else there had been in life before faded into an unimportant memory. Griff was, truly, for the first time in his life, "whole and alive." And with this exuberance, the heady taste of freedom that only the pilot knows, came a skill that was recognized quickly in his flying, but held even greater promise for the future when experience would more properly sharpen his piloting technique.

After graduating from advanced combat training school at Moody, Griff was assigned to an overseas tour for three years. He flew F-84 Thunderjets and F-86 Sabres in England and Holland. "Leona joined me in Europe," Griff said, speaking of his wife (who cooks a real mean breakfast), "and you might say that we have sort of an international family. Eddie was born in Holland, and Marie in England."

I think a word about those two Griffin children is needed. Marie is a quiet, beautiful child, but whatever she lacks in ferocity is amply compensated for in Eddie. My introduction to this bundle of vibrating young sinew, when I first walked into the Griffin household, was in the form of a small shape that flung itself happily at me, and with shrieks of joy swung its fists with delight. Whenever Griff brings home company, he first goes through a chore that he usually has to repeat on each occasion—ungently picking his son off any unwary visitor! "Tha's m'boy," he grins.

By now we've seen a lot of the Thunderbirds' Solo Pilot in our book; we know that he opens the show each time, using either the AB or the supersonic pass. "This AB pass, when I cut in that big stove back there," Herman explained to me, "came about by accident. It wasn't always in the show. Now we use it to let the crowd get acquainted with the sound of the AB."

He lifted the cover of a box on my desk, picked up a cigar, sniffed carefully. "This'll do for a starter," he chortled, and at once filled the room with smoke. "Now, back at Daytona Beach in 1957," he said, "before I was on the team . . . the boys were putting on a show before a few hun-

The USAF **Thunderbirds** demonstration pilots, 1968. **From top left to lower right:** Major Neil Eddins, Commander-Leader; Captain Mack Angel, Left Wing; Major Stan Musser, Right Wing; Captain Jack Dickey, Slot; Captain Tony McPeak and Captain Mike Miller, Solos.

With wingtips overlapping 36 inches, and vertically separated by less than 60, the **Thunderbirds** smoke-in for a wedge formation salute to Hoover Dam, near their home at Nellis AFB, Nevada.

The diamond pilots roll over the top of the Arrowhead Loop maneuver. The blue wings of the **Thunderbird** emblem can be seen on the belly of each aircraft, as well as other details of the sparkling red, white and blue paint scheme.

Bottoming out at 500 miles per hour, less then 100 feet above the ground, the six **Thunderbird** demonstration aircraft complete the Wedge Loop.

Thunderbird maneuvers are breathtaking exhibitions of precision flying.

The Calypso Pass is performed by the two Solo Pilots, showing the stability of the F-100 Super Sabre during inverted as well as normal flight. As they enter the demonstration area, the lead Solo rolls his aircraft inverted, and is joined on the wing by the second pilot.

Racing toward each other at a closing rate of almost 1,000 miles per hour, the **Thunderbird** Solo Pilots first hug the ground and then pull up to flash past each other into aileron rolls.

America's "Ambassadors in Blue," the **Thunderbirds** have flown more than 25 million miles to complete nearly 1,300 aerial demonstrations over the land of the United States and 39 other nations.

dred thousand people who had come down to watch the races on the beach. The team was to fly over the beach, but they were worried some about all those seagulls flapping around like mad."

He swung his feet to rest them on the desk, then went on: "John Bartley was the solo man then. Jack Broughton—he was the leader—called him over and said, 'Bart, there's a mess of seagulls down there along the beach. Go down and shake 'em up a bit; make a pass on the deck and see if you can scare them away.'

"Bart did just that. He screamed in right over the water, cutting the AB in and out—boom, boom, boom. The crowd loved it; they thought it was the actual opening of the show. It was so successful that we've used it ever since with the team."

I watched Griff make his AB pass during the races at Daytona Beach early in 1960. The crashing explosion of the afterburner shook up the seagulls, all right, including one that was smeared along the side of Griff's airplane. Seems this one bird went straight up in front of the airplane. "There was a bit of a bump"—Griff smiled—"but that was all. No damage."

Most observers are convinced that when Griff races in before the crowd for the AB pass, he has the F-100C wide open, throttle rammed right up against the last stop. Actually, this isn't so. Nor do they realize that Griff makes his run before the audience along a flight path that has been calculated with precision, with the safety of the viewing crowd affecting all movement of the airplane. His fighter moves along a path that allows Griff always to plan a course taking him away from his audience in the event of mechanical failure or any other emergency.

Griff plans his moves with the accuracy of his extraordinary pilot skill, long hours of practice, and a flight path established by Fitz. He begins his run in front of the crowd so that about a mile out of the show center point, the F-100C is at its minimum altitude and in level flight. From this point on Griff is through with any maneuvers—any changes from his flight course or flight attitude.

"A good pass is one where the airspeed is just about four

161

hundred knots directly in front of the crowd," he explains. "At this speed I've got the best possible positive control of the bird, and I can get a maximum number of afterburner lights right where the people can best see and hear the effect.

"I come in about seventy knots slower than I'll be doing when I reach a point directly before the audience. Everything here is a matter of timing. Just as I begin to light the AB I trim the aircraft nose down and hold a positive back pressure on the stick. This keeps me from porpoising from the sudden changes in power.

Opening afterburner pass.

"There isn't much use in making an ineffective AB pass, and the way to create the best sound—the series of AB explosions—is to hold absolutely level flight during the reviewing pass. We've even worked things out to where we know the audience best receives its impressions from the sight, and the smell, of the smoke oil.

"The intention is to get as many lights on the AB as possible during the pass—that's the purpose of the whole thing. The moment the AB lights, I pull the throttle inboard and the same moment that it goes out I shove that throttle right back into AB range—it's on and off all the way through the run. At this speed, four hundred, I generally get about five or six lights. By the time I end up on the run I've gained at least a hundred and ten knots over the entry speed."

I sat in with Griff and Bob Cass, the new spare pilot, while Griff was working with Bob on details of the solo man's flight maneuvers. Griff is an irrepressible, smiling individual who seems always to have a chuckle or a laugh struggling to burst free. The other pilots love nothing so much as to "knock" their Solo Pilot on every occasion. He's either a "madman" or they keep him as Solo Pilot because "he sure can't fly formation; it ain't safe to be in the same sky with that rebel boy."

But no one has more respect for Griff's slide-rule precision than the men with whom he flies. I kept a tape recorder going while Griff worked with Bob, flying the maneuvers in his office with an F-100 model.

"Now we got this four-point roll," he explained, "and make no mistake about it. It's a precision maneuver that requires more practice than you're going to want to do, and it also demands that you've got to know every last aspect of the airplane. The key to successful—and safe—low-altitude aerobatics is positioning prior to the maneuver. . . ."

It was hard to believe what I was watching. Bob Cass is a skilled veteran of flying fighters, yet he listened in complete absorption to every word Griff said.

"You should always try to be at minimum altitude in level flight, indicating about four hundred fifty knots, at least two thousand feet before you reach the point where you pull up to start the roll. When you're in position you pull up sharply and immediately you establish your initial point, just as the nose passes through twenty degrees nose-up attitude.

"Now, right here, you've really got to be riding hard on that bird. You make your movement with hard stick forces, and no question about being positive about it, to about half aileron deflection, and then right back to neutral as ninety degrees of roll is completed. As she begins to roll"—he turned the model slowly around through a halting circle—"you apply a smooth top rudder force. You hold this pressure, because this lets you stop right on a point without any yaw, and you maintain just that nose attitude that you want.

"As you roll into the first point, you smoothly release the back pressures and allow the stick to move into a neutral elevator position. And right here, boy, is where that proper

163

trim setting becomes the most important thing of all. The aileron action for the remaining points is roughly the same as the first point—except that the stick forces are slightly lighter on the third and fourth points because you've lost some of your airspeed.

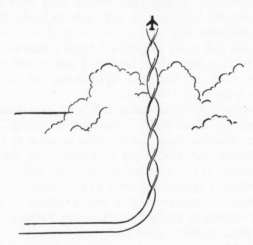

Solo vertical rolls.

"Here's where you've got to be extra careful. These lighter stick forces give some pilots the tendency to overshoot that last point, or start something that I guess could be called backlash. You've really got to stay on the wire to prevent overcontrolling those last two points. She can get away from you without your knowing it, and it means a sloppy maneuver. Fitz doesn't go for that sort of thing; he's liable to make you wash that airplane two or three times every morning."

"Sho 'nuff?"

"Sho 'nuff! That Irishman, I tell you, he got a penchant for clean birds." Herman grinned at Cass, then continued:

"Now, the thing to do is to be sure you release your rudder pressure back to neutral as you complete the second point. During your roll into the third point, you apply smooth

164

top rudder pressure. This way you keep the nose attitude right where it belongs.

"You'll need about half rudder deflection at the completion of the third point. Things get a little tricky here. While you hold the third point, and then begin to execute the fourth, you've got to play your rudder pressures to maintain a proper clearance for terrain, and keep that smooth, even arc going through the rest of the maneuver. Usually you'll require full rudder pressure while you execute the last point—this is to be sure that you get a sharp roll out. When we try it this afternoon, you'll notice that trim is really important here.

"Now, this four-point roll, it's really pretty easy. It's the eight-point roll that is the *real* precision maneuver of the solo routine. . . ."

That was enough for me. I left Cass to the mercies of the quiet, balding, ex-school teacher.

We've discussed the inflexible demands of safety under which the team operates during its demonstrations before watching crowds; Griff acts, as I said before, as a high-flying top cover for the diamond formation during their maneuvers. But even his every move is made with exacting requirements of safety. When he comes in past the audience, for example, Griff always—terrain permitting—breaks away from the crowd in a steep, climbing left turn. The idea of this maneuver is to permit his airplane to break out behind the crowd. And that pullout that looks so smooth and easy to the audience actually imposes a punishing load of from five to six g's on Herman. Doing this for every show, every practice session, day after day, in the kind of beating the average man couldn't sustain. Yet skill improves, if at all possible, and safety is never compromised.

We have seen this word—safety—crop up again and again in this book, yet it is not at all repetitious to the team. Safety is the ultimate law itself to these men, and they never forget their responsibility. During a conference of the team, Fitz took advantage of a break to answer several of my questions on specific points regarding this matter.

"Well, the troops fly the F-100C," he began. "You can summarize this machine by saying that it is a high-perform-

165

ance, powerful, supersonic fighter airplane. It is a machine that, despite the skill of the engineers who made it possible, flies in a performance region so demanding that it must be *flown*—at all times. Unlike the private airplane, flying at speeds and under conditions where the very design of the airplane permits the pilot to be forgiven some of his mistakes, the supersonic fighter airplane is a craft demanding constantly of skill and unflagging attention.

"No airplane is foolproof, and the greater the degree of complexity built into any machine, especially the high-performance military airplane, the greater the chance that, at some time, equipment may fail. It may be a flameout, it may be a fuel line rupture, it can be the failure of an electronic system—anything. But whatever it's going to be, it can happen during the demonstration of the team before an audience. And that fact is never forgotten by the men who fly the airplanes of the Thunderbirds ... they do not permit themselves, ever, to forget the responsibility of safety."

The other pilots listened to our conversation; on this matter all wise-cracking is completely absent. Safety to the team is almost religious.

"Above all else," continued Fitz, "we plan every step carefully. Every move we make, every step that is taken, does not take place without first considering every aspect of safety. For this reason, as an example, when we perform before an audience in a public show, our airplanes never make a pass directly at—into—the audience.

"All maneuvers are so flown that they are on a quarter-line—we approach along a quartering course—rather than along a line that would send us directly toward the audience. Because of this stringent and self-imposed safety consideration, no matter what happens or may happen, the aircraft, singly or as a group, never endangers those people who have come by the thousands to witness their Air Force in action. They've come with trust in us, and we've got to uphold that trust. There are no excuses, no alibis, no reasons for ever deviating from this policy."

Way back in Herman Griffin's military flying career is an episode of a damaged fighter airplane, and the easiest, most gentle bailout in flying history. Griff was practicing a low-

166

level, high-speed strafing pass, and made a sharp pullup with a speed of approximately Mach .89. Suddenly he felt a "slight jolt; at the same time something in the bird went *clunk*."

Some pieces had torn loose from the airplane; the sudden pullup, for reasons unknown, overstressed a part of the landing gear system. The six-*g* force of the pullup yanked the two main gear legs out about 15 degrees beyond a normal extension, toed out sharply. The nose gear extended about one-third its normal movement, as other pilots who flew close to Griff reported the condition of his aircraft.

"Hearing that *clunk* was more than enough," Griff recalls. "That bird doesn't go around making strange sounds unless something is happening. I pulled up for altitude and headed for open spaces. Didn't want houses or people below me if anything went to pieces—fast."

He talked the situation over with the other pilots. "You can't land in that thing, Herman," one of them called. "You'll have to punch out."

Griff acknowledged, and made his plans to abandon the crippled fighter. A check with the nearest radar controller enabled him to aim the airplane at a large area of empty fields.

Griff then trimmed the nose down, stopcocked the throttle, and went into a glide indicating 250 knots. At 4,000 feet he would "flip my lid and punch out"—jettison the canopy and eject.

The future Thunderbird pilot ejected, and everything worked exactly as the bailout manual said it should. The seat kicked him up and away, and he tumbled slowly. As he completed one body turn, he released his belt and shoulder harness, and pushed the seat away. One second later the parachute streamed out and billowed open.

It was all remarkably gentle. Everything stayed where it belonged, except that a pack of cigarettes and a lighter fell from an open sleeve pocket. Griff drifted slowly to earth, grinning and waving at the other pilots circling his parachute.

Trouble loomed suddenly as he drifted toward a power line; Griff prepared to spill the chute, but it was unnecessary as he drifted more than a dozen feet over the poles. As he dropped, however, the canopy draped over the power lines.

Griff came slowly to a stop with his feet about eighteen inches above the ground. Then, gently, the canopy slipped from the power lines, and Griff settled to earth as easily as a feather.

"I didn't even get my shoes dusty," he said. "I just unbuckled the harness and stepped out. I pulled the chute clear, spread it out on the ground as a marker, and sat down to wait for the chopper. I'd seen the airplane hit in a field of weeds. It tore the ground and the weeds some as it came apart, but that was all. So there wasn't anything to fret about. Except those cigarettes, and I wanted a smoke."

A farmer drove breathlessly to the scene, and Griff greeted him with a casual "Halloo, there!" The farmer stared in disbelief at the relaxed, grinning pilot.

"I'd sure be glad if you had a cigarette," Griff said. Unable to say a word, the farmer shook his head, but pulled out a cigar. Griff lit up and puffed away happily. Ten minutes later the rescue helicopter was on the scene.

Griff shook hands with the farmer, waved good-by to some other people who had come running up, and was on his way back to the airport, still puffing clouds of smoke.

That's our boy Herman. I think his son is going to be just like him. Whenever the team flies a show at Nellis, Eddie is always on hand to watch. But somehow, when Mom tells him the diamond is coming over, he just lolls around. Then the magic words. "Look—here comes Daddy."

And Eddie is on his feet, shouting and yelling with pride and joy. "That's my Pop!" he screams happily.

He sure is, Eddie, he sure is!

10 Left Wing

Bob Janca and another fighter-bomber pilot of the 67th Fighter-Bomber Squadron in Korea had a pact. Though it might seem to people outside the close circle of men who flew sweptwing Sabres against the Communists that the ritual was just a bit ridiculous, no pilot ever thought it very funny. It was just something, another element, of the life of the combat pilot. And little things can be very important when every flight you make could well be your last.

As fighter-bomber pilots, Bob Janca and his friend flew into a hornets' nest almost every day. The Chinese weren't just good at defending their targets, they were superb. They knew how to conceal every kind of gun, large and small, in gullies and thickets. So almost every trip into their side of the Korean fence meant a reception that was somewhat heated.

Rituals are important things to some pilots, and to Janca and his friend their particular ritual was very important indeed. They went out on missions together and, they hoped, they would always return together. When they did, taxiing their wicked-looking fighters back to the flight line, gun ports streaked black, their ritual began.

They climbed down from their planes. Each man filled out his post-flight form, handed it to his crew chief. But neither man said a word. The crew chiefs understood; there weren't any questioning stares.

The pilots met on the flight line, and the two men walked to a jeep. They never talked. It didn't matter if one of the airplanes was shot up or badly damaged by a flak burst. No matter what happened, silence was the rule. They climbed into the jeep and roared off, headed unerringly for the officers' club. Here they walked to the bar, selected stools, and sat down.

The bartender didn't ask questions or so much as raise a quizzical eyebrow. He could see the Sabres coming back, he watched them taxi to the line, and park. That was his cue to go to work. His part in the ritual?

Two very dry martinis. Before each pilot he placed a napkin, and atop this he carefully set down a martini. The two fliers picked up their drinks, nodded briefly to each other, and drank.

And then, not until then, did they speak their first word to each other—which might have been a quiet, "What happened to you out there today?"

And the answer, surely punctuated with a long, pent-up sigh of relief, "I don't know for sure, but those Chinese are improving their aim. I got me some hemstitching in that bird of mine. . . ."

I heard the story of Bob Janca's pact—more properly it was a solemn agreement—with his pilot friend during an evening at Janc's home. He emphasized that the pact stated specifically that a martini had to be served. Any other drink wouldn't do.

"Why?" I asked.

"Can't remember why," he said. "But whatever it was, it must have been a good reason."

"It's a funny thing, the way the guys will establish some sort of ritual when they're flying combat," he continued. "Anywhere else, at any other time, it seems ridiculous. But not under those conditions. Maybe it's our lucky charm, like an amulet. You're all too aware of the fact that a rabbit's foot doesn't stop anything, but what the devil . . .

"It makes a guy feel better, and you observe that pact with religious care. And besides"—he laughed—"we had a couple of real good missions with a lot of fireworks, but we always came back for that martini."

When you first meet Bob Janca he isn't at all what you expect. Janc flies the Left Wing position in the diamond, and there's little need here to explain in detail what all this demands. Just take all the problems of Chuck Maultsby on the Right Wing position, modify them slightly because of the opposite position, and you have Janc's story in the air.

It is needless, also, to stress that like the other members of the Thunderbirds team, Janc is a superb pilot. But the disarming thing about him is that boyish face and grin. You take a good look at Janc, and you think he's out of place because he isn't wearing Ivy League clothes and carrying around an armful of college books. Even after you've been with this guy and watched him move an F-100C around the sky like he was designed to fit into the airplane, you shake your head and wonder.

Except for a preoccupation with building model airplanes and reading aviation magazines, Janc's background doesn't point at all to flying. Like Neil Eddins, however, Janc went out for sports with all his might. There's a slight difference here; Neil is a strapping six-footer, and Janc is one of those pilots who fits the size of memorable flyers like Bob Johnson (twenty-eight kills as an ace) and Pete Everest (World War II ace and one of the world's greatest test pilots). Small, but packed with power.

Janc never flew until he entered the Air Force in 1951, but his skill with building models led many of his hometown folks in Cleveland to predict that one day he would become a fighter pilot. In 1943, attending Junior High School in Cleveland (he was then thirteen years old), Janc built several airplane models that looked so much like the real thing that he received a writeup in the high school paper.

"It wasn't much at all, of course," he explained, "just a couple of paragraphs, and as I became more interested in sports I forgot all about it. Until 1952, that is. I had just received my commission and my wings, and I flew to Tonawanda, New York, to visit a favorite aunt. The first thing she did was to drag out a scrapbook with that little article from the school paper, and she had underlined the first line of the article. It said: 'If some day you see Bob Janca in the cockpit of an Air Force Fighter, don't be too surprised—' "

Most men reach a certain crossroad in their lives that determines their future path. For Bob Janca the future seemed to lie in the field of athletics. In Cleveland's Lincoln High School, and later at Xavier University in Cincinnati, Janc applied a grim determination to his sports. In high school he played halfback on the football squad, and filled the position of safety man on defense with his college team.

Then he went hard at baseball. He was good at football, but superb with a bat in his hands and on the baseball field. A scout for the Pittsburgh Pirates took a hard look at Janc and immediately tried to sign him up for a tryout with the major league team.

That was the point where Janc had to decide, and after much deliberation he politely thanked the scout for the offer, and just as politely declined. "If I took any money from the Pirates," he explained, "I'd have lost my amateur status in sports. And I went to Xavier to study coaching. I was working for my bachelor of science in physical education. It was simply a matter of deciding on a goal and sticking to

171

it. That was my decision. But then that little fracas over in Korea got all fired up.

"I just couldn't stay out of it. I found out I qualified as an aviation cadet, and presto! there I was, in uniform and in pre-flight. I came out of Bryan Air Force Base in Texas, in December of '52 with lieutenant's bars and my wings. Then I took combat fighter crew training here at Nellis, and received assignment to Korea."

The North American F-86 Sabre, direct predecessor of the F-100C Super Sabre that Janc now flies for the Thunderbirds, is usually associated with the aerial fights against the Russian MiG-15 fighter high over North Korea. Janc didn't get into that kind of air war, he became one of the few pilots to use the Sabre specifically as a dive- and fighter-bomber.

"One mission above all the others I'll never forget," Janc recalls, "and not because of any narrow escapes or anything like that. Everything fitted into the groove on this trip. We were out to hit a marshaling yard, and this was a mission on which I really lucked out. I had two one-thousand pounders, and I came almost straight down over the target. They both went *plunk! plunk!* and the whole world blew up.

"I must have hit right in the middle of an ammo train. Boy! You should have seen that place—the whole rail yard lifted straight up from the earth, freight cars went flying in all directions, and the mountainside along the yard was covered with flaming debris. Those two bombs and what they set off finished the whole place; there wasn't anything left for anyone else to bomb."

Janc returned to the States with an assignment to McConnell Air Force Base as an Instrument Instructor Pilot. This one assignment reveals much about the man who now flies Left Wing for the Thunderbirds, for to become an instrument instructor in jet fighters demands a truly brilliant ability to fly with precision in the air.

From McConnell Janc moved to Nellis, and received a new assignment as a fighter-gunnery instructor—and his only real "close call." Janc refuses to consider it as such, but I've spoken to the other pilots, and they're unanimous in their belief that only Janc's lightning reflexes and his ability

172

to make the right moves in an emergency kept an incident from becoming a headline.

It was on July 17th, 1956. Janc was flying the instructor's chase position in an F-100A, with a student on his first F-100 solo flight directly before him, taking off on a south heading from Nellis. The takeoff was uneventful until just that critical point where the wheels bang up into their wells and the doors snap closed. Janc was airborne, wheels up, and using full afterburner to overtake the student in front of him.

He accelerated rapidly, closing in fast, and then chopped power back out of the AB range to prevent overrunning the other plane. And right then and there the big fire went out. Janc was without power, just above the ground, going like mad—and too low to get out of the airplane.

His hand snapped out, flicked the air start switch to ON, and jockeyed the throttle. To his amazement, the big engine rumbled a few times, and then caught. But only partially. His instruments read sixty-eight per cent power, and Janc could barely keep the heavy fighter airborne. Somehow he managed to mush along just above stalling speed while he called out his emergency.

Then, with infinite care, unable to climb, and just scraping the ground, he eased one wing low and began a gentle, wide turn. It was critical every foot of the way. If he could have climbed, then there was a case of punching out of the bird. But he couldn't. If he dropped any lower, the belly of the airplane would be scraping desert rock, and the result of that would be a ball of fire streaking over the naked earth.

Janc nursed and babied that fifteen-ton airplane all the way around its turn, flying with all the skill at his command. And then the runway came into sight at the side of the canopy, swinging around slowly. There was almost an irresistible urge to drop the wing and just cut short the approach, but that would surely have meant a stall. Janc played it carefully, skillfully, and finally the runway was dead ahead of the laboring Super Sabre.

He held up the nose with his minimum airspeed, snapped down the gear, and pulled the throttle back a hair. So fine was that balance of minimum flying speed that the airplane

173

simply quit flying and dropped in for a landing. Janc let her roll for a while, then applied the brakes and ground to a stop.

Even as he rolled down the runway, fire trucks and the meat wagon were rushing to keep up with the airplane. No sooner did he stop than the fire crew threw a ladder on the side of the airplane to get Janc out.

Releasing drogue chute on landing . . .

But the young pilot didn't move. The firemen stared at Janc as though he had gone completely out of his mind. Janc held his helmet in one hand, and howled with laughter. He choked and spluttered uproariously; finally he managed to point to his feet. The fire chief leaned over the cockpit and stared.

"I thought his eyes would pop right out of his head." Janc smiled as he remembered the scene. "It was my feet. They were trembling like a bush in a windstorm; they were absolutely uncontrollable.

"And do you know when *that* started? Not during the flight or coming around while she hung upon the edge of the stall. You expect this in a fighter, and you're ready in your mind for whenever it happens. None of that bothered me. But just before I came to a stop I saw the chaplain running across the field to where I was slowing down. And when I thought he had come on hand ostensibly to review the remains of one Robert Janca, well, that was it. Everything went ape, and my legs started to tremble like crazy, and then I laughed and laughed. Cripes, they had to help me out of the airplane."

That night we discussed Janc's flying with the Thunderbirds since he joined the team in April of 1959; Janc insisted that since I had Chuck's story of flying, then I knew as well what he had to do.

"Actually, all the guys feel that there is one real working hero of this outfit," he said. When he didn't continue, I took the bait.

"All right, Janc," I said. "I'll bite. Who?"

He smiled and nodded at his wife. Ginny stared at her husband, then looked at me and shrugged.

Janc pushed back his chair and motioned for me to follow. First we looked in one bedroom, and then in another.

When we returned to the table, he said, "Janis is four years old, Bobby is three, and the twins—Marta and Melissa—they're two years old.

"You think flying that bird is rough, Marty? Well, I used to think so too. Then for one full day I got the job of taking care of all those kids in there. Man, we got it easy. Ginny's the one who really works in this family!"

11 Every Man A Thunderbird

We have met the first string of the Thunderbirds—Bob Fitzgerald, Chuck Maultsby, Bob Janca, Neil Eddins, Herman Griffin, and Dick Crane. But there's still one more man to go who completes the lineup of the seven Thunderbirds fighter pilots—Captain Robert L. Cass, who flies as the Spare.

I have never been able to equate Bob Cass in his new position as the Spare Pilot. On the Thunderbirds team, the Spare is the neophyte, the newcomer who still must be put through his paces. The team never considers a man truly a member of the inner circle until he has flown with the Thunderbirds for at least six months—and Bob Cass came to the precision demonstration team in February of 1960. Since we all flew and traveled together, I had the good opportunity to see Bob competing with several other pilots to be chosen for the coveted team membership.

The difficulty with this process is that every man is so good that immediate selection is virtually impossible. Exactly what decides the final choice is something the pilots find almost impossible to define themselves. And it's not a

175

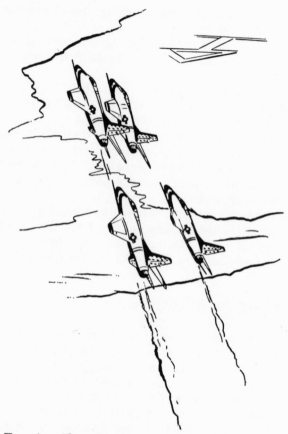

Entering Cloverleaf Turn . . .

matter of deciding on the basis of flying or appearance or experience. They are all great, and only some very small difference finally allows the team to point its finger at one of the men—as the boys did with Cass—and say, "Okay, you're it."

Despite his position as a "Thunderbird Trainee" when he sewed on his patches, Bob came to the team with more than ten years of military flying experience behind him.

The Korean War began while Bob was in college, and he

applied for the Aviation Cadet Program. On September 29th, 1950, he was sworn in and immediately entered flying training. By February of 1953 he was in Korea, assigned to K-2 Airfield (Taegu), and flying a Republic F-84G Thunderstreak fighter-bomber.

This man—whom I met as a "Thunderbird neophyte"—flew 101 combat missions in Korea with the 8th Fighter-Bomber Squadron, 49th Fighter-Bomber Group. The background of Korean air fighting—Bob's missions in close air support for the Army, strafing, bombing, firing rockets, and deep penetration attacks against the Chinese—makes it difficult to think of Cass in any respect except that of the experienced, highly-skilled, veteran fighter pilot. Which, of course, he is.

After a thirty-day leave following Korean service, Bob flew to Bitburg Air Force Base in Germany, and served there as a fighter pilot for four years. In February of 1960 he crossed his last hurdle, and became a member of the Thunderbirds.

"This is the apex of my career, Marty," he told me. "It's something I've always wanted, ever since the Thunderbirds first got under way. If I never do anything else with my flying career, this will have been *it*."

"Bob, do the pilots in the Air Force—you know, the guys who are hot flyers themselves—do these people talk much among themselves about the Thunderbirds?"

"And how they do," he exclaimed. "All through the Air Force they talk about the Thunderbirds, the way they fly, the precision they maintain. The pilots are worse than the kids who watch the shows. This is the elite of flying in the entire service. It's something that every fighter pilot wants badly, because when you make this team, boy, you've really climbed to the top of the heap."

SECOND TEAM

Bob Cass completes the list of the first-line Thunderbirds pilots—the official demonstration team of seven men.

But there are more, of course, and there isn't a pilot who has ever flown in that first string who thinks of the team as anything else but the entire complement of sixty-five men who are listed on the "Active Personnel" sheets.

The list includes the demonstration pilots; support pilots and their crews; ground crews and mechanics; maintenance teams; administration and supply units. Let's meet some of these men who enable the precision team to demonstrate with a record of on-time appearances that has never been broken in some eight years of precision flying.

Captain John C. Donohoe joined the team in March of 1959 as the primary C-54 commander, although when he first came aboard it was to fly the C-123 attack transport and the big, twin-boomed C-119 that was then used for support operations. For several months Johnny ran around on a schedule that knew no beginning or end, since he was the *only* transport pilot available. According to the tall, slim captain, however, this was perfectly normal to him. He'd been doing a bit of frenzied flying for years, and it was simply a matter of accelerating his routine. "Who needs sleep?" He shrugged.

John Donohoe has a tremendous storehouse of experience behind his transfer to the Thunderbirds. His Air Force service dates back to the old AAF in March of 1944. In addition to his transport, helicopter and amphibian flying, he flew B-17 Flying Fortresses with the Strategic Air Command as late as 1949—the last SAC outfit to fly the famed old Queen of the Bombers. Then, on up to the powerful B-50 Superfortress; and in late 1950 he went to Harmon Air Force Base in Newfoundland to fly every type of rescue aircraft in the region.

Down the line from Donohoe is his Assistant OIC for the Thunderbirds Transport Section, Captain Raymond F. Kayea, Jr. Ray *looks* like he belongs in the cockpit of a transport; he is physically a very big man, and it's natural to think that it takes all that beef to wrestle transport planes around. There's another reason why Ray seems to fit so well behind the wheel of a big airplane—this is the type of flying he likes best of all.

"I did all my early flying as a navigator," Ray explains. "But then I got that itch to fly; an itch that wouldn't stop. So I filed away my slide rule and applied for pilot training."

By 1953 Ray was on active duty as a transport pilot, and by 1955 he had more than 2,000 hours in his logbook. For the next several years he flew four-engine transports to Goose, Sondestrom, Thule, Newfoundland, Churchill, England, and throughout Europe. In December of 1959 he applied for the team and was accepted immediately.

During my stay with the team, I flew a good many hours in one of the two Fairchild C-123 attack transports. In the pilot's seat was 1st Lieutenant Chester R. Golka, who joined the Thunderbirds in May of 1959 with nearly seven years of C-119 experience in his logbook. To Chester, flying has been a natural, unhurried part of his life stemming from boyhood days. He grew up in the small town of Brooklyn, Pennsylvania. The fact that his uncle owned the airport near the town had a lot to do with his flying, and Chester celebrated his sixteenth birthday by making his first solo flight. It was a bit anticlimactic, since he'd already been flying for years.

The C-123 isn't the fastest-flying airplane in the world, and more than one pilot has turned up his nose at the twin-engine powerhouse. It's a high-wing brute with 5,000 horsepower, designed strictly for close troop support in rough field operations. In this respect the C-123 knows no superior, for it can be "dumped" into a field and come to a stop within less than a thousand feet—seconds later jeeps and troops come boiling out of the rear unloading ramp.

But the C-123 does represent a sharp contrast to the dazzling jet world of the Thunderbirds. Since it was designed for its specific field operations mission, little care was given to making it an airplane that would be convenient or comfortable over long trips. Chester, who usually flies with a co-pilot assigned from Nellis for a trip, cruises his brightly colored brute at a speed of 160 knots, maintaining 6,000 to 10,000 feet. The maximum nonstop flight never exceeds 1,100 miles.

I've flown the C-123 with Chester, and I'll say right off that you fly this airplane *all* the time. Because of its flat belly and slab-sided fuselage, it has a tendency to wallow happily through the air. Relax pressure on the wheel, and she slides off on a wing. She yaws like a wounded whale, and yet Chester and the other pilots who fly the Provider with the Thunderbirds like the airplane. For the life of me I don't know why. With the short, narrow-tread landing gear and the towering single tail, the C-123 is a pilot's enemy on the ground. In a strong crosswind this airplane will tip over while it's parked on the ground, so Chester has to fly the bird *after* he's landed, or even taxiing out to the runway for takeoff.

Thunderbirds' C-123 transport.

"Our job is to carry ground-support equipment for the F-100's," Chester said as he explained the details of his assignment. "We have a flyaway kit; it's a complete parts kit that we simply shove into the airplane and fly away. With the parts in there, the mechanics can take care of almost anything wrong with the fighters except major overhauls and repairs. There are extra tires, wheels, brakes, drag chutes, engine removal equipment, tools, smoke-oil servicing equipment, line servicing equipment—just about everything. It all comes to about four tons, which is much less than the maximum the 123 can carry."

On each mission there are about six to eight men aboard the C-123; Chester, a co-pilot, two flight engineers, and mechanics. Often the airplane looks as though it were flying the personal equipment for a theatrical group, for the F-100 pilots, and the men who will be flying in the C-54, often stow their personal gear aboard the C-123.

"Let's say there's a show about a thousand miles from Nellis," Chester said. "We go out first so that we'll arrive at the field shortly before the F-100's land. This way the ground crews are ready and waiting to assure their immediate servicing.

"First, however, there's got to be co-ordination between ourselves and our destination so that the people there will know just what our requirements are. Crane handles this job; he first sends ahead a requirement sheet, letting them know exactly what we will need. When we land in the C-123, the boys set up a parking area for the F-100's. Immediately they prepare for servicing. They round up whatever equipment they'll need. Essentially, they take whatever steps are necessary to assure that the 100's receive the same attention as they do back at Nellis.

"When we're all through, on our way around the country after shows, we tag along behind the demonstration pilots, following the same route. We always stay in radio contact, too; if not directly, then by calling communications stations or our fields. We make sure that all the 100's have taken off from whatever field they've landed at, and without difficulty. If there is a problem with any airplane, well, we're right behind them and the boys are ready the second we land to go to work."

The team has three transports—two C-123's and the single C-54. Chester Golka is assigned as the commander of each C-123; on field missions he takes one plane and leaves the other behind to be used for base support duties.

In a team of fighter pilots, it would seem that the airplanes that earn the greatest pride of the Thunderbirds are the sleek Super Sabres. But this isn't so. It's that four-engined C-54, an old, once weary veteran of international airairways that has become *the* pride and joy of the team.

Chief Warrant Officer Myron France clutched my flight jacket in a greasy hand, and half dragged me up the stairs of the C-54 transport. "C'mon! I want you to have a real good look at this phoenix of ours."

181

Fifteen minutes later, in the cockpit, after having minutely inspected various sections of the airplane, noted its careful interior workmanship, its living-room spaciousness, I got the chance to ask Myron, "Why do you call this thing a phoenix?"

Myron grinned and waved his arm to encompass the big Douglas. "Personal title on the part of all of us, I suppose, because this took us out of the bucket-seat class and put us into something we could honestly—and happily—call comfortable. But that's only part of it. We put a lot of personal attention into the airplane, almost a pet project for off-duty hours work as well as what was necessary for maintenance and so forth. A lot of the guys are proud of what they did with this ship.

"Let me go back to the beginning. First of all, we've needed four-engine dependability for a long time. There's also a morale factor involved, although this doesn't receive public attention. On short trips, the C-123 is fine. But who wants to go on long cross-country hops in that ear-beating monster? It became difficult for us to have our own people to the point where they wanted to go in the 123 for long hops.

"When the crews are stuck inside a C-119 or the 123 for eight to ten hours, they're bushed. It's really a physical beating. They were so worn out and fatigued from long flights that they couldn't give their best for intricate maintenance work. There are other reasons, too, but that's about the gist of it.

"So, finally, in June of '59, the Air Force relented, and sent us word that we were being assigned a C-54 Skymaster."

To the ground crews, the C-54 could become a heaven-sent transport. On long trips it would haul the mechanics, the support people. It meant enclosed spaces for clothing and personal gear and luggage. They could stow a smaller version of the flyaway kit within the hold. Long-distance flights of up to two thousand miles, cruising at a true airspeed of 190 knots—all this was possible. The airplane could be made comfortable, it would be insulated to bring the sound level down to a minimum. To a man, the entire team rolled up their sleeves and went to work.

182

Many of the items they needed to repair the C-54, and to build into the airplane the facilities they wanted, just weren't available through normal channels. Some of the history of this airplane since it joined the Thunderbirds is a matter of dim and poor memory, since the airplane was rebuilt with the aid of some truly remarkable midnight requisitioning. Not only the ground crews, but the fighter pilots as well pitched in. Material was scrounged out of nowhere. Items "impossible" to obtain would show up in the hangar one morning, and no one could—or would—explain how they got there. Mechanics called friends in other fields, and parts that hadn't been seen for years would show up miraculously.

What had been a weary-looking airplane began to grow into a beautiful machine. The mechanics tore apart the entire cockpit deck. They ripped out the controls and all equipment, threw away what was worn, and installed new equipment. If it was impossible to find the parts, they built the equipment in their tool shop. The radio equipment was taken out, refitted into new mounts, and suddenly the flight crew had two comfortable bunks for sleeping.

Then the men created an "executive compartment," primarily for the Thunderbirds pilots' office when they went along in the C-54. They built a table with four comfortable, deep seats. A couch appeared out of thin air, and was modified to fit into the compartment, and to take the seat belts. The table in the compartment is of beautifully finished wood. Special lights were installed in the cabin; their source, too, was a dark mystery.

Aft of this executive compartment the men built a whole new passenger cabin. Here they installed the closets for clothing bags, and emergency tools and parts for the F-100's. Determined not to lose an inch of space, they even built a wide comfortable bunk atop the closets. They installed racks for magazines and books, and these were always kept full.

On all previous trips, the ground crew had always traveled on bucket seats, or simply sprawled on equipment wherever they could find room. The men were out to get airliner-type seats for the passenger compartment. But where? Some midnight meetings were held, and somehow, without questioning, the seats were "scrounged up." Twenty-six comfortable reclining seats went into the compartment.

They wanted this to be an airplane with the least possible noise and vibration. From "somewhere" they got their hands on roll after roll of thick Fiberglas batting, and this went against the cabin wall. Then, from some equally mysterious source, there came beautiful birch plywood paneling. This went over the insulation.

When the men were through, they looked upon their "new" airplane and cheered. The C-54 has a beautiful, warm interior. It is quiet, comfortable, and largely vibration-free. It means that the support team can move out into the field, rest en route, and be prepared to go to work efficiently and immediately upon landing at any base where the fighters have flown.

"And it didn't cost the Air Force a red cent," one mechanic said in triumph.

THE TEAM

"The Thunderbirds demonstration begins," Dick Crane said, "the moment the guys step into the cockpit, and the Thunderbirds are performing their show until the last plane is taxied in, on the line, brakes locked, and every man has climbed down and walked away."

And all this is true. But to understand their close co-ordination, you must actually watch the team as it maneuvers on the ground. This is precision taxiing with a vengeance, it seems. Having done a fair amount of taxiing my own airplanes around runways, I am constantly amazed at the way the pilots handle their fifteen-ton fighters on their ridiculously tiny wheels.

Watching them return to the flight line is almost like an orchestral movement. The five fighters always return to the exact positions they occupied when the engines were started. But that term, "orchestral movement," is the key to their final few inches of maneuvering. It is a great sense of pride to the Thunderbirds pilots to be able to stop their airplane *literally* on a dime. And that precision would be impossible without the men who start the engines, give pilots their signals to move out, and guide them unerringly back to their starting points.

The pilots are the brass, the eleven men who meet them at the return of each flight the conductor, and the rest of the organization completes the "sixty-five-piece orchestra."

As the Super Sabres begin their turn off the taxiway to their parking positions, they parallel a line of five men—each is the crew chief of his particular fighter. They stand at rigid attention awaiting their jet airplanes. Behind each of these men is the assistant crew chief, and standing behind this row is one man—the flight chief of the Thunderbirds.

Formation taxiing . . .

Once they have turned off the taxiway, each man keeps his eyes glued to his crew chief. Remaining in one place, the chiefs signal by hand movements the exact positioning of the fighters. By no more than small hand signals the heavy airplanes are jockeyed exactly where they are to be parked, and when they are all stopped and the switches out, the airplanes are aligned as neatly as if the men had spent hours pushing them by hand into the exact line desired.

The key—the amazing co-ordination of pilots and ground crews. And this is carried further than parking these fighters on five individual dimes, of course—it is the backbone of the entire organization.

CWO Myron France—or Myron Maintenance, as he is more frequently called by the pilots—has approximately fifty airmen under his command. Every one of these fifty is a career man, and the majority are high-ranking noncommissioned officers. They are stable, adult, intelligent people, the very best of the enlisted ranks in the Air Force.

Most of the officers live on Nellis in base housing; Neil Eddins and his wife prefer a home directly in Las Vegas. Chester Golka, as the last bachelor holdout of the officers, lives in the Bachelor Officers' Quarters on Nellis in happy and unmarriage-like disarray.

But because base housing is at its very minimum at Nellis, the married airmen have experienced no small difficulty in acquiring base housing. Despite the fact that they observe no set working times, and perform their duties on a killing schedule, their positions as Thunderbirds personnel brings them no special privileges. It is not the best of situations, for off-base housing means paying rents considerably above the norm for the rest of the country. Despite these domestic tribulations, however, every man has struggled to achieve his place on the team.

The Thunderbirds team has its own hangar at Nellis about midway along the flight line, and smack in the heart of line operations of the busiest military airfield in the world. Nellis is 1,800 feet above sea level with excellent runways, the longest stretching to 10,500 feet. Except for about eight to twelve days of the entire year, there is either good or excellent flying weather.

To a major extent, the Thunderbirds team maintains its own line and hangar facilities. This is about the only outfit in the entire Air Force that operates on what its own men like to call a "closed cycle maintenance system." Except for major or heavy maintenance operations, or major depot repairs such as completely overhauling an engine, the team is on its own. The men use the facilities right at their doorstep that are normal to everyday Nellis operations. The intention, and the continuing rule, is to use everything directly within the "closed cycle" of the team, which operates much on the same basis as a World War II advance fighter outfit that is virtually self-sustaining in the field.

For example, the team has its own skilled hydraulic specialists, its own engine specialists. It maintains its own electricians, electronics experts, and just one lone radioman. But Airman 2/C Richard W. Rennie (married, one child) "is

186

worth his weight in a half-dozen experts," according to Myron France.

Watching these men operate on a day-to-day basis as I have is a complete education in itself. Despite the fact that the Thunderbirds comprise an aerial demonstration group, they operate on the same minute-to-minute conditions of a group right on the line of combat. And as I explained in Chapter Two, the F-100C Super Sabres can be quickly returned to full combat status. It is fully justified to repeat that this is a combat-ready organization that enjoys a tightly-knit skill which serves only to enhance greatly its efficiency. And the enlisted men are the key to that happy state of affairs.

We've learned that the demonstration team must operate on literally a second-by-second timing schedule. Griff as solo pilot flies his part of the show on the basis of two seconds plus-or-minus, and the four-plane diamond on a scheduling of five seconds plus-or-minus. Now, I don't care how good those pilots are, they aren't going to achieve anything remotely approaching their critical time requirements without a really hot maintenance team behind them.

This means that when the airplanes are fired up and ready to go, any last-moment technical or mechanical defect or emergency *must* be attended to right there on the spot—and no excuses, please. Airman Rennie, as an example, once changed a defunct radio system in Maultsby's airplane even as the rest of the team halted in their formation taxiing; Rennie rushed to the Right Wing airplane, yanked out the malfunctioning set, clipped in a new one, and restored full radio communications. And in barely three minutes! This is a fantastic performance. The moment Rennie signaled to the other mechanics, the men snapped down and sealed the nose covers, and Chuck shot away from the line to join the other pilots.

At this particular writing, the Thunderbirds have flown a total of 552 official demonstrations—and the team has *never* aborted a show because of any aircraft ever suffering a mechanical failure! That kind of performance just doesn't come easily.

You've got to see these airmen in action to appreciate

their amazing skill, ability, and intense drive. First of all, every one of these men is a volunteer, and no man ever joins this team without first making it a clear point that he wants to become a team member more than he wants to do anything else. Every man is a highly skilled specialist in his field, and he is a career airman. To join the team means to give up much of his personal and family life. He is on the road almost constantly with the demonstration team. He takes no bows, he has no specific working hours, and he doesn't hesitate to work stretches of sixteen to thirty-two hours without a break, if this is necessary—as I have seen them do.

This reaches right into something as prosaic as administration. Dick Crane and I often burned the midnight oil in the Thunderbirds' administrative building—a rebuilt tar-paper shack—and the three airmen assigned to duty here more often than not would continue working to eight or ten o'clock each evening. Technical Sergeant Robert W. Brandy doesn't know what the words "quitting time" mean, and he has about forty-seven jobs to do other than filling in as Dick Crane's assistant. Staff Sergeant Tim J. Heffernan is the Administrative NCOIC for the team; "Heff" runs a tight office, and brooks absolutely no nonsense. Often blithely ignoring any requirements of enlisted protocol is Airman 2/C Thomas P. Murphy. "Murph," I suspect, is somewhat incorrigible, but no one cares—since his usual routine is to do the work normally fulfilled by three or four airmen.

The airmen of the maintenance teams gripe, all right, and no enlisted man is ever worth anything unless he does know how to gripe. But it's in the nature of grousing that bodes only good. These men are fiercely proud of the Thunderbirds, and they consider themselves beyond any argument as the absolute elite of the Air Force. They don't think they're the best—they know it. Ask any man, and you're sure to have your ears chewed off by a sergeant or corporal who views his questioner with absolute disdain.

There's little basis to support an argument, for the record stands proudly by itself. Other teams—those in fighter squadrons and so on—may have carved out a maintenance record the equal of the Thunderbirds, but the team simply considers this to be a closed corporation of the best maintenance men in the whole Air Force. In other words, there are a very few who are as good, and they're welcomed into the conclave, but "sure as hell they don't come any better," growled one sergeant.

The flights these men make aboard the C-123 aren't the most comfortable in the Air Force. The C-123 is slow and unstable, and its performance is a mixed blessing and a curse for its role with the Thunderbirds. To gain its outstanding tactical abilities as a combat transport, it plays its mission with the Thunderbirds in extreme discomforts for its airmen. Chester Golka has his problems, but he has only sympathy for the men who fly in that cratelike space behind his insulated flight deck.

The machine, in addition to its wallowing gait, has no soundproofing, no pressurization, and too few seats. It has countless sharp edges and protruding pieces of metal. The interior is always jammed with working equipment, tools, spare parts, parachutes, personal gear—whatever the team needs to sustain itself on the road.

"Aboard one of these airplanes," explained Staff Sergeant Mike Ashcraft, "you can receive a really outstanding example in how to achieve bodily comfort under the worst of conditions. Now, this thing works itself down to a science. The major purpose on a trip is to 'rack out,' to get some sleep. The hangup bags with clothes make some of the best mattresses for covering up the sharp edges and knobs of equipment—but you sure gotta get that bag back on its wire before you land. The guy who owns it might not appreciate the way you're using it, that's for sure!"

When the team stopped in Taegu, Korea, the Korean Base Commander presented the men with several cases of succulent Taegu apples—for the pilots as well as the airmen. Unfortunately (for the pilots), the airmen hadn't had a decent meal in days, they had been on the go hour after hour, and, in their own words, "We were darn near starved."

The crates were loaded into the rear of a C-130 Hercules which the team used for this portion of the tour, and were wedged in the high, aft section of the attack transport. The men climbed in for takeoff in mid-afternoon—without food since six that morning. Then one sergeant roared his delight at the sight of those crates. A wrecking bar came out of thin air, wood splintered, and apples flew through the air into the eager hands of the men. "I wouldn't say it didn't take long for them apples to disappear," the sergeant sheepishly told Crane later. "I guess there was a good fourteen seconds between when I opened the crate and they were all gone."

In Taiwan, Formosa, the practice of living off the bounty of local high-ranking officers was continued. Again it was a gift of fruit being presented to the team. When the transport touched down at its next base, almost overloaded from the unexpected new cargo of several cases of ripe watermelons, there was a unanimous decision. "Let's have a watermelon party!"

Only, the watermelons were warm, and "whoever heard of eating warm watermelons?" The next scene was reminiscent of World War II improvisation, when bomber crews mixed ice cream on the ground, dragged it into a bomber, and flew to 20,000 feet where thirty degrees below zero temperatures assured a proper consistency upon landing.

"The trouble," explained one airman, "is that the Air Force would sorta take a dim view of our burning a few thousand gallons of kerosene just to cool off our watermelons. It surely would! So one of the boys had the watermelons placed in a big tub, and dragged beneath the hose of a liquid-oxygen generator. Real careful-like, he sprayed the fruit a couple of times until all the melons were taken care of this way. Those melons, they were just as cool as ice cubes. . . ."

I strongly recommend that the housewife doesn't follow this procedure, despite the speed with which the melons can be chilled. Liquid-oxygen is the same supercooled stuff they pour into giant rockets so that they can kick away from the earth at about 25,000 miles per hour. It is cold—unbelievably and impossibly cold. It boils at 297 degrees—*below* zero.

NO ONE IS OVERPAID

The F-100C is a big, extraordinarily complicated hunk of

190

machinery. To keep it flying in reasonably good shape demands twice the maintenance effort and the personnel that were required to maintain its predecessor, the F-86 Sabre of Korean air fighting. The F-100C is "far more complicated, sensitive, sophisticated, and twice as much trouble," groused a mechanic.

During normal show scheduling, each Super Sabre flies about fifty hours each month. Every one hundred hours the men tear down—completely disassemble—both the airframe and the engine for a complete and exhaustive checkout. This little job requires five highly skilled men working a total of three to four days (with overtime) for the airframe only, and another three men at least three days for the engine. That's eight men working steadily over a period at least of one full week of normal working hours.

An Airman First Class, with three stripes on his arm, who is highly skilled and has four years of active service, will earn just about $160 per month. On this amount, plus allowances and fringe benefits (the latter continue to shrink yearly), he may have to support his wife and several children.

Overseeing the complete maintenance spectrum is CWO Myron France, and he is another clear index of the only motivation for duty with the Thunderbirds being pride and morale. Because, to put it bluntly, it sure isn't money.

Myron has been in the Air Force for thirteen years, and has the rank of Chief Warrant Officer. He is a responsible, skilled man, as adept at working with his hands as any man, but much more valuable as the watchdog of Thunderbirds maintenance. For his thirteen years service, and his responsibility for approximately ten million dollars' worth of equipment and assuring the safety of the pilots and crewmen, the Air Force pays Myron—*including* all allowances—the lordly sum of $5,485 every year.

At one time or another every pilot on the Thunderbirds team has expressed to me in the strongest terms the extraordinarily high regard they hold for the maintenance crew. Dick Crane perhaps summed it up for the rest. "These are the people," he said, "who really deserve the lion's share of the credit for our show. Without the maintenance and support troops giving us everything they have—and I'll use the term *dedication*—why, we couldn't even begin to put these airplanes in the air.

"They are the Air Force's *finest,* and I'm not making any speeches now. Every one of us considers them to be the stars of our show. You know us now, Marty, and the way we feel about these men.

Diamond over Lake Mead.

"And there isn't the slightest question but that many of these same career airmen could easily multiply their annual salaries by anywhere from four to eight times. They are tremendously skilled in the most complex jet machines, and there is a crying demand for them within the manufacturing and airlines industries. The airlines especially would love to have their services, for they have skill where it counts the most—in the bankbook. They're the best men in the world for working against the plague of the airlines—meeting specific time schedules with their big jets.

"When we visit an airbase for a show they stand out there on the flight line in their white uniforms, with exactly the same status as the pilots. They are just as much an integral part of the show as the pilots. I'm pointing this out with a great deal of emphasis. They work as a beautifully co-ordinated and highly-integrated team in getting these airplanes started, prepared, and launched, in the absolute minimum of time with the maximum amount of efficiency.

"Now, these are perhaps fancy words in describing what these men do. But people have to see, just as you have, how these men operate. We have watched them year after year, doing their jobs in all kinds of weather, under every possible condition, without additional compensation, volunteering to give up much of their home life. Often they're dead tired— too tired even to eat. They're working when the rest of us are asleep. And they have chalked up a record of reliability that is fantastic.

"They've given us more than skill—they give the team their devotion as well. We think they are a tremendous bunch."

FROM BAYONETS TO SPARE PARTS

Technical Sergeant James W. Lafayette fulfills the unlikely position with the Thunderbirds of Supply Sergeant. Lest any veterans in the reading audience misconstrue the term to mean what it did many years ago, when the Supply Sergeant's responsibility consisted mainly of blankets, GI woolens, and shoes, let me hasten to explain that with the Thunderbirds this job has assumed rather larger horizons.

Jim Lafayette's job is quite simple—to supply all the necessary parts that keep the Super Sabres and transports of the team in the air. Supply Sergeant today means a highly technical job, for which Jim went to a special school. It demands skill and complexity, the ability to organize, and above all, to find things quickly. For Jim in his department keeps tabs on no less than 150,000 separate items (this figure is arrived at by actual inventory count), ranging from nuts and bolts to electronic parts, tires, subsystems, canopies, wire and cable, solenoids, ad infinitum.

Being able to improvise in times of need is an art that has not yet been relegated to electronic robots digging parts out of bins. Not only does Jim maintain his elaborate parts system in the Thunderbirds hangar, but he keeps a complete set of emergency parts (several thousand) in each C-123, and a lesser set in the C-54. Whenever something goes wrong —"and one of those birds starts to grumble a little bit, and it turns out old Jim hasn't got the part," said one sergeant, "then the fun begins. He starts things jumping; it's like tossing a hand grenade into a quiet room. But it gets results. Jim starts burning up telephone wires. He has only one goal in mind—get the part, and keep the airplanes flying."

When the team was at Langley Air Force Base in Virginia for a demonstration, the bottom sort of sagged beneath maintenance. Suddenly the mechanics needed two hydraulic pumps. The odds were greatly against the simultaneous need for two such items—but, here it was. Landing gears on two of the F-100C airplanes were malfunctioning because of hydraulic pump troubles.

Since it's impossible to keep many spares of every item, because of the size of the inventory, somewhere in the Air Force a man had punched buttons on a computer, and come up with the result that the Thunderbirds would never need more than one pump at a time for an emergency. And that's all that Jim Lafayette had on hand.

He issued his one pump to a crew chief, and then started on telephone calls. Jim has his own private little black book, but it isn't one that leads to femmes fatales. Inside of six minutes flat Jim knew where there was a spare pump; he yelled into the phone, "We'll be right over!" and dashed out of the hangar, grabbing Dick Crane's arm on the way. "Let's go, Captain!"

They climbed into a T-33, were in the air several minutes later. Dick said that "I had just enough time to get out of the airplane and stretch when Lafayette was pounding on my shoulders and asking me what the devil was I wasting time for? So we climbed back in and off we went back to Langley. The maintenance crews worked all that night, for twelve straight hours. But by show time the birds were in perfect shape, and they flew the demonstration right on the button."

I said that Jim Lafayette was an unlikely man to be a supply sergeant, and the more I think about him taking care of those seemingly limitless parts and spares in his shop, the more valid this seems to me. Jim is a husky man, standing six foot three and weighing in at a flat-stomached 200 pounds.

He simply doesn't look his age—thirty-four years old—nor is it easy to believe that Jim Lafayette has eighteen years of active military service behind him. In March of 1942, at sixteen, Jim walked out of his home in Colorado Springs and signed up with the Marine Corps. Six months later, as a ground-pounder with the 1st Marine Division, he was on his way overseas.

Getting any details out of Lafayette about his Marine Corps service is nigh unto impossible. Jim went through the campaigns of Guadalcanal, Cape Gloucester, New Britain. He found out firsthand what a full-scale jungle island invasion was like, he fought against stiff and murderous Japanese opposition that never wavered for three consecutive months. It was a time of fire-fights in the jungle, of hand-to-hand combat, of constant foot-slogging through thick undergrowth and swamps. Jim's own comments are somewhat away from the point. "It sure was a rainy hell-hole," he recalls.

Palau Island—with Jim now a corporal—was a vicious, deadly fight over coral reefs. Jim fought his way along Bloody Nose Ridge, and suffice to say (he won't say *anything* about it) that with other advance units he engaged in murderous hand-to-hand fighting. At one point of the battle he was moving up a path under a steady stream of fire, headed for a Japanese strongpoint in a cave. A jagged piece of steel from an exploding shell penetrated his skull, the world blew up, and that was all that Jim knew. He regained consciousness aboard a troop transport, his head swathed in bandages. The shrapnel hit along his temple just above the ear, digging deeply as it ripped through. An inch closer and he would have been dead.

But it was a long war, and Okinawa rolled around on the schedule, and Jim was back in the thick of the fighting. He participated in the followup fighting after the invasion, slogging his way across the northern part of the island, then down around the escarpment by Naha, the capital. He fought at Sugar Loaf Hill and Shuri Castle, and again it was the familiar scene of savage hand-to-hand fighting. Everything reached a peak when Jim was in a small patrol that rounded a turn in a path—and ran smack into a larger Japanese patrol. Lafayette ran one soldier through with his bayonet, shot another. Then the fight dissolved into a furious gun butt, bayonet, and fist-swinging struggle.

With the war over, Jim shoved his decorations into a bureau drawer, hung up his uniform, and tried to forget about it all. But there was another war in the books, and he ended up in Korea. This time it was the Chinese soldier, but everything seemed to blend into memory. There was a mass charge, a human wave that engulfed the Marine positions, and Jim was in the thick of the furious hand-to-hand fighting. He "sort of cleaned up the area" around him, and then a Chinese bayonet struck home. Jim was soon on his way back to the States with his third purple heart—a medal he would gladly never have "won."

For Jim Lafayette his cherished Marine Corps in peacetime simply failed to supply him with the means of living with his family. Jim and Lillian have three daughters, and by 1956 the couple had had enough of struggling to provide a proper home. Not only did Jim have his extensive combat experience behind him, but in every spare moment he had studied to improve his technical capabilities.

In 1956 he enlisted in the Air Force. To him, and to Lillian as well, the rewards were immediate, and they encompassed much more than the life they craved with and for their children. Jim took a short but accelerated technical course in maintenance and services, and spent his free evenings studying at home for his college degree.

"Then I saw the Thunderbirds," he said, "and as far as I was concerned they represented the very top of the heap. They were the elite, just like the first squad of a powerhouse football team. I wanted in, and bad."

When Jim filled out his application forms to join the team, he was distressed to learn that there were seven other men—everyone of them a ranking noncommissioned officer with many years service, and highly skilled—also applying for the same position with the Thunderbirds. But on April 15, 1959, he received the word for which he was so anxiously waiting—and he was "in."

Typical of Jim Lafayette, however, is the manner in which he describes his job with the team. He wraps it up in the single statement that "keeping those airplanes in the air is my job, pure and simple. But those troops of mine, they really do work. There's Ed Paul who's the manager of my spare parts kit and flyaway kits, and Morris Rasmussen who handles tech supply for me.

"Those two guys are always on tap. They're on demand day and night to meet any contingency. Whenever the crews are working, whether it's day or night, they have to be on hand to meet all parts requirements. They're quite a pair."

"And what about yourself?" I said. "You aren't down there with them, all the time? What about the fact that you make the trips, that you put in more time than anyone else?"

So help me, the big guy actually blushed.

12   It Began in 1953

By 1953, jet fighter planes had been operational in the Air Force for eight years. The first Lockheed P-80 Shooting Stars were on overseas duty in Italy in 1945, and the future of fighter operations with jets looked dazzling indeed. But there were problems created by the thin-wing, howling new machines. The jets demanded more of pilot skill than the propeller-driven fighters. Because of greater weight, higher wing loading, faster top speeds and higher stalling speeds, the jet was a machine in which the pilot had to assert his mastery all the time.

Operational fatalities began to climb. There was so little margin for error in these sleek new fighters! They flew so fast that a pilot in trouble stood barely a fifty-fifty chance for getting out of his airplane. Ejection seats were new and untried, and many fighters lacked even the primitive models. A forced landing promised all kinds of trouble; the airplanes came in fast, and the big engine behind the pilot could easily rip free and hurtle forward to crush the hapless flier in his cockpit. Not only could these things happen—they *did*.

To most Americans, therefore, the jet fighter was a machine that demanded nothing less than a three-headed genius, weightlifter, and daredevil to fly. The concept of the Air Force pilot being able to fly jets with competence, based upon experience and excellent training, withered on the public vine. The jet fighter gained stature as a beast difficult to fly, and too often fatal to new pilots. Bad enough that this feeling flourished with the public, but it also pervaded the thinking of new student pilots. And a man who is afraid of his machine simply isn't going to "hack it" as well as he could on the basis of his own skill.

How best to dispel the mixture of rumor and fear that had

blossomed into being? A meeting in the Pentagon resulted in the decision to form an official aerobatic team, a group of pilots who would, *in formation,* demonstrate to the public (and to neophyte cadets) the fact that the jets not only could do anything attributed to the older propeller fighters, but could do it faster, better, and with greater control and precision.

There is little need, this late in our book, to present the full mission and responsibility of the Thunderbirds; Chapter Two attends to that requirement. But in 1953, as the nation approached its celebration of the first half-century of flight, the problem was not quite so simple of solution.

Once the decision was made, however, the rest became an administrative problem. The immediate need was obvious —get some crack jet fighter pilots, preferably with past combat experience, and give them jet fighters that were then in widespread operational use. Keep the airplanes in basically their combat configuration. Stay away from any gimmicks or gadgetry that would simplify the maneuvering of these fighters in demonstration before the public.

Brigadier General Charles F. Born, Commander of Crew Training Air Force, was given the problem of forming up the team. Born selected Luke Air Force Base, then the site of advanced Air Force training, as the natural home of the demonstration team. He called Colonel Levi Chase to his office, and told Chase to select the men.

Chase went at his job shrewdly, for the first step he took was to yank Dick Catledge, a Training Squadron Commander at Luke, out of his job and appoint him the leader of the new team. Catledge not only could handle a fighter with fabulous skill, he was a natural leader of men—and that last requirement was, and still is, vital to the success of the team.

His qualifications were outstanding; he was an award-winning athlete, college graduate, experienced combat pilot, all-weather fighter pilot, a graduate of courses at the Air University; several times a commanding officer. He was, in brief, everything the new team would need at its helm.

Catledge selected his own men with care. For the Wingmen nothing could serve the demonstration team better than the Pattillo twins, Buck and Bill, who were not only outstanding fighter pilots, but men who had been decorated for their precision formation flying with the Skyblazers team. The Pattillos flew for three and a half years with the Sky-blazers across Europe and North Africa before an aggregate audience of ten million people. And they helped create the most famous maneuver of the new team—the thrilling Bomb Burst finale.

Into the Slot position of the diamond Catledge decided to use for the formation, went Bob Kanaga, a jet flight instructor, Korean veteran, and a pilot experienced in a variety of jets. At first the Solo position wasn't a regular of the team, and Bob McCormick joined the other pilots as a spare who would learn to fly all positions and be on tap to fill the role of any man who could not fly a mission. That practice is no longer applicable to the Thunderbirds, but it formed the basis of thinking as the team was slowly created. McCormick was perfect for the role; he'd flown Right Wing with the Sabre Dancers demonstration team, and had 100 missions scored in Korea.

The sixth pilot would back up McCormick as an alternate, and would function as a maintenance trouble shooter. "Brownie" Brown was a Korean veteran, a Master Maintenance Officer, and a pilot who was later to fly both the Solo and Wing positions. He selected a lead team of ground personnel—made up of fifteen skilled mechanics, who had the task of not only maintaining the jet fighters, but also establishing requirements that as yet were basically a big question mark.

Then there was the problem of the airplane, and by unanimous choice the Republic F-84G Thunderjet was picked. It had all the characteristics for the team—the F-84G was a rugged performer that had gained fame in Korea for its ability to absorb punishment. It was not as fast as the North American F-86 Sabre, but it had more than enough speed for a demonstration team. It featured excellent stability, and not at all last on the list of requirements was its ease of maintenance. The F-84G afforded still another advantage, since it was the primary aircraft for advanced training at Luke, and every man was well experienced in handling the bird.

Then, too, it carried across the message the Air Force

wished to stress—that the aerobatic machine people would see was a *weapon*. The Korean performance spoke well enough of the airplane, and it was also the first production fighter to go into midair refueling operations. The fact that it was also officially the first fighter to be assigned atomic weapons didn't hurt at all.

The pilots liked the idea of the straight wing. They were going to try and "squeeze it in tight," and the F-84G offered excellent stability and control for bringing the airplanes as close as possible. Another item, of course, helped. The airplane was available in number and would present no problems in terms of supply.

Final member of the new team was Bill Brock, an Academic Instructor at Luke, who was selected to fill the job of Information Services Officer and Narrator. From the outset the team required that this position be carried by an experienced pilot—and this Brock certainly was, with P-51 combat in Europe during World War II. He was also an instructor in fighter aircraft and tactics, and an experienced public speaker.

Then, what about the name? Meetings were held in the Pentagon and also at the Republic factory at Farmingdale, Long Island. The pilots came up with the title of *Thunderbirds*. Everyone seemed to like it but Ken Ellington, Republic vice-president and the man who has since the first day of the team been one of its strongest guiding spirits. There won't be much said here about Ken Ellington, because he prefers to remain in the background. But for a long time he has been a major figure in aviation, and by his own words there's no question but that he has maintained a constant vigil over the team to this day, as he will do for years to come. When special problems spring up, the boys usually put in a phone call direct to Ken, and his sage advice invariably contains the immediate solution.

The boys wanted Ken's approval of the *Thunderbirds* name. But Ken shook his head and said, "I don't like it."

One of the pilots leaned forward. "Look, Ken," he explained, "this is really a natural for us. We've studied the background to this name pretty carefully, and Thunderbirds fits the whole picture beautifully. First of all, the Thunder-

200

bird itself is one of the most famous deities in American Indian folklore. Between all the tribes that are involved, it seems to have been empowered with all the forces the Indians could imagine. But, basically, it was that of good overcoming evil, and light over darkness.

Thunderbird insignia.

"The way the legends go, the birds were enormous, and they would cause both thunder and lightning. The flapping of the wings created the thunder, and the arrows carried in its talons and bolted on down to the earth was the lightning. Now, the thing looked like a huge eagle or a hawk—and that's perfect for us! Even the colors are a natural—red, white, and blue."

Ken looked at the speaker. "It certainly sounds like you've gone into this thoroughly."

"Then you agree with us? You like the name—the *Thunderbirds?*"

"Nope. I still don't like it."

But today, Ken says, "If ever I was wrong about something, the name of this team is it. I was the only one who didn't like the name—and the only one who was wrong."

The airplanes were painted and assigned to the team, and pilots began an extensive training and practice program to work out their routine. It was apparent quickly that the Solo position was needed, for reasons explained earlier in the book—he filled in those moments between formation maneuvers. On June 1, 1953, the Thunderbirds flew an "off the

201

record" demonstration at Nellis, and worked themselves into shape for their first official exhibition on June 16th, 1953, at Williams Air Force Base, Arizona. This was the date when the late General Hoyt Vandenberg, Air Force Chief of Staff, performed his last but immensely satisfying official duty—participating in the ceremonies that marked the graduation of his son as a jet fighter pilot.

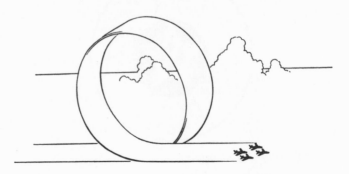

Loop.

Still working the bugs out of their operation in the air and on the ground, the new team launched itself on a whirlwind tour of airbases that resembled the frenzied scurrying of a vaudeville or circus troupe from town to town. For twenty-one consecutive days the men worked fourteen hours a day or more.

Ninety days after the first show, the record book showed its first bulge—thirty-four official demonstrations. They kept flying, and in September, at the National Aircraft Show in Cleveland, the team performed before daily audiences of more than 300,000 people. The Thunderbirds were now veterans.

Immediately after the Cleveland shows, the team began its first changing of personnel. Bob Kanaga ended his tour of service, and the Slot was filled by McCormick. Brownie Brown forgot what free time was, as he alternated between his two positions of Solo Pilot and Engineering Officer.

For the rest of the year the team flew its demonstrations on a steady, clocklike basis. In January of 1954, the Air

Force decided to see how the Thunderbirds would do with seven-league boots, and scheduled the team to join a special task force that would take in most of South America on a goodwill tour. The pilots and ground crew members were unceremoniously jabbed with medical and booster shots, and took off from MacDill Air Force Base in Florida for Mexico City, the first scheduled stop on a tour that would extend for 18,000 miles. It was quite an excursion—five F-84G and two F-80 fighters, three two-seat T-33's, and two giant C-124 Globemaster transports. All together there were 105 people along.

Because Bill Brock was fluent in Spanish, he received the additional chore of Operations Officer; on January 18th he filled his job as narrator by addressing a crowd of more than 300,000 people who jammed Mexico City Airport. This was a tremendous audience, but the hills that surrounded the area were black with onlookers—estimated by Mexican police to exceed 1,200,000 viewers!

Then on to Managua, Nicaragua; in a town of 65,000 people no less than 50,000 crowded the airport to view the team. The pilots flew their precision aerobatics next at Panama, then on to Lima, Peru. At Santiago the audience numbered 75,000 people, and there was a bit of a flurry when the city fathers introduced to the Pattillo twins two beautiful dancing girls—identical twins, of course.

At Pistarini Airport in Buenos Aires the crowd swelled to reach a half-million spectators. A quarter of a million showed up at Montevideo, Uruguay. Then on to Rio de Janeiro, Brazil, for a show at Guailano Airport one day, and over the Copacabana the next—before an audience officially stated by local authorities at one and a half million people! The pilots performed at Maracay, and Caracas, Venzuela; in the Dominican Republic; and finally over the harbor of Havana, Cuba, before 450,000 people.

And so began the years of an amazing flying record that continued to stretch out "on time and no failure" performances that to this day remains unbroken. Pilots filled their two-year tours, departed for new assignments. New men were carefully screened, accepted into the ranks, and put through their paces. Dick Catledge turned over the leader's chair in late 1954 to Jack Broughton, who started flying with the Thunderbirds on October 10th, and led his first airshow on the 16th.

By the first months of 1955 traditions had been created, and some of them stand to this day. But the Thunderbirds is an outfit that must change; their policy is intrinsically that of the Air Force itself. After 130 airshows and over 300,000 miles flown, with air demonstrations before some ten million spectators in North, Central, and South America, the team decided it was time for a change.

Since they presented the best foot forward for the Air Force, this meant a requirement for flying the shows in a late model operational aircraft—and the faithful old F-84G was slipping in performance against its new replacements. Team officials talked to the Pentagon, test-flew a variety of fighters, then went into a huddle with Ken Ellington and his engineers. Soon after the orders were given—the team would change from the straightwing F-84G to the more powerful, faster, sweptwing F-84F Thunderstreak.

The new fighter presented problems. Heavier than its predecessor, the sweptwings of the F-84F complicated tight formation precision aerobatics; the closer an airplane flies to the speed of sound the more severe are compressibility and stability problems. But these were matters to be taken in normal stride, and they were. If anything, the show performance seemed a little crisper, a bit faster and co-ordinated just a bit finer.

INTO THE CENTURY-SERIES FIGHTER

In June of 1956 it was time for another change, and the Thunderbirds retired their F-84F fighters for their entry into the supersonic realm—taking delivery of the big, powerful North American F-100C Super Sabres. The F-84F was powerful, fast, and heavy—the F-100C, as we have learned, was all of these things, only "a hell of a lot more," as the pilots put it.

By October of 1957 the Air Force wanted a repeat of the tour of South America. In ten days flat Major J. A. Robinson, who had taken over the helm from Jack Broughton,

204

was ready to leap off on *Operation Longlegs,* the USAF participation in the 12th Annual Aviation Week celebration in Buenos Aires, Argentina. The flight of the F-100C fighters would mark the first appearance of truly supersonic aircraft in South America, and tremendous crowds were expected.

Captain Bill Scott was then Narrator (unique in that position because of a beautiful, bristling, waxed mustache which, at last report, is being flourished with great success in France). "The moment we got the call from the Pentagon," Scotty told me, "we started the ball rolling by checking out information on the fields we would use. We had a standing requirement that the F-100C aircraft must have a 7,000-foot runway as a minimum, but one field had only 6,800. The boys said it wouldn't be a problem, and Washington gave us the go-ahead on that.

"The whole thing had plenty of headaches for us. The Pentagon wanted estimates on every last possible phase of the trip. Maintenance would be rough, but we could handle it. Supply, however, gave us nightmares. We even had to draw our own maps. Now that may seem to be a small thing—but first we had to locate them, and any time you've got to have something in a real hurry it always disappears and can't be found for a month.

"We drew up a couple of flight routes, but finally decided that the best way to stage down would be along the east coast, into Ramey in Puerto Rico, and then on down to the continent. Fuel problems drove us nuts, because all the legs from Ramey on south exceeded a thousand nautical miles, and we didn't have alternate fields, or those that were available were too short. So the mechanics loaded two 275-gallon external tanks on each bird.

"Then we found out that the JP-4 fuel we needed was in real scarce supply after we left Ramey. At that time no one on the team had ever done any air-to-air refueling, and it was too late to learn now. We would have to have fuel sent down by tankers, and have it waiting for us at our stops.

"We did some juggling with figures, and the results weren't good. It looked as though the Air Force would have to involve up to eighty tanker airplanes to give us the fuel for the whole trip and the shows at our destinations. They couldn't do it—

not without hurting standby combat capability. Someone came up with the idea of using aviation gas for the J-57 jet engine —and you should have heard the free-for-all *that* set off among the pilots, the engine manufacturers, the Air Force and the tech reps from North American.

"It simply had never been done, but the requirement proved to the Air Force that both the J-57 engine and the F-100C were a bit more versatile than anyone had believed. We used high-octane gas that was mixed with two per cent, by volume, of grade 1100 engine oil. It cut down our range just a bit, but it worked real fine otherwise. We used the JP-4 for the actual shows, and although the fueling crews went slightly nuts, we met all our requirements. All in all, we had some pretty knotty things to work out. Just say that the boys were really on their toes."

This is a great understatement on Scotty's part. Three days before the team left, they were notified that they would have to fly an F-100F, a two-seater, with the team (Scotty's job) in order to provide supersonic flights for government and Air Force dignitaries of South American nations. Warrant Officer Floyd Pulley, then engineering officer, had just torn out all his hair meeting all spare parts requirements for the F-100C's, and the F model, which has many parts and systems foreign to the C, nearly drove him to distraction.

Then the team learned that there wasn't one single piece of UHF radio equipment in all of South America. The pilots whipped this little problem by using the support aircraft (two C-119's and two C-124's) as en route checkpoints, and sending one plane ahead to each field to act as a field tower for landing and takeoff. Weather reporting facilities in South America simply failed to meet the requirements of the supersonic fighters, and the Thunderbirds took along with them two meteorological officers who begged information from everyone—including Pan American Airways.

"When we landed at Zanderij," Robby recalls, "it was like a scene out of a movie. The runway was constructed from bauxite—our first landing on an 'aluminum strip.' But that was all that was good about it. The operations shack was, so help me, nothing more than a thatched hut, and natives wandered around right across the runway, never looking where they were going, and carrying giant bundles on their heads.

"We had almost no ramp space for parking the birds, and then the ground crews had to refuel us from an underground storage tank. But the tank filled only about two planes. So they filled the tank, added the oil that was necessary for the mixture, and then started to fuel two fighters. Then they had to refill the storage tank, pour in the oil, recirculate the whole thing to be sure of a proper mixture, and start all over again. The crews worked all afternoon and all through the night without a break. They really put out for us on the whole trip, snatching a few hours sleep in the airplanes between stops."

The pilots didn't at all appreciate the long-distance hops. They flew not only over long stretches of water, but also over thick, impenetrable jungle filled with snakes, alligators, and a teeming variety of jungle life that seemed to exist only to tear to pieces any hapless pilot who might parachute into its midst.

Several of the runways used by the F-100C airplanes had the pilots almost wringing their hands. They encountered loose rock and gravel. At one field they found half the runway, plus one side of the entire runway, under construction and covered completely with sand and gravel. Small rocks and sand showered the planes, even with extra spacing. At Galeao the runway was 6,000 feet of concrete and 1,800 feet of asphalt, but that's only the conditions at first glance. The entire field was "rough, and in many places the concrete was sinking," Scotty said. "The runway was on an island, and both ends of it dropped into water. And wouldn't you know it—at both ends of the runway someone had shoved high poles into the ground. It was tight getting in and out of *that* place."

At Buenos Aires the team performed before a packed throng of more than a million spectators. Scotty "stole the show" and became the hero of Argentina when he flew the President of the country, Pedro E. Aramburu, through the sonic wall—making him the world's first head of state to fly faster than sound. On the trip many dignitaries received their first supersonic flights, and Scotty grabbed some more headline space when he flew the President of Brazil, Juscelino Kubitschek, and then his Minister of Air, Francisco Assis Correa de Mello, at supersonic speeds.

The record book bulged more and more—in four shows the team performed before more than three million people.

REMINISCING

The official history of the Thunderbirds doesn't carry everything that happened to the team in its years of demonstration flying, but the boys managed to bring to light a few of the more memorable moments as they racked up air miles and hours. One of the problems that plague the Thunderbirds are other birds—all kinds and sizes of birds. They insist, it appears, that they were in the air first and fooey on the Thunderbirds, who are latecomers. Most of the boys have had their share of running into the feathered flock, and finally they came to disregard their aerial opponents. Until they ran into a swarm of giant condors in the Panama Canal Zone, and then everybody kept a sharp eye out.

A B-57 jet bomber ran into one of the monsters which, fortunately, hit his external fuel tank instead of the cockpit windscreen. At that, it caved the tank halfway in and threw the airplane out of control. The Thunderbirds pilots took an awed look at the smashed metal tank, and vowed from that moment on to give the condors the right of way.

Problems arise from the most unexpected places. In the fall of 1958, Robby took the team to Guatemala and the boys flew some very successful shows. But the ground crews greeted them with haggard eyes and weary expressions. "Those poor guys," Robby said. "It was their first chance to sleep a full night in a bed that they'd had for weeks. And you know what? That night they had a beaut of an earthquake, and everybody was sent flying!"

Homer Whitlow has gone into the Thunderbirds roster with no small wonder and affection at his flying abilities. "Homer could fly a show lefthanded," Robby explained, "and take home movies at the same time and never move so much as an inch out of position. He was incredible, and I think he was the most natural pilot the Thunderbirds ever had. You

208

ask Fitz about him. He helped break Fitz in to the routine. Homer never flew an airplane; he just put it on like his flight jacket and went off into the blue."

Robby gave me the word on Bill Pogue; he set fire to a cigar and dug into his memory book. "Marty, did I ever tell you about Bill Pogue and his expensive convertible? Well, we were out practicing near Nellis one fine sunny day, and just as we broke out of a Bomb Burst we hear someone call

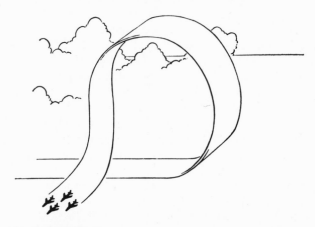

Cloverleaf Turn.

as if from the center of a wind tunnel, saying that he had lost his canopy. It was Pogue, and we all latched on to him and escorted him back to the base. And you should have heard those guys pouring it on old Bill; they razzed him silly about his expensive convertible, that he'd never again have a chance to ride in a million-dollar convertible with the top down. But he brought her home just as pretty as you please."

There's another story I managed to dig up on Bill Pogue. This was a show in South America, with hundreds of thousands of people waiting while the weather steadily deteriorated. A cloud deck moved in, but it was patchy and the conditions looked good enough for the demonstration, even though it might mean breaking up through the clouds and then coming on down again. The weather improved and the entire show went without incident—until the Bomb Burst.

The diamond bored on up through a great big hole in the clouds, and the four planes broke away in perfect view of the spectators. Three of them remained in view, but then as Bill Pogue came around and down on his recovery the airplane disappeared into the soup.

Pogue let the airplanes get away from him for a moment, and the next thing he knew he was in a whirling spin. The Super Sabre spun out of the clouds, but Pogue calmly brought her out of the spin, never moving out of his track, *and made the precision crossover exactly on time!* None of the other pilots knew what had happened until Bill told them about it later. As far as he was concerned, it was all in a day's work.

Major Jack Broughton recalls his "hairiest of all moments" when Captain Ed Palmgren, then in the Slot, proved he had full rights to his nickname of Lucky. The team was practicing over open country for a demonstration to be flown near Montgomery, Alabama, when Palmgren flamed out.

As I've explained before, the F-100C has hydraulic-boosted controls, and for every pound of pressure that the pilot exerts on the stick, those controls add another thirty-four pounds to the control surfaces. But you need power for this, and that comes from the jet engine. When Palmgren flamed out, he lost that hydraulic boost. There's a standby engine power system, but this proved useless because the jet engine had "frozen."

That's why the Super Sabre has still a third emergency control system. Palmgren yanked at a control, activating a small ram-air turbine. A small door moved, and a scoop inside the the air intake diverted the inrushing air against the turbine, allowing limited control action.

Under these conditions the recommended procedure is for the pilot to set up his aircraft for ejection, and then get out —fast. But Palmgren refused to do this. Even though he was over open countryside, he felt that there was *some* chance, however remote, that the ship might hit one of the scattered homes in the area.

So Palmgren calmly notified the nearest tower of his difficulty, and added that "I'm going to ride her down." In a heavy jet fighter this is an extraordinarily difficult feat to accomplish safely. Behind the pilot lies that massive jet engine, and the sudden, sharp decelerations of bellying in the airplane over open country means that sheer inertia can rip that mass loose and hurl it forward like a boulder into the pilot. And Palmgren couldn't dump his gear and deadstick it to a runway.

He had two choices—eject and assure his own safety, or ride the bird down and, although endangering his own life, assure the safety of the public. To Palmgren there was only *one* choice—and he stayed with the fighter.

He dropped into a glide and headed for an open area southwest of Maxwell Air Force Base. Three miles from the base, the fifteen-ton aircraft settled down to the ground. Palmgren held up the nose, hanging on the edge of a stall as he tried to reduce his airspeed to the lowest possible speed before contacting the ground.

At 170 miles per hour Palmgren aimed for a small cornfield, rocketing in right over the ground. The big fighter streaked in just above a set of telephone wires, ducked beneath another power line, and slammed into the ground. A terrific roar burst from the airplane as it scraped over the earth, hurling dirt upward as it slewed from side to side.

At a hundred miles per hour Palmgren ran out of cornfield. The airplane crashed over a railroad track, bounced wildly against a road embankment that tore out the gear. It shot across the road, bashed through a fence and left part of the tail behind, rammed into and tore down two telephone poles (leaving part of one wing behind), careened into another field, and then skidded another 200 yards in a cloud of dirt, dust and flying bushes before grinding to a halt.

Lucky Palmgren climbed out, grinned at the people dashing to the scene. The next day he flew a complete show.

THE BIG YEAR

In 1958 the Secretary of the Air Force presented to the Thunderbirds the *Air Force Outstanding Unit Award* for "exceptionally meritorious service of great national significance." This is the highest peacetime award that can be given to a unit of the Air Force for outstanding service and achievement.

Looking back on 1959, however, it might seem that the Award was just a bit premature. For whatever the Thunderbirds had accomplished before that year, it paled against the more recent achievements that exerted the greatest demands on the team in its seven-year history. More shows were requested and flown than ever before as a direct result of congressional, diplomatic and international interest.

The Thunderbirds were acclaimed everywhere they appeared as the "American Ambassadors in Blue." It was an accolade that was earned the hard way.

Stepped down . . .

It's doubtful that the team will ever easily exceed their 1959 performance. In 1958 the Thunderbirds flew a total of seventy-seven air shows, of which thirteen were held at Nellis—and that means no travel. In 1959, however, they flew ninety-four shows, and ninety of these were on the road.

International travel increased as well, for the number of shows flown outside the United States jumped from seven to thirty-eight. More spectacular was the total number of spectators that watched the team perform—from 2,566,000 in 1958 to a new annual total the following year of 10,061,000! And that brought the total at the close of 1959 to some 31,000,000 people who have watched this amazing team in the air.

Now, these are statistics, but I know of no better means of emphasizing the tremendous team performance. In 1958 the pilots flew a total of 125,000 air miles to travel to and from their demonstration sites; the following year this jumped to 173,500 miles. The crews groaned when they had to spend 272 days away from Nellis in 1958, but in 1959 they were on the road a total of 302 days.

Dick Crane's shop sagged under its accelerated work load. Fifteen thousand brochures were requested by the press, and 18,000 photographs went to magazines and newspapers around the world. Twelve thousand airshow posters in a half-dozen languages were tacked up around as many countries, and the men as a team made 752 public appearances on radio, television, at press conferences, and so forth (compared to 231 in 1958).

There were some memorable "firsts" that went into the record book. More people watched the team than in any other year, the pilots flew the greatest yearly number of shows, flew more air miles than ever before, spent more time away from Nellis than ever before—and scored their single largest audience to ever watch an air show—*any* airshow. On July 5, 1959, at Chicago two million people craned their heads back to watch the Super Sabres flashing in the sun.

The year 1959 saw the first appearance of the Thunderbirds in the Far East, and it was also the first time the team utilized air-to-air refueling to expedite their mobility and range.

It was also the first time that the team ever flew its demonstrations with a top cover of fighter planes armed with "hot guns." During all shows on Formosa (Taiwan), fighters of the Chinese Air Force flew top cover against the possibility of an attack by Communist MiG fighter attacks from the mainland.

The demonstrations flown in Korea provided yet another intrusion into the intricate and demanding task of precision, formation jet aerobatics. Communist radio stations jammed the UHF radio frequencies used by the Thunderbirds in an attempt to prevent interplane communications.

The demonstrations were flown as scheduled.

Fitz and Chuck Maultsby set a new record of shows flown by any team pilot in one year—they both flew a total of eighty-seven demonstrations, and this does not include the practice shows that bring the total to several hundred.

The team itself set a new record of shows flown in one thirty-day period. Between November 11th and December 11th, the pilots flew twenty-nine official air demonstrations before millions of people—and that doesn't count the sixty-two practice shows flown in the same period.

Team enters vertical 360° Turn.

The tour of the Far East brought to a total of twenty-three the number of countries that have been visited by the Thunderbirds. In November and December, for a total of fifty-five days, the Super Sabres of the team covered more than 25,000 miles, and flew thirty-one shows in forty days throughout Okinawa, the Philippines, Taiwan, Korea, Japan, and Hawaii before a total audience that reached to 4,624,000 people.

During the tour, the Thunderbirds demonstrated dramatically the rapid and long-range deployment capability of the Air Force. With show sites often located great distances from

214

each other in the Far East, and time factors being so critical, air-to-air refueling was necessary to meet the schedules laid down by the Pentagon. In one instance, the team flew a scheduled performance and, without landing, departed for their next show site which was more than 1,200 miles distant. This is a feat unparalleled by any precision team anywhere in the world.

The seven pilots refueled from two tankers in just seven minutes while en route, and arrived 1,200 miles away within *five seconds of their scheduled time to give another demonstration—before landing!* "The impact of this demonstrated capability," states an official report to Washington, "repeatedly awed millions of people in the Far East."

The statistics are dazzling, and they demonstrate also the constant on-time and in-the-air reliability of the Thunderbirds. In the Far East tour the pilots flew a total number of 400 sorties; accumulated 500 hours on the F-100D fighters; made 250 air-to-air refueling hookups during ten missions— and twice had to completely secure the entire unit because of full-scale typhoons.

It is impossible to put down on paper all the accomplishments, for there are certain results which cannot be measured in statistics. The millions of people who watched the Thunderbirds gained a deep-rooted new appreciation of what our Air Force means in terms of performance, dependability, skill and precision. This cannot be stated in terms of numbers, for good will defies such impression.

But the Thunderbirds files are crammed with letters that leave every pilot—and the rest of the team—with the feeling that they have performed in a manner that brought to their country respect and admiration—and that is, really, the kind of success that leaves a man feeling awfully good.

Brigadier General E. S. Chickering, Commander of the Pacific Air Forces Base Command, wrote to General Frank F. Everest, Commander of the Tactical Air Command that: ". . . I have seen the Thunderbirds perform on thirteen occasions, mostly under near perfect and fair weather conditions in the States. However, despite the fact that they were working in and out of extreme turbulence, coming off the near-by mountain range, and had flown twenty-nine performances during the preceding thirty-five days, their Hickam, Hawaii, performances were, without doubt, superlative.

"The team . . . has made the word Thunderbirds synonymous with perfection here in Hawaii."

Millions of spectators . . . open house.

The Commander of Pacific Air Forces, General Emmett O'Donnell, Jr., wrote to General Everest: "Dear Hank: I want to take this opportunity to express my admiration for the manner in which your Thunderbirds executed their mission throughout the Pacific area during recent weeks.

"I personally saw them at Okinawa and Hawaii. In each instance, their performance was outstandingly fine. It really was gratifying to see the remarkable impression that the team made upon the people of the countries they visited. They left in their wake a tremendous amount of admiration for themselves and good will toward this country. . . .

"Would you pass to Major Fitzgerald and those who accompanied him my congratulations and appreciation. While the team's total contribution to the President's People-to-People Program can never be accurately measured, be assured that their performance while on this tour, both in the air and on the ground, will stand as a monument to their own skill and to the mission on which they were sent to perform."

13 The Price

Captain Charles "Fish" Salmon was—as one of the Thunderbirds' wives put it—"a terrific-looking guy who made women stop and turn around." The pilots only thought of Fish behind the stick, but that was thinking enough. For Fish Salmon was one of those men who are called great pilots. He started with the Thunderbirds in January of 1958, worked as the Solo Pilot through most of October, and when Sam Johnson completed his tour, began to fly the Slot.

"It's too bad you never met Fish," Dick Crane said. "People instinctively liked the guy. He looked like a Hollywood version of a fighter pilot—handsome, winning smile, that sort of thing. He was six foot one and weighed about 210 pounds —a big, happy guy who had a tremendous sense of humor. As a solo pilot, he was almost the twin brother of Griff—he had flair, timing, and the execution of his maneuvers were cut with a razor they were so precise."

I learned that Fish didn't exactly take kindly to being stifled, and he had his own way of pressing home a point. During a show at Eglin Air Force Base—"home territory" without flying restrictions—Fish wanted to open the show with a supersonic pass. He'd been held back on this so long he was aching to come before the crowd on the deck with the bird wide open and howling.

To his astonishment the local brass poured cold water on the idea. "There are too many sonic booms going on here all the time," one officer snapped. "It's about time we started to put a halt to this nonsense."

Now this is a strange statement. Eglin is a proving ground, and there is a constant war under way here. Observers to the Aerial Firepower Demonstrations at Eglin have seen more shooting going on than a good many veterans of actual combat. The din at times becomes deafening, with supersonic strikes, cannon, machine guns, napalm, high explosives, and simulated atomic blasts being the order of the day.

Fish didn't say a word, but he set his jaw in a way that foretold that he just might alter his opening pass slightly. As

217

he explained to the team before the show, it "was a good time to teach a few people a lesson or two."

At Eglin, the proving ground personnel mark a large, clear white line with chalk dust along the ground. This moves from the rear right of the long reviewing stands, so that an airplane approaches from this position, passes directly in front of the crowd, but goes away to its front left. With so many planes coming in with all their armament blasting away, the chalk line is a vital reference point that erases all positioning doubts for the pilot. The brass pointed out the line to Fish, told him to scrub the supersonic pass, and to fly over that line with the "afterburner opening."

Fish took his fighter down to barely three feet off the deck. Just under sonic speed, he rocketed without warning (except to air traffic control) from the left rear of the crowd, afterburner blasting on and off in a series of crashing explosions. Fish was so low as he beat up the deck that every time he slammed the throttle into AB a streamer of fire lashed the ground, sending the chalk flying in all directions in clouds of white dust.

The thousands of people in the reviewing stands watched breathlessly as Fish shot across their view. Usually the solo man makes his pass to the end of the field or a designated line, then hauls up and around in a swooping, steep, climbing left turn. But Fish reached his line for the pullup, and just kept right on going.

He dragged the Super Sabre away from the reviewing stands, still at his three feet of height, and disappeared into the fields beyond, the afterburner still blasting—BOOM, then silence; then, another BOOM, and silence, and again and again.

The crowd jumped to its feet. Six thousand people stared in amazement (except Crane, who was almost fit to be tied at the reaction of the audience), and every one of them, including pilots, was convinced that Fish was going to prang that bird right into a wall of trees.

But at the last possible second (it seemed that way; Fish had plenty of room), the fighter lifted her nose and screamed skyward in a tremendous, soaring left chandelle. It looked death-defying and all that, but it wasn't; rather, it was a combination of superb flying, precise timing, and all the effects of optical illusion because of the increasing distance.

The timing was the most important thing, because as 6,000 people kept their eyes glued to the hurtling solo airplane, Robby led the diamond over their heads directly from the back of the crowd. And just as they crossed over all four pilots lit the afterburners.

I was in the stands that day, and it was the most marvelous sight of a crowd I've ever seen. The four afterburners went off like a salvo of giant bombs directly over the reviewing stand, and that audience (half of them military pilots!) just collapsed back into their seats. The Thunderbirds call that episode the day of the famous One-Two.

On March 12th, 1959, the team was practicing in its private amphitheater of Thunderbird Lake. They had flown the entire demonstration, and then came down on the deck, using an old dirt road for a reference line, to practice precision pitchouts for landing. Fitz was the new leader, and had recently taken over the reins from Robby.

It was a good practice session, and the boys came in for the pitchout in a solid diamond formation. Halfway down the "runway," at a height of one hundred feet, Fitz pitched out and up cleanly to the left, swinging into the steep vertical bank that brings him into his tight 180-degree turn.

Exactly one second behind the leader, Gayle Williams (then flying Left Wing) snapped his wings over and followed. And hard on his tail from Right Wing position was Chuck Maultsby. Flying in trail, coming out of the Slot, was Fish Salmon.

It's difficult to fit everything into its exact place because of the speed, timing, and g-forces involved, but it seemed almost certain that Fish came out of the diamond a little too fast and just a bit hard. Chuck, watching the airplanes in front of him, couldn't see Fish as he rolled into his pitchout; Fish, in turn, positioned himself on Chuck.

Both fighters were in their vertical banks, pulling those punishing g's, when suddenly Fish saw that he was overrunning Maultsby—and in another second would collide with his airplane. The instant that Fish noticed his excessive closing speed, he reacted. He tried desperately to dump full stick and to kick hard rudder. This was a top rudder movement, tramping down on the right rudder in the left bank, which would move him off and away from Chuck's fighter.

But despite his instant reactions, the minute error of judgment was compounded by speed and the one-second pitchout interval into an inevitable collision. Actually, Fish moved so quickly the other pilots later said it was an almost impossible pilot reaction, it was so fast. And the attempted corrective action saved Fish from entangling both airplanes in a mass of wreckage that would have killed both Salmon and Maultsby.

The margin of a complete miss, or a collision, narrowed down to just about a tenth of a second. But Fish didn't have that fraction of time, and he couldn't skid his airplane clear. Despite his frantic efforts, momentum carried him almost in front of Chuck's airplane.

The F-100 just missed slamming broadside into the other fighter; instead, it struck a glancing blow. The vertical stabilizer of the Slot fighter hit Maultsby's Super Sabre at the long pitot boom and the nose scoop. The impact ripped away the pitot boom, leaving Chuck with no airspeed reading, and also damaging the underside of the nose scoop.

Chuck felt a sudden, sharp vibration—pieces of metal and parts of the boom ripped back through the intake into the engine. Almost in the same instant, the force of the impact hurled Chuck's fighter out of control into a half-cartwheel.

As the big airplane whirled on its wing, Chuck heard clearly in his earphones the distressed voice of Fish: *"I've hit Chuck!"* He seemed absolutely disgusted with himself for committing an error that he felt was unforgivable; and relief was obvious a moment later when Chuck snapped his airplane back into level flight.

The collision sheared the top eighteen inches of the vertical stabilizer from Fish's airplane. Both planes were back in level flight immediately, and Fish wisely pulled back on the stick and went into a fast climb.

220

The other pilots reacted like a well-oiled machine moving through a dress rehearsal. Gayle Williams skidded in to take up a wingman's position on Chuck so that he could visually check the damage. Homer Whitlow, flying that day as an observer for a final checkout of Maultsby for the Right Wing position, immediately lit his afterburner and rocketed after Salmon's climbing airplane. Hot on his tail was Fitz, who had racked his airplane around in a wicked turn to reach his Slot man.

Williams radioed that he had Chuck under control, that the airplane was flyable, and in no immediate danger. The F-100C was under full control, and Williams stayed glued to Chuck's wings, calling out the airspeeds. They headed back to Nellis, flying a wide pattern in formation, and landing as though they were tied together.

Fish, of course, wanted altitude. At 30,000 feet he leveled off and set his course for Nellis. The closer he got to home, the better. He didn't know the full extent of the damage to his airplane, and although it responded well enough to the controls, it vibrated badly through the rear section. Altitude was insurance—to get back to Nellis, and if necessary to eject from a safe height.

Fitz checked out Salmon's airplane from every possible angle. Despite the vibration, she continued to fly, and Fish reported normal control response was being maintained. All engine instruments operated normally, he had no power loss. Except for that vibration, he seemed to be in good shape.

"Thunderbird Leader from Four," Fish called, "I think I can bring this bear in. She seems all right. I'll lower the gear and drop her back to approach speed to check the reaction. . . ." By following this procedure at 30,000 feet, Fish assured himself plenty of room to recover from any unusal response of the airplane to his lowered airspeed.

Whitlow and Fitz dropped back and to each side to fly a loose trail, watching every move that Fish made. Nellis was in sight, about twenty miles to the southeast of the airplanes, right over the last ridges, when Fish eased back the power and lowered the gear. He was going to fly the full approach procedure at altitude with the throttle back and the gear down; if the fighter responded well, there would be no problem in saving the airplane. Fish called out every move he made in the cockpit.

The other pilots reduced power with him, decelerating to the same speed. At 225 knots, Fish lowered the gear.

Just as the right wheel was halfway out of the well, and the left gear was a third out of the well and coming down, the airplane reacted to the sudden change in pressure and airflow. Coupled with the loss of the upper vertical stabilizer, the fighter got away from Salmon; the loss of the top of the vertical stabilizer proved too much to maintain contol.

Instantly the F-100C pitched up to the right, whipped over on her back, and then whirled into a spin. . . .

At once Fish snapped up the gear and started his spin recovery. Fitz and Whitlow were in a wide spiral about the spinning airplane, hauling it in close to watch everything that was happening. By the time he had dropped to 23,000 feet, Fish appeared to be in control again, and seemed to be just about out of the spin.

But suddenly the nose pitched up violently again, and she clawed over and into another spin. Fish fought her out of it the second time, but again she broke away and entered a third spin. In seconds the fighter fell below 20,000 feet.

Whitlow called anxiously, "How is she flying, Fish? Can you get her out of the spin? Can you recover? *Keep your eyes on your altitude!* If you can't bring her out of that spin, give yourself plenty of time to bail out."

Fish called his leader. "I'd like to stay with this bear for a couple of more recoveries, Boss. I can get her out of this spin. . . ."

Twice more Fish brought her out, and twice more there came the violent pitchup, and the whip into the spin. When the three airplanes passed through 15,000 feet, Fitz decided that this was more than enough.

"Get ready to get out of that thing, Fish—"

Homer repeated the message, more and more concerned with the vanishing height.

The big Super Sabre whirled sickeningly through four more turns.

"Fish, let it go!" Fitz ordered. "Get out of there—bail out, *NOW!*"

Fish didn't waste any time. Immediately after the leader's call, the canopy blew off the airplane. It was followed at once by Fish in the seat. In the next moment the pilot disappeared from Fitzgerald's sight, behind his airplane. But Homer Whitlow was right there as Fish fell out of sight from the Leader.

What no one knew was that Fish didn't have a chance to switch his parachute mechanism from the zero lanyard position for low-altitude flight to the one-second setting for greater heights. Immediately after the collision he had climbed to altitude; in his preoccupation with checking out the airplane the detail escaped him. In the spin, it was impossible to change the setting, for centrifugal force from his rapid rotation prevented the movement.

Homer saw the parachute stream out. But it did not open fully. He watched Fish in the partially-opened chute fall out of sight. Homer never saw Fish separate from his seat; he kept watching, but nothing happened.

"We're not sure of what happened, not exactly," Chuck Maultsby explained. "But because of the chute opening instantly, and the effects of the spin—well, whatever it was, for some unknown reason the heavy seat drifted up and tore right through the canopy. The chute never opened fully, although it did slow Fish's descent. . . ."

Fish Salmon, unfortunately, had run out of luck. Actually, everyone at this time was convinced that Fish had made a successful ejection. Even as he was blown free of the spinning fighter, Fitz ordered a helicopter dispatched on emergency call from Nellis. His parachute streaming behind him, Fish fell for three miles.

"At the base we heard only that Fish had bailed out," Dick Crane said, "and that a chopper was on its way to pick him up and bring him back. We didn't know at the time that Captain Ted Baer, the flight surgeon assigned to the team, was the doctor on crash duty that day, and was in the chopper flying to the scene.

"Fitz and Homer were circling the area where the plane

crashed, and they were trying to locate Fish by his white parachute. While they looked for their pilot, Baer was coming in. The doc didn't know the details, didn't know who was down. Only that the bird was from Nellis.

"Fitz and Homer were running low on fuel. The moment they saw the chopper moving in, they had to run for Nellis to land."

The helicopter crew searched the area around the crash scene. Then, several miles away, across the desert floor, the pilot saw a parachute. It was at the base of a 3,000-foot cliff. The fighter pilot, they saw, had landed at the bottom of a small range of hills.

The helicopter dropped to the ground at the bottom of the hill, and Ted Baer and the crew started to rush up the steep incline. Baer is not a big man, but he scrambled up that rocky, sharp slope in fifteen minutes (it later took the experienced search-and-rescue parties thirty-five minutes to cover the same ground).

Baer ran as fast as he could toward the body that he saw crumpled on the ground. He still didn't know who the man was.

But as he clambered breathlessly over the last boulder, he saw the Thunderbird helmet. . . . The doctor stopped as though he had been struck a physical blow. The shock was terrific; it was the first moment when Baer knew that the crumpled form on the ground was one of *his* men.

A doctor in a business where a crash can, and usually does, mean a flaming holocaust, becomes hardened to his job. At least they're supposed to be hardened. But Ted Baer admitted later that it took almost all his will power to force himself forward, then, to bend down, and turn the body over to see who it was.

He knew, from the moment he saw the body, that it couldn't be Fitzgerald, or Maultsby, or Crane. It was a big man. The realization that it had to be Fish Salmon, or Gayle Williams, or Homer Whitlow, flashed through his mind.

Then he discovered, with mounting shock and horror, that the body in his arms was that of one of his closest friends. Without thinking, he immediately checked for pulse and heartbeat. He stood up slowly. Fish was beyond all earthly help.

Ted Baer stumbled to the nearest rock, and sat down, his senses numbed. He fought to keep the tears from coming out of his eyes. He was still there, numbed by grief, when the rest of the party found them. It took the rescue crew an hour to return the body to the helicopter.

They flew back to Nellis Air Force Base with the only pilot who has ever been lost to the Thunderbirds.

14 Rendezvous at Angels Thirty

The Thunderbirds' tour through the Far East had been a smashing success, and with the cheers and applause of millions of people still ringing in their ears, the pilots prepared for the long flights home in their fighters. Seven pilots would fly the F-100D-15-NAA combat airplanes from Japan across the vast Pacific to the United States. Fitz was leading, and with the team on the extended trips through the Asian countries were Neil Eddins, Chuck Maultsby, Bob Janca, Herman Griffin, Dick Crane, and Gayle Williams.

No one was sorry to come to the end of the road for the Far East tour. The pilots were bushed. They had just flown twenty-nine shows in thirty-one days as well as the practice missions and the flights from one airbase to others many miles distant. There had been refueling practice, flybys, photography missions, and many, many personal appearances. The men were tired, and even the airplanes seemed weary. And there were yet two more complete demonstrations to fly on the way home, during the stopover in the Hawaiian Islands.

But on December 16th, 1959, the pilots were at Yokota Air Force Base, about thirty-five miles southwest of Tokyo, and ready to leap off. At the base were many bombers, transports, tankers, support aircraft—and thousands of men who had come out to bid the Thunderbirds farewell.

The pilots were anxious to roll. Their schedule called for takeoff on the 15th, but a thick fog rolled in from the Pacific and blanketed the runway. The 16th dawned with a

2,500-foot ceiling. But the day was promising; the sun gleamed off the wet runways, and the air was crisp and clean from the front that had moved on through.

The seven fighters taxied into position, each plane loaded to its maximum gross weight with four heavy fuel tanks slung on pylons beneath the sweptwings. Two tanks each held 275 gallons of fuel; the other tanks, each 200 gallons. Aboard each fighter airplane was a total of 13,900 pounds of fuel alone.

With this weight, the Super Sabre demands a longer roll, more speed, before she will fly. She doesn't respond as quickly, as gracefully, as she does when this heavy weight is cast off. Sluggishly, she builds up speed slowly, but there's still that authoritative grip of the air when the nose does come up and the wings bite solidly for their lift. The pilots planned to climb out, away from Japan, with a speed of Mach .72. Everything would be flown by slide rule and exacting computation. At low altitude Mach .72 figures out to about 375 knots, and with all the tanks aboard, this would be the maximum speed flown. With all those tanks aboard, there was the chance that higher speed might warp a tank, and interfere with the proper flow of fuel to the flaming engine.

The diamond moved into position, lining up on Runway 18 for a takeoff directly to the south. A crosswind of fifteen knots blew across the runway, but this was no problem to the heavy, powerful airplanes. The smoke poured from each fighter as the pilots advanced the throttle; then, at a signal from Fitz, the four leading Super Sabres began to roll. Three seconds later four spears of flame shot back, and the roar of afterburners boomed across the airbase. Faster and faster they rolled, accelerating with every second, the tires bumping in a steady rumble over the tar strips on the concrete.

Fitz held the planes down longer than usual. At 155 knots he lifted the nose wheel and, magically, with exact timing, three other sticks moved back and the wheels came up. But they held down for a moment until the needle read 165 knots. Exactly 5,800 feet from the start of the roll, a remarkable distance, the four Super Sabres were airborne, and began to shrink in size as they bored away to the south.

226

The second formation of three airplanes, Gayle Williams, Dick and Griff, rolled onto the runway, lined up, and began to send their shrill whine of increasing power across the field. The dials read maximum power, but just before the signal to release brakes was given, Crane saw his crew chief, Airman 2/C Donald Thomas, running toward his airplane, and pointing to Dick's wing. He looked down and immediately chopped power. From the cap opening of the left inboard tank, which was under feed pressure, a spray of fuel shot out.

"Thunderbird Five, this is Thunderbird Seven," Dick called to Gayle, "I've just blown a left tank cap and am shutting down."

Gayle immediately contacted Fitz. "Thunderbird Leader from Thunderbird Five. Thunderbirds Five, Six and Seven are aborting. Number Seven has blown a left inboard cap and we'll try to get off as soon as it is fixed."

Gayle then switched to the tower. "Yokota Tower from Thunderbird Five. We've got some trouble, but we think we can fix it quickly. Please keep our flight plan open and extend our weather clearance."

The pilots pulled back the throttles, and the deep roar of the jets subsided to a descending shriek, and then silence.

By now Technical Sergeant Daniel R. Cane, the jet flight chief, had looked over the situation. He knew the time problems involved, that getting a new cap from supply would take so long that the three planes would have to cancel their flight, and plan an entire new mission to catch up to the diamond.

Cane rushed over to a pickup truck and tore off down the flight line. He screeched to a halt by a B-66 jet bomber, grabbed a cap from a wing tank, and then scribbled a note: "The Thunderbirds owe you one 200-gallon tank cap. Thanks a lot, fellas." He jammed the note into the opening, making sure it would be seen during the B-66 preflight inspection, and raced back to the three fighters. In a few seconds the cap was screwed tightly to the tank. Dick started the fighter, all instruments read in the green on pressure and fuel flow, and the three pilots were ready once more for takeoff.

Gayle called the tower, and a few minutes later the Super

Sabres were taxiing to the active runway. "Thunderbirds, you are cleared for immediate takeoff. . . . And from all of us up here, thanks for a wonderful show. Have a good trip home, happy flying, and have a Merry Christmas."

"Those words, with our takeoff roll, were the first real step toward going home," Dick said. "Each mile and each minute after that brought us one more step closer to home. It had been a wonderful, albeit a grueling tour, with so little time in which to relax; there had been so much work and so many things to do, that it seemed as if in the last few weeks everybody had been going strictly on the basis of pride and inner strength. . . ."

AIRMAN'S WORLD

The three sweptwing jet fighters roared from the runway and tucked in their gear. In a perfect Vee formation, they accelerated away from Yokota, then increased their speed and climb just a bit more as Gayle called for maximum climbing thrust. Outside the pressurized cabins the winds that streak over Japan were building in intensity, and as the three airplanes began to ease into the base of the broken clouds over Japan, a low jetstream rushed faster than a hundred miles per hour; it was unseen, unheard, and recognized only by the slight compensating moves of the fighters as they maintained their course.

The world vanished into a blur of grayness, and the three pilots reacted from long training. Dick Crane and Herman Griffin each eased down on a rudder pedal, and the Super Sabres effortlessly widened the distance between them. Gayle Williams at the head of the Vee maintained a constant course and rate of climb; his wingmen stayed glued exactly to the same figures. Unseen by each other, hearing only the hiss of the radio in their earphones, they bored upward through the mists.

The pilots for the past two days had seen nothing but gloom and murk; there were two days of rain and fog pressing upon the men who were already weary. This is an emotional blanket, a stifling psychological fog that brings the fighter pilot to the point of acute irritation. He becomes fret-

228

ful and quick to react to any affront. He doesn't like the weather, and even if he fails to realize the yearning, he seeks the clarity and breathless vistas of the world, the air-man's world, which so many times in the past has brought him peace of mind, a feeling that all is indeed well with the world.

The three men literally burst from the gloom over Japan. Two miles above the picturesque, storied coastline, they exploded into that glorious freedom, into a great ocean of gleaming, golden light. No matter how many years of flight there are behind the pilot, no matter how many times Nature has bared its richest treasures, it is always a rich thrill, a wonderful experience that begins again. This is how these men felt at that moment, in words that differed but carried the same intrinsic emotions.

It always happens, but today the miracle was a bit brighter, the heavens of earth and sky, of land and clouds, blue and gold, all this gained a new perspective, a touch that had never quite existed before. The stunning world of white stretched away beneath them, falling gently as the jets rose higher into the thinning air; beneath them through wind-torn canyons in the clouds that tumbled away in swoops and folds, there could be seen flashes of the Philippine Sea lying outside Tokyo Bay. Then Tokyo and Yokohama drifted past, to their left, visible in hurried snatches as a gray mass lying sullenly beneath the blinding clouds.

But beyond all this, Japan bid the airmen farewell in her own fashion, as only the physical beauty of the islands can do. The sacred mountain, Fujiyama, inspiration of poets and lovers, of stirring martial songs and nationalistic fervor, godsend to artists and musicians, lay gently on the surface of Japan, most of its startlingly graceful lines hiding from view within the clouds. But the last esthetic lines of the peak, shimmering in blinding light from its mantle of snow, thrust gently upward, through the clouds, as though aloof from the world below, and sharing with the three flyers the wonder of what had been captured in this timeless moment.

"Fujiyama had become a living thing," Dick said softly late one night, as he recalled when time itself stood still. "It became to us, in that sudden and truly rich moment, what the mountain had been for all those centuries to the Japanese. Sacred Fuji ... the sacred mountain, the most beautiful, graceful sweep of rhythm that has ever graced the skies. Revered because of its esthetic lines that are unapproached by any other worldly work of nature.

"If all this, the golden light, the dazzling valleys stretching away to infinity, the depth and clarity, the infinitely soft sweep of that peak ... if all this is what they call the airman's realm, then we were blessed at that moment to know truly what they have meant all these years."

Water flashed through a gap in the clouds, and the three fighters arrowed past Yokosuka, the former mighty naval base of wartime Japan. Then across the small peninsula that juts into the Sagami-Wan, lying to the southwest of Tokyo Bay. Following the invisible electronic pulses of their navigational equipment, riding the invisible beams that crisscross the skies, the fighters climbed steadily into the heavens. Thirty thousand feet above the blue of the Pacific— Angels Thirty—racing along under maximum power, the seven airplanes rendezvoused. Fitz and the team had throttled back to low power and speed, waiting for the three.

Now, all together, the seven airplanes became as one, an entity in the skies interconnected electronically and by voice, flying with precision, comforting in their presence with one another. It was a day for flight, glorious and sparkling. It was magnificent, the vaults of heaven reserved for them only, it seemed, and for none other. They climbed easily another two thousand feet, and six and a half miles above the earth streaked southward. The navigational grids drew them with exact precision to a point in the sky directly over the island of O-Shima, an inhospitable chunk of land with a volcanic peak jutting from the outer bay waters to 2,477 feet, and still growling deep in its bowels with sufficient energy to spit forth ashes and smoke.

The pilots went to work, each man trimming his airplane for level flight. The seven planes eased out again into their respective formations of four and three fighters each, Fitz leading the diamond, Gayle the trio. The course now lay direct to Iwo Jima, on a heading of 189 degrees.

The broken clouds began to vanish over O-Shima, and in

the aftermath of the storm that had only the day before lashed the ocean into a heaving, angry fury, the Pacific now lay sparkling like a sea beyond imagination, a heaving ocean of small jewels. It was a slow breathing of a limitless surface, a rhinestone tableau whipped with light. O-Shima and its grumbling volcano passed far behind. Sliding with jet fighter speed over the water there appeared clusters in the sea, black volcanic outcroppings. Islands spawned of fire from hell, bleak, fuming with gases, arrogant of all life.

But from on high, painted generously with the miracle brush of height and distance, even these savage rocks gained a magical quality. The pilots looked down in wonder, banking their wings to expand their view, looking through sun visors and plexiglas canopies as light from the sun crashed into wings suddenly turned, and reflected blindingly.

T-Shima and Udone-Shima; then Nii-Jima. Strange names unnatural to our language, but bearing ominously their relationship to a name no longer strange or unnatural to Americans. Iwo Jima, now another name in history books, taught with patience by teachers to students who see Iwo Jima only as another episode in a great and complicated war. To them it is a name, and nothing else. Here, they˙are taught, men fought, men suffered, men died. But it is numbers, and textbooks can never capture the smell of blood.

The pilots thought of the name of the island, and they realized that theirs was the very same route that only thirteen years before had become a graveyard. Japanese pilots in fighters and bombers, then in kamikaze planes, had flown through these same skies. So had the great B-29's, and especially two of the Superfortresses, bearing the only atomic bombs ever dropped in war.

The Super Sabres flew through the sky that Fitz had once known from a B-24. Here too there had been B-17's, and all manner of fighters, and rescue planes searching for the crews of bombers who had ditched in the sea, and looked hopefully to the skies for succor. Perhaps one of these pilots in the Super Sabres remembered O-Shima, where the last American bomber to be shot down by Japanese fighters had crashed into the sea.

Miyake-Jima slid beneath the wings, and then Mikura-

Jima. Framed in sparkling water, there appeared the larger island of Hachijo-Jima, with its volcanic peak stretching upward for 2,803 feet above the waters.

Time and space and distance began to blend into one another. Until now the air had been mildly turbulent; not uncomfortable, but enough to impart to the fighters a gentle rising and falling movement, boats cruising slowly through placid waters. Then even this vanished, and the air became glass. The fighters no longer flew; they were fixed in the heavens, rooted immovably to some invisible bed of granite. Beneath them the seas slid slowly past their wings.

Then some clouds crept over the horizon. Fishing boats appeared as specks on the Pacific. Someone spotted a freighter, and then all eyes turned to watch a big military transport floating beneath them, Tokyo-bound. And then, again, everything disappeared from sight, and there was only sea and sky.

The circles on the maps were around Tori-Shima, the next checkpoint. Fitz called on his radio to *Duck Butt Bravo;* the call-sign for an Air Force SA-16 rescue amphibian, flying far below them, providing a navigational and rescue checkpoint. The voices drifted into their earphones, bid the Thunderbirds Godspeed, and then faded away.

"Halfway to Iwo, when there is nothing else," Janca recalled, "all of a sudden you look down, and there is the damndest sight you have ever seen in your life. I couldn't believe my eyes. I called *Duck Butt Bravo,* and just blurted out. 'What—is *that?'* "

"That" is a sliver of rock, an impossible, jagged, twisting, deformed volcanic needle. It is a spike born, it seems, of some savagery, stabbing malignantly out of the water. It is not an island, not a reef or an outcropping that shoots hundreds of feet from out of the ocean. It is a ghoulish jest of some past cataclysm of the subterranean deeps that thrust this stark symbol from the ocean. It is alone, an obscene, naked finger.

More water, and then Iwo Jima, with its bloodstained slopes of Mt. Surabachi, where Japanese soldiers had dug in carefully and then killed Marines who clawed and crawled their way to the top. It seems impossible to accept this sav-

232

age, bloody history that was fought barely a decade ago—and that now is little more than checkpoints that slide quickly away beneath the powerful metal wings of the seven jet fighters.

Directly over Iwo Jima, Fitz leads the formations in a gentle turn; when they ease back to level flight they are on a heading of 165 degrees. The Thunderbirds contact *Duck Butt Whiskey Alpha* for winds aloft reports and radar contact checks. Then they are beyond the halfway point to their destination at the island of Guam.

The minutes slip away. Then, far ahead of the airplanes, more than a hundred miles in the distance, there is a touch of green. No more than a smudge, really, a shadow on the horizon, the first betokening of clouds that provide the sign of the island beneath. Saipan, even richer in history and tradition if not soaked so deeply in American blood as Iwo. Saipan, home of the great B-29's; nest of the enormous iron birds that smashed Japan's cities and forced the war to grind to a halt.

But now, years afterward, the names so once well known, so vital to the crews of bombers sweating out their last precious drops of fuel—but no discomfort to these slash-winged fighters—are forgotten. Mardi Point—*Abandoned* is the listing on the chart. Kobler is abandoned, as is the most famous of all, Isley. Kagman Point, too, is closed. Only the Tanapag seaplane base knows signs of life.

"You look down and a feeling of distress crawls over you," said Chuck. "The buildings have collapsed to the years of onslaught of rain and wind, of salt and corrosion and rust, to jungle that never quits. Those buildings we saw down there, for which people fought and bled and sweated, and then defended—now they are rotted hulks of decay. The quonset tops have caved in, there is rot and filth and decay. It was like looking down on a sordid and dirty page of history. It made me feel unclean; it besmirched the accomplishment of what had once been done—by men whom we would never know—for us, and for our kids, too."

Just beyond Saipan there lies Tinian. Home of the *Enola Gay,* carrier of the first atomic bomb, destroyer of Hiroshima in a terrible, impossible, searing crash of light. The chart shows two big fields: North Tinian and West Tinian. They are both *Closed*. The pages of history collect dust here.

But not immediately to the south. Here looms an inhospitable outcropping of rock, the island of Aguijan. The chart reads *Warning Area*. It is a range for bombing, for firing rockets and cannon.

Another island—Rota. Here, too, the great airfield is *Closed*.

Only Guam lies ahead now.

The long descent begins. Imperceptibly the fighters give away their altitude, ease gently from the sky. The great airplanes still smash through the sky, but so overwhelming is this miracle of jet flight that to these pilots, veterans all, it is the gentlest of motions. It is obedience to the gentle manipulation of controls. Everything is as it should be; the sun is bright, the sky clear, the Pacific sparkling and blue.

Two hours and fifty-six minutes after taking off from Yokota on the island of Honshu, the seven fighters pitch out over the runway of Andersen Air Force Base on the island of Guam, and slide in to land.

The Thunderbirds ground crews were waiting for them, and the weary pilots left their airplanes with relief. They tumbled into cots in a barracks and fell asleep almost at once. They were too tired for conversation—takeoff time would come around all too soon.

The next destination—the tiny dot of Wake Island. Since this would also be a direct flight, without air-to-air refueling, each airplane would have to rely upon its 13,900 pounds of fuel for the pilots. The men climbed into their cockpits, fired up the birds to check all instruments and controls, then shut down. Small tugs dragged them to the runway, the tanks were then topped off to their maximum capacity, and then the pilots restarted the engines.

Seven sweptwing fighters raced down Runway 6, stretching eleven thousand feet ahead of the brake-release point, a comforting feature to pilots in airplanes loaded to their maximum weight of more than seventeen tons. It is a peculiar runway. The planes raced along, then, still on the ground, followed a tremendous dip in the runway; this came

234

up sharply and then leveled off for the final four thousand feet. At the end of the runway there was no doubt about flight; a sheer cliff dropped away for 350 feet to the water.

The Super Sabres turned eleven degrees after takeoff, took up a course heading of 071 degrees. They climbed to 32,000 feet, but never wavered from that original heading—all the way, 1,036 nautical miles, to Wake Island. The winds were calm, but gave a slight eight-knot push to the fighters.

The airplanes descended in a long, flat glide, preparing to land straight in. Just off Wake a black cloud loomed, and suddenly the fighters were in the midst of a blinding rainstorm. Each man was immediately blotted from sight. Then they were out of the blinding rain, the runway on Wake Island rushed toward them, and the pilots were answering the waves of the ground crews—another group that had flown ahead to service the Thunderbirds. Time from takeoff on Guam to touchdown at Wake—two hours and forty-five minutes.

That was all the flying for the day. The next leg, from Wake to Hickam, in the Hawaiian Islands, was 2,169 nautical miles—and all of it over water. This called for air refueling with KB-50 tankers from the Tactical Air Command; one set would operate out of Wake Island, the others from Hawaii. There would be two separate refuelings, involving twelve of the giant tanker airplanes.

FILL 'ER UP, MAC

The Thunderbirds departed Wake Island at ten in the morning, on a clear, beautiful day. The takeoff was uneventful, and the seven big fighters bored to their cruising altitude.

Air refueling over the trackless wastes of the Pacific demands critical timing and co-ordination, in order to achieve a rendezvous between fighters and tankers that brings together the aircraft over a certain point, at a certain time, and a specific altitude. There is little room for error in these calculations, for fuel has a nasty habit of pouring relentlessly into the voracious chamber of the jet engine.

The planes use special refueling frequencies, and they

use a versatile homing system and sweep radar for locating one another. The altitude set for this rendezvous and refueling was 20,000 feet over the ocean, and it called for an airspeed of 210 knots by the formations.

This alone was enough to set every one of the Thunderbirds to doing some heavy thinking, for this low airspeed, with all the garbage hanging from the airplanes, at that altitude, meant that the Super Sabres would be right on the critical edge of the stall. The pilots would have to fly their F-100D's at a steep, almost excessive angle of attack in order to maintain the lift necessary to hold altitude.

Four hundred miles out of Wake Island the pilots spotted the first set of six tankers. The KB-50's were almost at their maximum weight, getting all the speed that was possible from their four-piston engines and two underslung jets. For the moment the picture looked brighter; the fighters were at 32,000 feet when the tankers first came into sight, there were no clouds, and the air was smooth.

All seven Thunderbirds were maintaining close formation at the first tanker radio contact; this was about 150 miles from the refueling point. Fitz called in on the designated UHF frequency, locked on the radio communications. When they were 100 miles apart the command tanker called that "We have you on our scope. Steer five degrees left."

"The tankers helped vector us in," Neil Eddins said. "They called out course changes that would bring us together. It's a remarkable operation, and the airborne radar systems enable the tankers to bring a flock of fighters in to them, whether or not it's the middle of the night or there is a complete cloud cover.

"Thirty miles out we began our letdown from thirty-two to twenty thousand feet. From here on in everything gets right on the wire.

"Five miles short of the tanker"—Neil was flying now with his hands, explaining every maneuver—"you start coming off on the power, and start to slow down from the cruise speed to about 210 knots. No—scrub that 'about.' The 210 knots is exact, because the tanker pilot is flying everything right on the needle.

"The refueling probe juts out of the fighter's right wing and

236

extends out for nine feet. We used the probe-and-drogue refueling system; you know the gadget, a large funnel at the end of the hose, and that is reeled back from the tanker. In any turbulence it can whip like a snake through the air, quivering and undulating its full length.

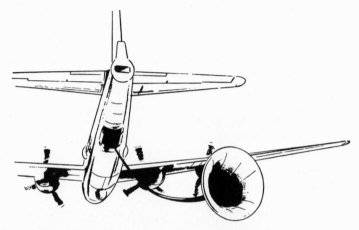

Air refueling drogue, early model KB-29.

"There are two lights on the fueling tank—this is where the hose reels out. One is amber and the other green. Now, when you're cleared in on the tanker, you see the amber light. This is the signal for the refueling pilot that tells him he is 'cleared on the hook up.'

"The trick is to come in with your probe, jab it right into the drogue, and make a positive contact. But it's not quite that simple in practice.

"We began to get some turbulence at twenty thousand, and it made things sticky for us. The hose reels out for sixty feet, and when you make your contact and continue to creep on in for another thirty feet, you end up snuggled in to the tanker. The big bird is only thirty feet away and it seems to fill the sky.

"There's wash coming off the tanker's wing, and there's turbulence from the props, you're fighting the edge of a stall, and the whole blasted mess just doesn't make for any relaxed flying, *that's* for sure!"

Each Thunderbird pilot creeps up on the tanker with a speed of 214 knots, just four knots over the speed of the big KB-50. Once contact is made and a hookup with the drogue is assured, the fighter pilot has to ease in enough power to drive the hose thirty feet back onto its reel in the wing of the tanker. Each hose is marked with white stripes to show the increments of push the fighter gives the hose. Marked every ten feet, it shows the pilot immediately just how far back he has shoved the hose.

All this time the refueling boom is quivering and vibrating like a thing that is alive; the drogue bounces around like a wild, gibbering creature that knows no rest. The F-100D pilot has to not only watch the probe and drogue out of the corner of his eye, but he must also keep a wary lookout on the tanker ahead of him.

Actually, the pilot does not watch the drogue itself. To get an accurate idea of just what these men were doing, Dick and I flew several simulated refueling missions in the F-100F, recounting every step of the maneuvers four miles over the Pacific. The KB-50's outboard refueling nacelle has a half-moon slit in the bottom, which is readily seen by the fighter pilot. The combat fighter has a gunsight system, and these pilots use that sight for a reference line. But these sights were removed for the Thunderbirds when they picked up the F-100D's in Okinawa. Crane took a grease pencil and marked off a series of vertical and horizontal lines on his windscreen.

As he came in he tried to remember a half-dozen things that all had to be blended into a single flowing motion. There were the rudder pedals to work, the stick and its operation of ailerons and the big slab tail, there was power, radio call switches, he had to read the engine instruments and the speed and worry about that stall. There was the tanker and the wash, the turbulence and the quivering probe and the snaking drogue. There were the lights and the fuel meters and the other airplane and a lot more things that he was doing instinctively.

And everywhere in the world, day and night, in fighters and bombers and tankers, in fair weather and foul, over land

and over ocean, somewhere and sometime during almost every minute of the day, there are Air Force pilots who are doing just this same thing. They are doing a magnificent job, and America hardly knows about it at all. I couldn't help thinking that as Dick Crane, the other pilots, and I pored over the charts and flight logs and the notes, so that we could put down on paper those dramatic moments so high over the Pacific.

"As you come in," Griff continued, "you know exactly the sight picture on that tank that you need in the windscreen in order for you to stick the probe into the drogue. If you miss, you're either under or over or short, or maybe two of them. Your feet and hands are like they're disembodied, working by themselves. You correct the sight picture constantly. You never look at the drogue, because if you do this and try to stab the probe in, you end up chasing the thing all over the sky, and that is no way to fly an airplane that is one shake away from stalling."

The three fighters, despite all this, moved in steadily, surely, with exacting precision. Each man snapped in his probe, and it was amazing how every pilot was hooked up almost at once. Fitz and Janca hooked up on the lead, Tanker One; Maultsby had Tanker Two all to himself; Eddins was solo on Tanker Three; Williams on Four; Griffin on Five, and Crane on Tanker Six.

Everything went smoothly. Then trouble fell all over Herman Griffin. He moved in like a key fitting into its groove, hooked up. Without warning "the hose came off the tanker, ripped clean away, and tumbled down into the Pacific twenty thousand feet below."

Cursing a blue streak, Griff eased over to Tanker Six with Crane, and plugged in for his second hookup. Each tanker has two drogues, one from each wing, and the six tankers left an emergency slot open for several of the fighters.

With the fighter plugged in, the pilot waits for the amber light to blink out and for green to snap on. But this is done with precision, and according to exact procedure. When every plane is in position, the tanker leader calls, "All Thunderbirds are hooked up, stand by to receive fuel."

Each pilot acknowledges, "Thunderbird Leader," then 'Thunderbird Two," and on down the line. Each man calls his own tanker. The entire process takes only seconds, but at this speed and height the system, which has been developed after years of experience, must be rigidly adhered to.

The individual tanker calls, "You can start taking on fuel whenever you're ready."

Crane squeezes the radio button on the throttle: "Tanker Number Six, this is Thunderbird Seven. On the right drogue. Give me a full fuel load."

"Roger, Thunderbird Seven. You're now taking on fuel."

The pilots look up at the light; the green is on.

Even as the Super Sabres fly their constant, close formation with the tankers, fuel pours into the thirsty fighters. The crew scanners in the blisters of the tankers call in steadily to the fighter pilots, letting them know when each two thousand pounds of fuel has surged into their tanks. The fuel transfer came to three tons of fuel per fighter, twenty-one tons of refined kerosene transferred miraculously in the midst of the Pacific—all in a brief few minutes.

The last pound pushes into the fighters, and the light switches back to amber, signifying the end of fuel transfer. Each man holds his position; the Tanker Leader always checks each of the fighters on his own channels. When he is certain that the fueling responsibility is met, he calls:

"This is Tanker Leader to Thunderbird Leader: Be advised that all aircraft have full loads. You're cleared to back off when ready."

Each Thunderbird pilot calls his particular tanker, "Backing off," and reduces power. He backs off gently, the Super Sabre sluggish at the great weight and slow speed, keeping his aircraft level, in a straight line so that he will not bend or break the probe, or cause the hose to whip suddenly.

Crane couldn't resist it: "Tanker Six, this is Thunderbird Seven here. Where's my green stamps, and while you're at it, would you please wash the windshield?"

The crew scanner in the blister thumbed his nose merrily at Dick, whipped out a sheaf of green stamps from his flight suit and waved them at the fighter pilot: "Here they

240

are, buddy, just come and get 'em!" Then he sprayed his own windscreen, and polished it lustily. Flying off Dick's wing, Griff watched the scene and howled.

The fighters eased away from the tankers, spread out in a great line-abreast formation, and climbed back to 32,000 feet. Midway drew steadily closer, and there came again the voice of a tanker formation commander—"We have you on our scope." The fighters rendezvoused at 20,000 feet, closed in and hooked up, and took on another three tons of fuel each. Back to 32,000 feet, and a course straight for the Hawaiian Islands.

Then came the first landfall, a strip of white beach against the blue-green ocean. In several minutes the white strip gained in size, revealing behind it the island of Niihau; farther behind, several times its size and almost as large as Oahu, was Kauai.

Far to one side and barely behind Fitz was Janca's plane, and then the rest of the team. Each fighter was separated by several thousand feet, a lazy, comfortable formation—well dispersed, but each man always within easy visual sight of the other Super Sabres. Each man had his own flight plan, did his own navigation, to provide a constant check. Neil Eddins, however, spoke for all the pilots when he made the position reports to the tankers, to Midway Island, and the *Duck Butt* rescue planes.

With Niihau in sight, Fitz called his men. "Thunderbirds, this is Lead. Give me a fuel count, will you?"

Each man radioed back in staccato fashion, reading off his fuel in terms of pounds. The fuel ranged from 6,600 to 8,800 pounds per airplane, amounting to almost a full internal storage for each fighter, the recommended tankage for the Super Sabres when they began their letdown.

"Okay, gang, we're all fat on fuel, so we'll start our letdown now. Let's get in some sightseeing on our way down to Oahu."

"Yassuh, Boss," chirruped Griff.

At this point the formation had only fifteen minutes of flight, if they headed straight toward Hickam Field on Oahu. But aboard each airplane was a full two hours of fuel. The airplanes would be over their maximum landing weight,* and it was necessary to burn some of this fuel before the fighters would be ready to pitch out and land. At low altitudes, however, the jet is a voracious creature, and gulps fuel in prodigious quantities. Coming in to the island on the deck would quickly burn off the excessive fuel weight—and it would also be a lot more interesting for the pilots.

"Okay, troops—Lead's coming back to eight-five on the power."

At 32,000 feet each F-100D was held to a throttle setting of ninety-two per cent power. Each man moved the throttle back until the tachometer gauge read eighty-five per cent. The fighters lost speed, and a slight reduction in lift. The airplane responds to the change in balance between lift and gravity, and the nose drops. It is a maneuver these men execute not so much with care but with a wonderful proficiency and an exact ease of movement that is afforded only by years of experience. No two jet fighters respond exactly the same, and therefore the figure of eighty-five per cent power called in by Fitz may be slightly greater, or less, in the other airplanes. But the flight speed and rate of descent *will* be identical, and that is what matters.

At 32,000 feet each Super Sabre cruised with a speed of Mach .82. This showed as 325 knots Indicated Airspeed, working out to a true speed in the air of approximately 500 knots.

Seven airplanes fall away from the upper reaches as one. The nose drops about seventeen degrees, and each F-100D slips into a shallow descent. The loss in airspeed is negligible, or none at all, because what was given away in the reduction of power is reclaimed by the descent. Nobody wants speed now, for every fighter is operating under a safety red line of 350 knots indicated because of the four heavy tanks slung beneath the sweptwings.

The airplanes slide in closer as they ease toward the ocean.

*Note: The fuel remaining was a very necessary flight-planning factor—in case of bad weather at Hawaii, the flight would have to "hold" at altitude until the weather improved for landing. Also, an internal fuel reserve was necessary in the event of malfunction of the external tanks.

242

Barely 200 feet over the water, Fitz levels out, and with him is a neat formation of the Thunderbirds. A wedge of red, white, and blue fighters sweeps toward Oahu.

The pilots look out to their left. Kauai, far from the main center of activity of the Hawaiian Islands, is a stunningly beautiful island. From their position, the high peak of 5,170 feet soared high above them. It is an old volcano, rising from the shores of the circular island and sweeping upward in an unbroken line, a rich green that is a growth of the earth itself.

Fishing boats flashed beneath the fighters, deckhands waving to the pilots. Several interisland freighters came into view, and again everyone in sight waved madly to the star-spangled Super Sabres.

Oahu lay dead ahead, but as yet no one had seen the island.

"Everyone was straining like mad to see Oahu," Gayle Williams recalled. "This was the last stop before debarking for home, and as such it held a special significance for us. Besides, this wasn't Guam or Wake. This was no sandspit or a jungle that was filled with the decaying rot of a war everyone was doing their best to forget. This was an island of beauty, part of America, and we were eager to catch our first glimpse of the mountains. It takes only fifteen minutes in the Super Sabre, even at our reduced speed, to reach Oahu from Kauai, but we were overanxious, and the minutes seemed to drag."

The men were dog tired. Not only because of the past weeks of hard flying and grueling schedules; they have been in the cramped cockpits now for five and a half hours. They have flown tight, precision formation for air refueling. They are hot, each man's legs and back feel the ache of cramps. Every man's arm is tired from flying the sensitive fighter along a specific route and altitude. No automatic pilot in these birds! And there's a sigh of relief, a feeling of pressure and tautness lifting. A lot of water lies between Wake to Midway to Oahu, and it is always a wonderful feeling when that water is behind the flight.

Neil calls Hickam and reports for the team. He advises approach control of the team's position, altitude, course, and speed; he requests that the Thunderbirds' flight plan be canceled, and advises that the pilots are burning off fuel to meet their landing weight requirements. His last call is that the seven planes will land in approximately fifteen minutes.

The seven fighters hold a course that takes them to the south of Barber's Point; coming in from west-northwest they angled into the Waianae Mountains that rear along Oahu's western side. Then, as they passed the southwestern tip of the island, they came into a perfect view of the Barber's Point Naval Air Station.

Everything that Oahu was supposed to be came to life. The sea changed color gradually as the planes descended until it had darkened to a rich, deep blue; then, as the fighters swept in closer to the land it faded to a lighter blue and then a startling, rich and clear green.

The sky that had been empty soon swarmed with activity. Bob Janca called out the first of the Lockheed picket planes, great Constellations pregnant with radar gear, bulging from top and bottom with round, electronic-packed plastic membranes. Fighters, transports, commercial airliners, flying boats, private planes—the Hawaiian area is a mecca for flight. The Thunderbirds formation swung around in a wide, sweeping turn to the right, still at 200 feet and well below any other air traffic.

Hickam Air Force Base came into view, crowded with its fighters, bombers, and military transports. Pearl Harbor, Ford Island, the harbor and docks ready to burst with the influx of commercial, fishing, private and military shipping.

Then Diamond Head comes in to view, not a towering peak, but high enough at 3,105 feet and a good half mile above the Thunderbirds.

The team closes its rank, and holds the altitude assigned by air traffic control. Four fighters edge into the familiar diamond, Gayle, Griff and Dick swing back into a precise, tight Vee. They are now "before eyes," and the Thunderbirds are on review.

But it's not so precise in the cockpits. The pilots are jazzing away merrily, calling out airplanes, manifesting their relief at the end of the flight with gay conversation. They swing around the island, whizzing over sailboats and cata-marans, waving back to the grinning people on the boats. Neil is in constant touch with Hickam approach control, and the team is being tracked on radar to assure complete air traffic separation.

The seven fighters are still too heavy to land, however, so Fitz calls his pilots, "We're still too heavy on fuel. Let's push it up to ninety-five per cent. We'll go into AB for a while and burn off this load."

"Roger!"

"Good idea, Boss."

"What you been waiting for, Bossman? My butt is getting awful tired."

Then from Griff: "Roast pig, heah we comes!"

"Thunderbirds ready ... AB's— *Now.*" The pilots in the Vee see the splashes of flame from the four fighters in front of them. All airplanes under AB, hurling a crescendo of sound along the boats over which they pass; they swing into a wide left turn, past Koko Head on the island's south-eastern tip. Then around to Makapuu Point, a wonderful sightseeing tour northward. The Koolau Range looms to their left, the beaches are gleaming white, the island lush and profuse with vegetation. Fitz, who once flew through here as a wartime bomber commander, points out the old airbases from which he once took off on his long flights to Australia and New Guinea.

Fuel load is down and weight is acceptable. The team cuts back across the northwest corner of the island, arrow-ing steeply into the sky to clear the mountains. They drop back again on the west side, coming once more into view of Barber's Point.

"Thunderbirds from Leader. Let's go to Hickam tower frequency for landing."

Everyone switches his radio control, and Hickam calls in with landing instructions.

Fitz calls for the diamond to tuck it in real tight, re-peats all the data on wind, barometric pressure setting, temperature, the runway. "The diamond will go in first. We'll pitch to the left."

The diamond swoops in, the tight formation drawing every

pair of eyes on the base as they pitch steeply to the left. Fitz has been asked to have the team make a Thunderbird pitch-out; tired or not, the boys snap it in and grease the Super Sabres around on that invisible sheet of glass. The 'Birds come in at 350 knots, almost scraping the runway, then ease up to 1,500 feet. Right on their heels is the Vee. Gayle pitches out, then Griff, and Dick in trail.

After landing, Fitz calls for the pilots to tuck it in for a close trail in taxi formation, and the big airplanes squeeze in tight, causing mechanics on the flight line to stare and shake their heads.

"The entire flight from starting engines to stopping engines," Chuck said, "took us six hours and five minutes. It was bad enough on your butt in the airplane, but about a half hour after you've climbed down, the numbness really begins to hurt, and everybody is rubbing that posterior and groaning in painful relief.

"The operations officer told us that the ground crews would be in at midnight to service the airplanes and release the tanks. Because we are right on schedule—and that means *two* complete shows to be flown the next day! While we're catching up on sleep, the mechanics will be working all night long."

The two complete demonstrations the following day are almost anticlimactic for the pilots. The second show is the last of the Far East tour; December 19th, 1959. The first was in the morning for top military and civilian officials at Oahu, and in the afternoon the team repeated the entire performance for the public during Open House at Hickam.

The pilots had a break on Sunday, not because it could be scheduled, but to meet maintenance requirements, and allow the mechanics to replace the four drop tanks beneath each fighter. They needed all Sunday for the task; they checked out the tanks, assured that they were all hung properly, carried the right amount of pressurization, fed fuel exactly as required. It was another day in the exhausting attention the boys paid to the airplanes.

The pilots hit the sack early that night—Hawaiian locale or not. Wakeup Monday morning was set for five o'clock sharp. Then there were meetings with the Ferry Command

Squadron for the en-route briefing, weather, tanker rendez-vous points, and general flight planning information. Each step of the leg for the long flight home came under briefing and control of the 4440th Aircraft Delivery Group. At nine a.m. sharp, the seven airplanes began their take-off. Everything was right in the groove, the weather fine, the Super Sabres operating with precision. The first rendez-vous with the KB-50 tankers was scheduled for 20,000 feet, on a heading of 048 degrees out of Hickam, 300 miles out from the field.

GOING HOME

"That first refueling went like we'd planned it for months," Griff told me. "We hit 'em at 20,000 feet, slowed down, came in with a fine line-abreast formation. We got the whole thing greased up real slick, no problem a-tall. And then we had only one more rendezvous ahead of us, and that was it."

The Thunderbirds dropped back from the tankers, eased away from each other, and lifted to their cruising altitude of 32,000 feet. So far everything had gone off with wonderful precision—the final refueling would be 500 miles closer to home. There had been only one incident; the tanker losing its entire reel-and-drogue system on the first refueling pickup. Other than that, the schedule had been met with perfect timing and co-ordination.

This entire aspect of the cross-Pacific journey was in every last detail the movement of a combat force, and entirely self-sustaining in respect to maintenance and repair. Alter the Thunderbirds' paint, fill the four cannon in each fighter with shells, replace the gunsights—and you had seven deadly combat machines.

The minutes moved by slowly, and then the planes were almost at the halfway point—and time for the second refueling rendezvous. Everything moved as it should; the pilots assumed their positions for formation with the tankers and began to descend to 20,000 feet.

But then came the first warning signs, the invisible but —to a pilot—sharp and significant sensations that ring an alarm bell that something is *wrong*.

It comes first in the tugs of the air at the descending fighters. This begins at 25,000 feet; the turbulence is more than should reasonably be expected. There are no clouds in the sky. It is clear, but with each hundred feet of descent the air becomes rougher. The bumps become shocks, the shocks turn to rapid, hard blows.

At 20,000 feet, the rendezvous altitude, the sky is violent; it is almost a shock compared to the peace and quiet of the sky 12,000 feet higher. But the immediate future boded even more ill, for as the seconds passed the turbulence increased in its severity. Now it was no longer just a matter of flying; the pilots were fighting merely to stay level.

"Even this didn't bother us too much," Janca explained. "Then the tankers began to grow in perspective to where we could really see, in the form of the tanker and its trailing drogue, just what was really going on. The drogues on all the tankers were bouncing around so violently they looked as if they were being dragged at high speed against the deep furrows of a plowed field, instead of moving through thin air four miles over the earth—thin air that *looked* smooth and serene."

And still the turbulence became worse. Every pilot was tense, senses alert, ready for any emergency that under these conditions could erupt without warning.

"As I looked at my drogue," Dick continued, "I kind of swallowed, a big hard swallow that didn't want to go down. Two thoughts immediately came to my mind. The first was: 'How am I ever going to get a hookup on *that* thing?' And the other was about what a nasty break we had gotten. Talk about the tables turning on us!

"Everything so far had gone so smoothly, the weather had been with us all the way, the air was clear. We thought we had it made, all sewed up with no sweat. But now . . . the airplanes were acting like skittish Cubs flying right through the middle of a summer thunderstorm."

"Holy smokes!" Janca cried. "Look at that thing *bounce!*"

"Yeah," Chuck added. "You're really going to earn your flight pay today, Dad."

The pilots were talking with the tanker crews. "Hey,

fellas!" Griff called. "It's about this freeway you're supposed to be on. How about getting off that cotton-pickin' dirt road and back onto the pavement?"

"Cripes, yes," grumbled Neil. "One thing is sure about these tanker boys. Their highway repair department does a lousy job. These chuckholes are pretty big."

Then the Boss cracks the whip, quietly. "Okay, Thunderbirds, let's get the show on the road. Each man is cleared to his own individual tanker frequency. Take your time. It's rough up here, and don't bust up any probes. Watch out especially for that drogue against your windscreen.

"Don't none of you characters lose any canopies—it's pretty cold up here.

"Okay, gang, move up."

There came a chorus of "Roger!" and the inevitable "Yassuh, majuh, suh!" from Griff.

Everyone moved in, carefully, flying right on the edge of their airplanes' maximum performance. Their speed is low, and the severe turbulence aggravates the danger of a stall.

Fitz comes on the air again on the command channel. "All right, troops, remember now—we're not in any rush. If some of you are having any trouble getting a hookup, the rest of us will hang on all the way to the coast if necessary and wait for you. So hang on. Don't bust up any airplanes."

Everybody moves to an individual airplane except Gayle Williams and Dick Crane. The pilots closed in and started to fly tight formation on the drogues.

"I was sure glad I had taken Fitz's suggestions, and marked those grid lines on the windscreen with the grease pencil," Dick said. "I knew if I ever had any doubts about my proficiency in air-to-air refueling, today was going to tell the truth. This was the big test.

"The old narrator, of course, sits on the ground a great deal, and his flying proficiency and capability isn't as finely honed from day to day as the rest of the team. So here was the test of calling on all the old skill I had, as well as experience and cunning. All the tricks I'd learned during flying in all kinds of planes under all kinds of conditions for more than eleven years. This was *it*.

"What it all boils down to in the final essence is that if you're a good pilot, you have confidence in yourself and in your ability under almost any circumstances."

The tanker commander calls Fitz: "Thunderbird Leader. We'll try the hookups here at twenty thousand first. There's a chance that we soon can get out of these layers of turbulent air. If not, we'll either try climbing or diving below this level, to see if we can find a smoother altitude."

There was no longer any jesting about the situation, and even the irrepressible Griff was working hard in his cockpit. The airplanes were being tossed about like chips on the surface of a stormy sea. It wasn't merely uncomfortable any more; it was, because of the refueling hookups, a dangerous procedure. The moment for jocularity had vanished. Every man flew with all his skill and grim concentration. A slip, a mistake, right here and now, could mean at the very least a dangerous accident and a pilot falling down into the Pacific, twenty thousand feet below.

Right here, for all the men, is where the training, the constant practice to improve skill, would either pay off or reveal its deficiencies. This is where, as Fitz puts it so well, you either make your nickels or go broke.

In training they taught the pilots *not* to watch the drogue, or else they would end up chasing it all over the sky, skittering about even in smooth air. But it is a natural tendency to watch the drogue, to see what is happening, what you're doing. It is so natural that the pilots have to fight, consciously, to overcome their instincts. It is almost like driving down a twisting road at seventy miles per hour, and guiding yourself only by alignment with the tops of telephone poles flashing ahead, never looking at the road. The urge for these seven men to look down was almost overwhelming, but it had to be repressed, to be shoved from conscious thought.

Each man forced himself to fly with disipline; there was no other way, and there is no other means of explaining what they did in those critical seconds. Many qualified men had in the past taught these same fighter pilots, giving to them the best of their own skill and experience.

Each pilot, therefore, disregarded the drogue. At first, it was a concentrated and determined effort, but within seconds the men became what the Air Force had trained them to be—a co-ordination of man and machine. They simply, and literally, pushed the drogue completely from their thoughts in respect to flying into the position for hookup.

Fitzgerald: "I put my windscreen lines on the tank, and flew my airplane into contact. Fighting the turbulence, even worse now than before, had become, as it does with all experienced pilots, no longer a movement of conscious volition, but actually of instinct.

"The pitot boom is fourteen and a half feet long. You fly up to maintain a lateral separation between the pitot boom and the drogue of three and a half feet, which is exactly the distance between the fueling probe and the fuselage. When this distance is held, the drogue parallel to the tip of the boom, and the pilot watching his half-moon slit on the reel nacelle along with the indicators, he is right in the slot. The key is to fly formation with the tanker's reel nacelle, and stabilize right on it.

"If the pilot is too far away, of course, no contact is possible without correction and this means falling back and coming in again. If the drogue is too close to the wash streaming back and to the sides of the fighter's nose, this puts the drogue into violent turbulence that whips the drogue around."

Each pilot comes up to his tanker, and he eases in to the point where he has the drogue just about directly across from the end of the pitot boom sticking out ahead of the air intake. This is the correct alignment. Right here the pilot stops jockeying the throttle, and stabilizes his heavy fighter.

He now must do three things. The first is to look out at his own probe, and then check the drogue for lateral separation. Is the drogue too close, or too far out? How is center alignment? Is it in too close, inside the probe—or too far outside? All these things must be evaluated with a glance—for the pilot is flying that wicked formation in the severe turbulence.

He stabilizes his position. Once this is done, he looks up and checks the sight picture obtained on the windscreen.

251

And this is the picture he wants to retain, for he uses it to fly his probe directly into contact and hookup with the drogue.

But this isn't all. If the probe hits the drogue too hard, the reel can't take up the slack fast enough, and the pilot suddenly has a vicious snake or whip of the hose that shakes and rattles his whole airplane. And if he goes in too slow, the turbulence off the nose agitates the drogue and causes it to bounce around and possibly to slam against the side of the airplane.

To Crane's amazement, the first call from the tankers was: "Thunderbird Seven, you have a good contact. You're the first one in—"

Dick was amazed. With all their experience, he had beaten the rest of the gang into position! Maultsby, Eddins, Janca, Williams—these were all experts at air-to-air refueling. (And it should be pointed out right here and now that Dick *never* allowed them to forget who hooked on first.)

"Much to my surprise," Dick said, "I heard the call and shouted 'Rog! Give me a thousand pounds, if you please.' It was just like I'd been doing this jazz every day before breakfast. The fuel flowed in at a rate that meant holding the hookup and flow for several minutes. It flowed in through the right wing and on up into the main fuselage cell, aft of the cockpit.

"Gayle called in next—he hooked up almost immediately after I got on. We didn't know what the other people were doing, and we sure weren't about to bother looking.

"Flying formation was brutal. We were all over the sky. It was the hardest flying I have ever had to do, and I don't expect it ever to be any worse. To keep that hose lined up and level with the tanker, keep it from getting twisted. Worrying about whether or not the entire boom may tear off.

"It took everything I had to give. I had a tiger by the tail, and I was afraid to let go, yet I had to hang on. Not only me, but the rest of the boys, of course. It was murder up there."

It didn't seem possible, but the turbulence increased. What had been violent became hell. Then the tanker allowed his speed to drop; it wasn't his fault, the pilots were fighting

252

madly to keep the big airplane level. They understood only too well the task of the men behind them in the single-seat jet fighters.

"But when his speed came down, we had had it," Neil said. "With all the power I had—using the AB, and flying at the highest possible angle of attack, I slowly started to fall back. I was using every trick in the book, but it wasn't enough. I couldn't stay with the tanker at the slow speed. The airplane fell back and unhooked."

Neil glanced to the side, just in time to see Gayle's fighter literally flung off the fuel line. Both planes had fallen behind the power curve; maximum thrust with the AB wasn't enough to keep them at that speed. They were stalling out.

Both pilots came in again, making two more attempts to hook up. They failed, but on the third try they were "on."

His patience rapidly disappearing, Gayle called the tanker. "Tanker Six—you've got to keep your speed up so we can hang on back here. We're behind the curve, falling off."

"Right, Thunderbird Six. We'll give it our best."

He did, but it wasn't enough. Four minutes later both Super Sabres fell off, stalling back from the tanker.

This was the moment when the situation was no longer just troublesome—it had become tense, and dangerous. The fighters were down to their minimum fuel load in mid-Pacific. And incredibly, impossibly, the turbulence lashed with greater ferocity at the Thunderbirds.

They prepared to go in for the third hookup. There was the real chance now that they might not be able to accomplish the refueling. The men couldn't help but think of miles-to-go and minutes-left-to-fly. They were at the point of no return—and the heavy fighters had only *six minutes of fuel remaining in their tanks.*

"Tanker Six from Thunderbird Seven. You're going to have to keep your speed up even if you have to dive that damn thing." Gayle echoed the call.

Fitz called to the tankers, "Can you climb and find smoother conditions at higher altitude?"

Immediately the tanker commander responded. "We're now going to all available emergency power. I'm going to initiate a very low rate of climb. Maybe we can find some smoother air."

In the cockpit of the KB-50 six throttle arms moved forward. Propeller pitch changed and the blades spun faster. The two jets wound up to maximum thrust. In several seconds the KB-50 was back to the required 210 knots speed, climbing slowly at 400 feet per minute, and easing into air that accepted without violence the presence of the heavy airplanes.

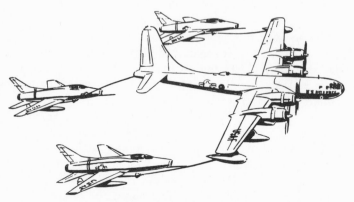

KB-50 refuels Thunderbirds over Pacific.

It made all the difference between success and failure. The Super Sabres hooked up, and now they could hang on instead of falling back.

Then came those wonderful, welcome words. "This is Tanker Leader. All Thunderbirds are hooked up. You're clear to take on fuel any time you're ready."

In moments the precious kerosene surges through the lines. The green light is a marvelous thing to see. But the fight is not yet won; not at all. The fighters have had difficulty hanging on while they were light, low on fuel, and at a lower altitude.

Now they must each take three additional tons into the

254

airplanes, and they cannot, they must not, fall off the tanker, even while their wing loading soars by a half-ton every sixty seconds. The higher altitude of 27,000 feet brings everything right to the critical point.

It takes more and more of what little power is left to hang on. Each man by now is wringing wet with perspiration. The pilots have been all over the sky, fighting with constantly rapid and shifting control movements to remain at the end of the fuel line. Each plane looks as though it were a bucket swinging wildly, being dragged through choppy water from a racing speedboat.

The pilots are forced to use afterburner as the fuel pours into their airplanes. They come in and out of AB, rushing in and falling back. The hose line stretches out, and the AB crashes back its flame. Then there is the rapid manipulation of the throttle to keep the Super Sabre from rushing like a bull up and under the tanker.

The tankers have been climbing slowly but steadily, and near the end of the refueling there is a minor but blessed relief from turbulence as the formations reach smoother air. The pilots mutter fervent thanks and close down the afterburners; they are no longer needed, for the tankers ease over into a gentle descent and gain even more speed.

The final words come: "Thunderbird Leader. All your aircraft have full fuel loads. Cleared to back off and disconnect when ready."

Not a pilot needs to back off. The men hold everything with maximum power just short of afterburner, and the big, heavy fighters fall off.

The sigh of relief can be heard all the way back to Hickam.

Fitz's voice comes over the radio. He speaks softly, but there's no question of what he feels: "Let's go upstairs."

The seven fighters ease away from the tankers, climb to 32,000 feet where once again the air is smooth and wonderful for flight. In each cockpit a man sags a little. The stick pressures are light now, and the airplanes are soon trimmed out. Once again they are in their element, sliding through the heavens with gentle beauty and great, subdued power.

The sky is wonderful, the sun bright and golden, and it sparkles on the blue Pacific.
All is well with the world.
The Thunderbirds set their course for home.

Epilogue

This is not the first epilogue I wrote for this book.

The first time, I wrote that *These are the Thunderbirds —
the men, the team.* I lived with these men, I said. Flew and
worked with them. I came away a man rich in new friends.

I have been writing of aviation and have been flying for
more than twenty-four years. Those years have been filled
with exciting and memorable events, flying over different
continents and oceans, in everything from fabric flivvers
and my own Messerschmitt, from jets to four-engined
aluminum giants. The time I spent with the Thunderbirds
I will always remember as the best I have ever been privileged to share.

This was all true the first time I wrote those words. It is
true now.

During these years the demands of flight under exacting
and rigorous standards have exacted their toll.

In the Foreword I wrote of the deaths of Dick Crane,
Bob Fitzgerald, and George Nial. In the story of the team
the reader learned of the death of Charles Salmon. You
read of the tragedy on October 9th, 1958, when a C-123
aircraft took fourteen members of the maintenance crew,
as well as its own crew, to their deaths.

In 1964 Eugene Devlin, Left Wing, was killed while a
member of the Thunderbirds. In 1966 Bob Morgan, Solo,
and Frank Liethen, Executive Officer, were killed in an
F-100.

Other events have claimed their toll. In May, 1965, Bob
Bell, who had flown Slot, was killed at Bien Hoa in Vietnam. He did not die in the air; a series of explosions on
the ground claimed his life.

In 1966, Russ Goodman, who had been the Narrator in
1964 and 1965, was shot down and killed during a mission
over North Vietnam.

In April of 1966, Sam Johnson, whom the reader will
remember as the Slot Pilot from March, 1957, to October,
1958, was shot down during a strafing run against North

Vietnamese targets. Sam Johnson and his rear-seat pilot ejected successfully from their Phantom II fighter. Chutes were seen. Perhaps Sam Johnson is still alive, a prisoner. We don't know yet.

Hank Canterbury (who flew Slot from January, 1965, to February, 1967) cheated the odds during a combat mission in Vietnam. He was flying a low-level mission when Viet Cong gunners riddled his F-100 and shot out his engine. Canterbury had just enough altitude to turn his crippled fighter over the sea where he "punched out." The ejection went smoothly and the former Thunderbird pilot landed in the water. He inflated his life raft and waited anxiously for helicopter rescue. Canterbury's eyes widened when he noticed a sampan pushing off for him at full speed from the shoreline. In this day of rapid-fire automatic weapons, the survival gun carried by Air Force pilots is about as effectual as a wide-calibre peashooter. Nonetheless, as the sampan drew closer to him, Canterbury pulled free his "trusty six-shooter" and blazed away at the vessel approaching him. He knew it was ineffectual, but to his amazement and delight the sampan turned away. Shortly afterward the rescue chopper blatted its way to him and snatched him to safety. . . .

Shortly after I left the team early in 1960, the Thunderbirds received one of the highest aviation honors of the United States — the coveted MacKay Trophy for 1959. This annual award is presented to the person, persons, or the organization that carries out "the most meritorious flight of the year." It was for their operations throughout the Far East, where in one forty-day period the Thunderbirds flew thirty-one shows in Japan, Korea, Okinawa, and the Philippines. To fly 24,000 air miles from show site to show site, the team called for air refueling 250 times, and on several occasions flew two shows in one day. In commemoration of that Far East journey, General Thomas White, then the Air Force Chief of Staff, made the presentation of the MacKay Trophy to the Thunderbirds on May 15th, 1960.

Nineteen sixty was a year to be remembered for the team

. . . not only for dazzling air demonstrations flown in sunny Colombia and El Salvador, but also for a winged debut in chilly Alaska. The F-100's performed at Fort Yukon, at different air bases, noting in their record book that the Fort Yukon aerial demonstration was the first of its kind ever flown north of the Arctic Circle. Before the year ended, the Thunderbirds tallied eighty-four shows before more than three million spectators.

They picked up speed and activities for 1961 by flying a total of 104 shows. During November and December the team capped off the year with another deployment — their fifth in all — to Latin America.

Their sixth deployment to the countries far to the south started off the 1962 year. From Panama to Guatemala, the Thunderbirds winged from show to show. Evidence of their energy-draining schedule was one week during which eight shows were flown. Then it was back to the United States in wide formation to begin the usual tour of flying the world-famed demonstrations from coast to coast. By the close of the year the record book showed an additional seventy-six shows for 1962 before enthusiastic audiences numbering more than four million spectators.

As we have seen clearly in the pages preceding, it's easy enough to become preoccupied with the statistics of the demonstrations flown by the Thunderbirds. Statistics provide a ready reference, of course, to accomplishment, but they throw a pall over the reality of what goes into the aerial shows in terms of planning, effort, and coordination. And what must never be forgotten is that statistical descriptions of tens of thousands of people disguise the true nature of the moment, the sensations of awe and the expressions of pride and delight, the outstretched hands for congratulations and the thunderous roar of acclaim that meets the appearance and the skill of the team.

Nineteen sixty-three saw the first deployment of the Thunderbirds to Europe and North Africa and a smashing success of precision artistry in the air that brought crashing cheers from more than two million people in Portugal, Germany, France, Libya, England, Luxembourg, Italy, and Spain. As part of Project Grand Play to demonstrate airpower, the Thunderbirds again and again went to air refueling to continue their swift movement from one show site to another. The entire episode was, in the memory of those who were present, a minor miracle of international timing and coordination.

When 1963 went into the history books, the Thunderbirds looked back upon their first full decade of demonstrations. For ten years they had performed with a precision and color that had earned them international acclaim and the respect of pilots everywhere. The team flew ninety-four shows in 1963 and notched their 865th demonstration since the first team flight. A figure of five million spectators for 1963 brought the grand total for ten years to just over 50 mililon people who had gathered to watch the Ambassadors in Blue.

Nineteen sixty-four took a toll in effort, time, problems, and the life of Captain Eugene Devlin in the crash of his F-105. The Thunderbirds flew but six demonstrations in the big Thunderchief. The availability of new models of the airplane was something that just couldn't be arranged; the F-105's were needed desperately in Vietnam (where many Thunderbird pilots had flown, and were yet flying them in combat). The annual total of shows, because of time problems in changing airplanes again, back to the F-100, fell to sixty-four, all of which were staged before audiences totaling two mililon spectators. The last five months of the year saw the team back in the flashy Super Sabre.

The "busiest year in team history" became the historical banner for 1965. "Busy" in this instance doesn't necessarily mean numbers of shows flown or numbers of spectators, but rather the effort involved for deploying the aerial demonstrations before the audiences assigned to the Thunderbirds. For 1965 the team carried out not the usual one, but *three,* overseas deployments. Operation Island Tide took the sweptwing F-100's to the Caribbean for appearances in Barbados, Aruba, Curaçao, and Puerto Rico. Then came Operation Big Wing and the second deployment for the Thunderbirds throughout Europe. In a grueling twenty-seven days, in airfields scattered from Turkey to England, the team put on twenty-two aerial demonstrations before wildly cheering crowds. They returned to the States and, for the third overseas deployment of the year, Operation Easy Road, flew a sixteen-day mission to carry out their eighth Latin America visit. The leaders and citizens of five nations gathered to stare in awe and delight at the world-famed aerial artistry of the Thunderbirds.

The 121-show schedule for 1965 left pilots and the support teams weary in every bone. But it had been a smashing success. Nearly seven million people in twenty-three different lands had gathered to stare at the precision display of American tactical airpower. There was yet another milestone for the year On August 11th, the team flew before 25,000 spectators at the Waukegan Boating Festival in Illinois.

It was the grand slam performance — the 1,000th aerial demonstration of the Thunderbirds.

One year later, at the close of 1966, the grand total of aerial shows climbed to 1,141. Ninety-two demonstrations were flown in 1966 and boosted the total of spectators to 62 million people.

Another year and the figure climbed to nearly 1,300 air demonstrations, the total of spectators to approximately 70 million.

The year 1967 closed out in a manner unexpected — and for the first time when the Thunderbirds had sent out their recall and visiting guests' signal for the reunion at Nellis Air Force Base, the red, white, and blue wedge of the F-100 Super Sabres was absent from Nevada skies. This was the first time the Thunderbirds played host in a manner unique — their guests flew *for them.*

For the team was, temporarily, on the ground. On October 21st, the Thunderbirds were flying a demonstration at Del Rio, Texas. Suddenly the fighter flown by Captain Merrill "Tony" A. McPeak in the solo performance suffered a wing structural failure. Tony McPeak stayed with the Super Sabre, fighting to get it clear of the crowd or any structures on the ground. Not until he had lost all control and fire was in the cockpit did he eject — to land safely.

Subsequent investigations of the wreckage, and of other F-100 fighters, showed that the aircraft were developing fatigue cracks. These were originating from bolt-holes just inboard of the gear fulcrum mounting on the lower wing stress skin.

Tactical Air Command grounded the Thunderbirds until the fix could be made. In retrospect the loss of that fighter flown by Tony McPeak may well have saved other lives. Immediate orders to all F-100 organizations restricted pilots to pulling a maximum force of four g's in flight until the remedy was carried out. Approximately 700 of the North American jet attack aircraft were in the active Air Force inventory — and they were all to be modified by the end of the year. The F-100 has been in continuous service with the Tactical Air Comand since the 1950's, and the fighter has been a major element of the U.S. Air Force strike force in South Vietnam, as well as being flown on missions over the southern portion of North Vietnam and Laos.

The Thunderbirds' aerial demonstrations have never constituted maneuvers which could be defined as unchanging — kept the same so as to guarantee that the pilots would not have to cope with variations in the performances. Through the years new maneuvers have been added; the aerial demonstrations changed as time and situations required or demanded. No longer is there a Solo Pilot; the one has become two — Lead Solo and Second Solo. The result is to enhance the effect of the demonstrations. The team also flies certain maneuvers with the familiar four-plane formation, but variations have added five-plane and six-plane maneuvers. The reader is familiar with such maneuvers as the Diamond Roll, Changeover Roll, Trail Roll, Cloverleaf Turn, Changeover Loop, and other precision demonstrations. Now there has been added the Solo Pilots' dual maximum performance takeoff and roll; solo four-point breakaway rolls; solo opposing Half Cuban Eights; solo opposing aileron rolls; the four-plane Arrowhead, roll, and roll back to Arrowhead; the six-ship Wedge Loop; four-plane Diamond Tactical Pitchup; six-plane Pass and Victory Roll; the Arrowhead Roll; solo opposing loops and solo opposing slow rolls with each Solo Pilot performing in crowd-shuddering passes. The solo performers' Calypso Pass is a guaranteed lip-chewer. In this maneuver the Solo Leader flies inverted and the Wingman in normal attitude. Because the Leader must throttle back to idle while flying and sustaining his inverted flight position, the Wingman has to extend his speed brake to keep from overrunning the Leader. It takes tremendous timing and superb flying, yet the "dynamic duo," as the Solo Pilots have become known, fly the maneuver with the same apparent ease with which the four-plane formation slides through the sky.

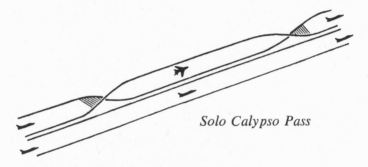

Solo Calypso Pass

In the Victory Roll, with the diamond and both Solo Pilots flying in a six-ship wedge formation, a level flyover followed by a left barrel roll is performed.

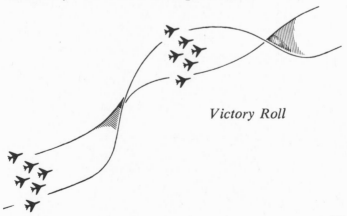

Victory Roll

The Five-Card Loop is flown with four Super Sabres in a square and a fifth in the center, resembling the pattern on a five from a deck of cards. It's quite a sight to see the five of diamonds going through a miles-high loop in the blue!

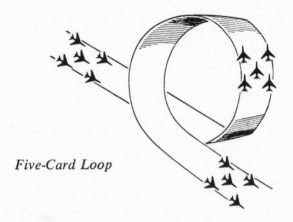

Five-Card Loop

In the solo opposing Half Cuban Eights, the two solo aircraft rush toward each other from opposite directions and, as soon as they have passed, begin climbing in graceful loops. They perform synchronized Half Cuban Eights with minimum lateral and vertical clearance over the top, as shown in the diagram below.

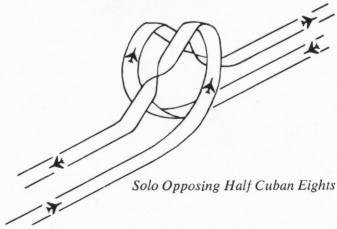

Solo Opposing Half Cuban Eights

There's another dazzler known as the *Bon Ton Roulle,* which was first flown in 1963. This consists of a slow, low-altitude formation pass in the conventional diamond formation, with the planes at their normal three-foot wing-tip overlap formation distance. On signal from the Leader over a preselected checkpoint, the formation explodes outward to where they are one full aircraft length apart. Simultaneously, the Leader and Right Wingman roll right and the Left Wingman and Slot Man roll left. The effect is startling — in bright sunlight it seems as if a horde of glittering knife blades were spinning around violently. Then faster than people believe it's happening, the team is back in the diamond, tucked in tightly.

The *Bon Ton Roulle* is a guaranteed crowd-stopper.

Bon Ton Roulle

Some of the Thunderbird routines, in the administrative and personnel sense, also have changed. Ed "Lucky" Palmgren, who walked away from an F-100 bellied to a landing in an open field, flew Slot from November, 1954, to September, 1956. In March, 1963, Palmgren returned to the team as the first Thunderbird pilot ever to finish his tour, spend several years away from the team, and return to its ranks. The former Slot Pilot became the new Leader early in 1963, and then went on to a new position as Commander.

Another change took place with Paul Kauttu who joined the team as Slot Pilot in September, 1962. Kauttu was the first four-year pilot with the Thunderbirds, moving successively from Slot to Leader to Commander.

As we mentioned in the Foreword, Neil Eddins, who joined the team as Slot Pilot with the rank of lieutenant in April, 1959, departed the Thunderbirds ranks in December, 1961, as captain — and in 1967, this time as a major — became the second pilot to return and to take the position of Leader. The reader who has come to know Neil so well in these pages may well understand that the team is flying as it has never flown before — it defies the veteran onlookers by getting better and better even while imposing greater demands on the pilots who fly in the aerial demonstations through an increased number of aircraft and precision-demanding new maneuvers.

Neil maintained a steady flying pace during that interval he was away from the Thunderbirds. The new Commander-Leader flew 100 missions in the F-105 fighter-bomber in Vietnam; in addition, he had flown in Germany with the F-105, had attended "a string" of special schools, and became project officer in the Operations and Training Evaluation Section (F-105) at the Tactical Fighter Weapons Center. It was during this latter assignment, just prior to rejoining the Thunderbirds, that Neil Eddins was selected as the TAC Pilot of Distinction for expert airmanship in an emergency. While assigned to the 4525th Fighter Weapons Wing at Nellis Air Force Base, he ran into trouble during an F-105 test mission. He noticed that his fuel supply was decreasing rapidly — *too* rapidly. Neil declared an emergency situation and set up the big Thunderchief for a long straight-in approach.

Five miles out from the runway the engine quit. As most pilots will be quick to tell you, an airplane like the F-105 without an engine has the tendency to glide like a piano. Neil was perfectly justified under the conditions in punching out — ejecting. He didn't; he stayed with the powerless fighter and brought it down safely, saving a valuable aircraft through the cool and skilled airmanship that for so long has marked Neil as a pilot.

But as *he* said it, "Why, I just acted like I knew what I was doing. . . ."

So at that big 1967 reunion, we took time out to get together just by ourselves. We were impatient for Janca to tell us of his shooting down a MiG-21 over North Vietnam. Chuck Maultsby, as noted, had finished 216 missions in Vietnam, but couldn't get home in time to make the scene at the reunion. Herm Griffin, that wild man in the Solo slot, was now an educational adviser to high-school students, and perhaps that was considerably more demanding than what he had done with the F-100. Bob Cass had been to several schools, served overseas for a few years, and for the reunion departed the Pentagon to join the ranks together. And, of course, Neil Eddins, who had picked up the traditions of old and who was giving them new and dramatic meaning.

He looks great up there at the helm.

Roster of Thunderbirds

Major D. Catledge	Leader	5-53/10-54
Captain Buck Patillo	Wing	5-53/ 3-54
Captain Bill Patillo	Wing	5-53/ 3-54
Captain B. Kanaga	Slot	5-53/ 3-54
Lieutenant B. McCormick . . .	Solo/Slot	5-53/10-54
Captain B. Brock	Narrator	6-53/ 5-54
Captain B. Creech	Wing	3-54/10-55
Captain B. Spalding	Wing	3-54/ 3-55
Lieutenant A. Brown . . .	Solo	3-54/10-55
Captain A. Davis	Narrator	5-54/ 9-55
Captain E. Palmgren . . .	Slot	10-54/ 9-56
Captain J. Broughton	Leader	10-54/ 3-57
Captain B. Ellis	Solo/Wing	5-55/ 2-57
Lieutenant B. Anderson . . .	Solo/Wing	7-55/ 3-57
Captain D. Ferris	Narrator	7-55/11-56
Captain P. Ross	Spare/Solo	7-55/ 6-56
Lieutenant B. Pogue . . .	Solo/Slot	10-55/ 9-57
Captain J. Bartley	Solo/Wing	6-56/ 2-58
Captain D. Brenner	Spare/Wing	8-56/ 2-58
Captain B. Scott	Narrator	11-56/ 4-58
Captain B. McIntosh . . .	Solo/Wing	3-57/ 8-58
Lieutenant S. Johnson . . .	Slot	3-57/10-58
Major R. Robinson	Leader	3-57/ 3-59
Captain C. Salmon	Solo/Slot	1-58/ 3-59
Captain H. Whitlow	Slot	12-57/ 5-59
Captain G. Williams . . .	Left Wing	4-58/10-59
Captain D. Crane	Narrator	1-58/ 7-60
Captain C. Maultsby . . .	Right Wing	10-58/ 8-60
Captain H. Griffin	Solo	8-58/ 9-60
Captain N. Eddins	Slot	4-59/12-61
Captain R. Janca	Left Wing	4-59/ 3-61
Major R. Fitzgerald	Leader	3-59/ 4-61
Lieutenant G. Nial	Narrator	3-61/ 4-61
Chief Warrant Officer M. France .	Maintenance Officer . . .	5-59/ 6-61
Captain R. Cass	Right Wing	2-60/ 2-62
Colonel J. Groom	Commander	1-62/ 4-62
Captain R. Everett	Narrator	5-60/ 5-62
Captain B. Gardiner . . .	Narrator	7-61/ 7-62
Captain R. Brooks	Right Wing	2-62/11-62
Captain R. Bell	Slot	3-61/11-62

Captain G. Larson	Solo	12-60/	8-62
Major R. Gibson	Leader	4-61/	3-63
Captain W. Hosmer	Left Wing	2-61/	3-63
Captain C. Husdale	Maintenance Officer	6-61/	7-63
Captain R. Moore	Solo	3-62/	9-63
Lieutenant Colonel W. Alden	Commander	4-62/	4-64
Captain L. Czarnecki	Narrator	4-62/	4-64
Captain E. Devlin	Left Wing	2-64/	5-64
Major E. Palmgren	Leader/Commander	3-63/	1-65
Captain R. Catton	Solo	8-62/	12-64
Captain J. Shockley	Left Wing/Slot	4-63/	12-64
Captain W. Higginbotham	Right Wing	1-63/	12-64
Lieutenant S. Sasaki	Administrative Officer	3-62/	2-65
Major L. Reder	Maintenance Officer	8-63/	8-65
Captain R. Goodman	Narrator	3-64/	12-65
Major P. Kauttu	Slot/Leader/Commander	9-62/	2-66
Captain C. Langerud	Solo	8-63/	2-66
Captain C. Hamm	Left Wing	6-64/	2-66
Captain A. Schreihofer	Information Officer	4-63/	5-66
Captain R. Morgan	Solo	1-65/	10-66
Major F. Liethen	Executive Officer	11-65/	10-66
Captain H. Dortch	Narrator	11-65/	12-66
Captain W. McGee	Right Wing	1-65/	2-67
Captain H. Canterbury	Slot	1-65/	2-67
Lieutenant Colonel R. Maglione	Leader/Commander	7-65/	7-67
Captain Bob Beckel	Solo	1-66/	12-67
Captain C. Patterakis	Left Wing	1-66/	12-67
Major E. Haney	Maintenance Officer	1-66/	12-67
Captain G. Scoggins	Administrative Officer	4-65/	7-67
Major Neil Eddins	Leader/Commander		
Captain Mack Angel	Left Wing		
Major Stan Musser	Right Wing		
Captain Jack Dickey	Slot		
Captain Tony McPeak	Solo		
Captain Mike Miller	Solo*		
Captain Doyle Ruff	Narrator		
Major Joe Moore	Executive Officer		
Captain Clyde Labell	Administrative Officer		
Captain Steve Murata	Information Officer		

*Mike Miller served with the Team as Narrator, and then moved into position as Solo Pilot, instituting a new procedure for the team. Each Narrator will now have a position open to him after completing his service as Narrator.

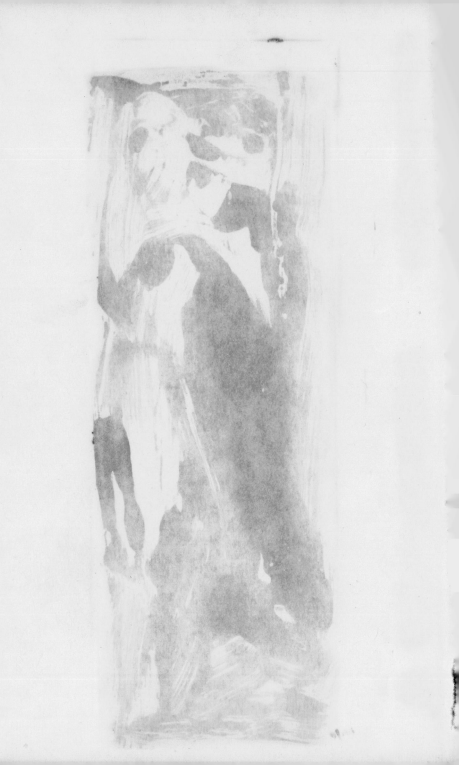